IBBOTSON ACADEMIC SOFTWARE MANUAL

INVESTMENTS
A Global Perspective

Jack C. Francis and Roger Ibbotson

JOSEPH F. GRECO
California State University – Fullerton

Upper Saddle River, New Jersey 07458

Executive Editor: Mickey Cox
Managing editor: Gladys Soto
Media Project Manager: Torie Anderson
Production editor: Wanda Rockwell
CD Duplication: Failsafe Media Company
Manufacturer: Victor Graphics

ISBN 0-13-060939-0
10 9 8 7 6 5 4 3 2 1

TABLE OF CONTENTS

PREFACE

At the present time, we are confronting a tidal wave of information thanks to the electronic highway we call the Internet. The wave of information that continues to be generated in the investment industry was formally available in the not-too-distant past to only the wealthiest investors, giant pension funds, or the largest brokerage houses. Unlike the physical destruction from an ocean tidal wave, the information tidal wave can leave the small investor immobilized and confused. Today, one of the greatest challenges for any small investor is the challenge to collect and process the seemingly unlimited data available from the markets in such a way that he or she makes an informed investment decision with the same expertise as the broker from the largest firm supported by a backroom of specialized software and multiple analysts.

The purpose of this book is to give the reader information about the EnCorr software and to provide applications drawn from the field of modern portfolio theory. You will find in the following chapters a step-by-step description of how to research, analyze and find an optimal portfolio and to manipulate the software to illustrate many of the concepts found in the text *Investments A Global Perspective* by Jack Clark Francis and Roger Ibbotson. The prepackaged software is the same software used by the largest investment houses and the most sophisticated investors. The exercises provided in the chapters are just an introduction for those who wish to make practical use of this valuable software. The most rewarding part will come when you learn to integrate the software and its techniques in the capital markets in order to make an informed investment choice and to assist you in developing your optimal portfolio.

Joseph F. Greco
College of Business and Economics
California State University Fullerton

Part I

The Ibbotson Associates Software

1

Getting Started

INTRODUCTION

Ibbotson Associates, the Allocation Company

Ibbotson Associates was founded by Professor Roger Ibbotson in 1976, and the Company has become one of the leading authorities in the world on asset allocation. The software provides services to help investment professionals make the best asset allocation decisions for their clients. With the purchase of the text *Investments, A Global Perspective*, you have at your fingertips the same software used by these professionals.

Professor Ibbotson was the first to collect the requisite data to quantify the benefits of diversification and model the concepts underlying asset allocation. He published his findings in a landmark study, *Stocks, Bonds, Bills, and Inflation,* which has become an indispensable annual reference tool for investment and finance professionals.

Getting Started

The Ibbotson Investment Analysis software combines the latest in financial theory and practice with innovative software development and robust performance. Just as money managers, plan sponsors, consultants, and mutual fund product developers find the tools they need to meet the challengers associated with the investment analysis process, you will have many of the same tools and be able to conduct much of the same type of analysis.

The two components of the software that we will use most often are found in the EnCorr Analyzer and EnCorr Optimizer. Chapter 1 will provide information about the tools and commands found in the two components that you will be using in later chapters. This chapter includes:

- System Requirements
- Software Overview
- Installation Instructions

The examples and exercises presented here give just a small fraction of the scope and flexibility of the Ibbotson Associates software package. Although you will be shown a wide variety of uses for the software that correlate to concepts developed in the Ibbotson and Francis text, keep in mind that there are many more applications that you can develop on your own.

System Requirements

Minimum Requirements

Hardware

- Microsoft Windows compatible PC
- At least a Pentium 75 processor with 16MB of RAM for Windows 98
- At least a Pentium 90 processor with 32 MB of RAM for Windows NT
- 100 MB of available disk space
- Windows-compatible mouse
- VGA or SVGA graphics card compatible with Windows
- Access to a local or network CD-ROM drive

Software

- Windows 95
- Windows 98 or Windows NT 4.0 or 3.51 (with Service Pack 3 or 4)

Preferred Configurations

- Pentium 166 processor with 32 MB of RAM for Windows 98
- Pentium 166 processor with 64 MB of RAM for Windows NT
- Office 97 Service Release 2 (SR-2)

How The Products Interact

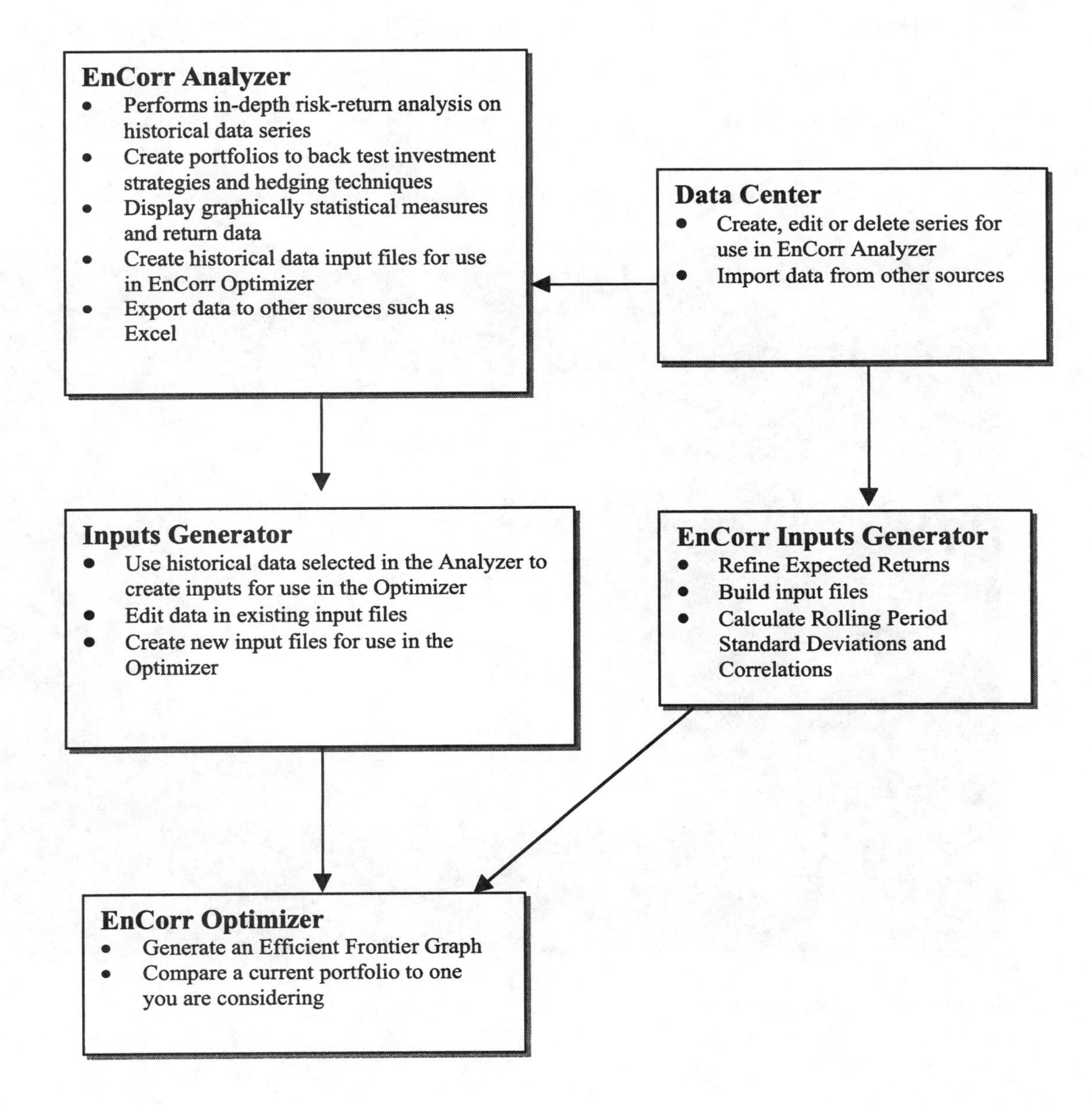

EnCorr Analyzer
Performs in-depth risk-return analysis on historical data series
Create portfolios to back test investment strategies and hedging techniques
Display graphically statistical measures and return data
Create historical data input files for use in EnCorr Optimizer
Export data to other sources such as Excel
Data Center
Create, edit or delete series for use in EnCorr Analyzer
Import data from other sources
Inputs Generator
Use historical data selected in the Analyzer to create inputs for use in the Optimizer
Edit data in existing input files
Create new input files for use in the Optimizer
EnCorr Inputs Generator
Refine Expected Returns
Build input files
Calculate Rolling Period Standard Deviations and Correlations
EnCorr Optimizer
Generate an Efficient Frontier Graph
Compare a current portfolio to one you are considering

Software Installation Instructions

Follow these steps for installing Ibbotson Software version 8.1 Software. It is best to close any open applications before you begin the installation process. During the installation process you will be prompted to install the Borland Database Engine. This program must be installed in order to view data in the Ibbotson software and run other programs.

1. Insert the Ibbotson Software version 8.1 CD into your CD-ROM drive. The installation program automatically begins. (Or insert the CD, select **Start, Run,** type **D:\setup.exe**, where **D** denotes your CD-ROM drive, and click **OK**.)

2. The Welcome box appears (**Figure 1.1**, below). Click **Next**.

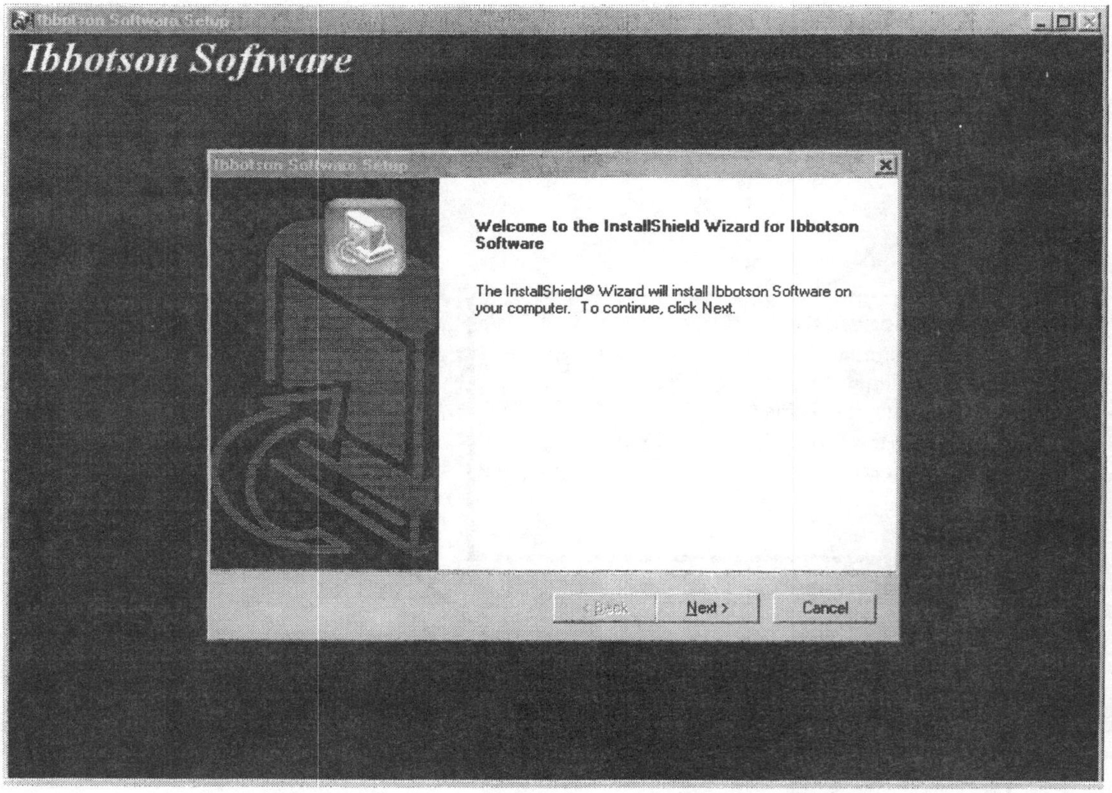

Figure 1.1 Welcome Dialog

3. The License File Location dialog box (Figure 1.2, below) appears. Select the location of your Ibbotson License File.

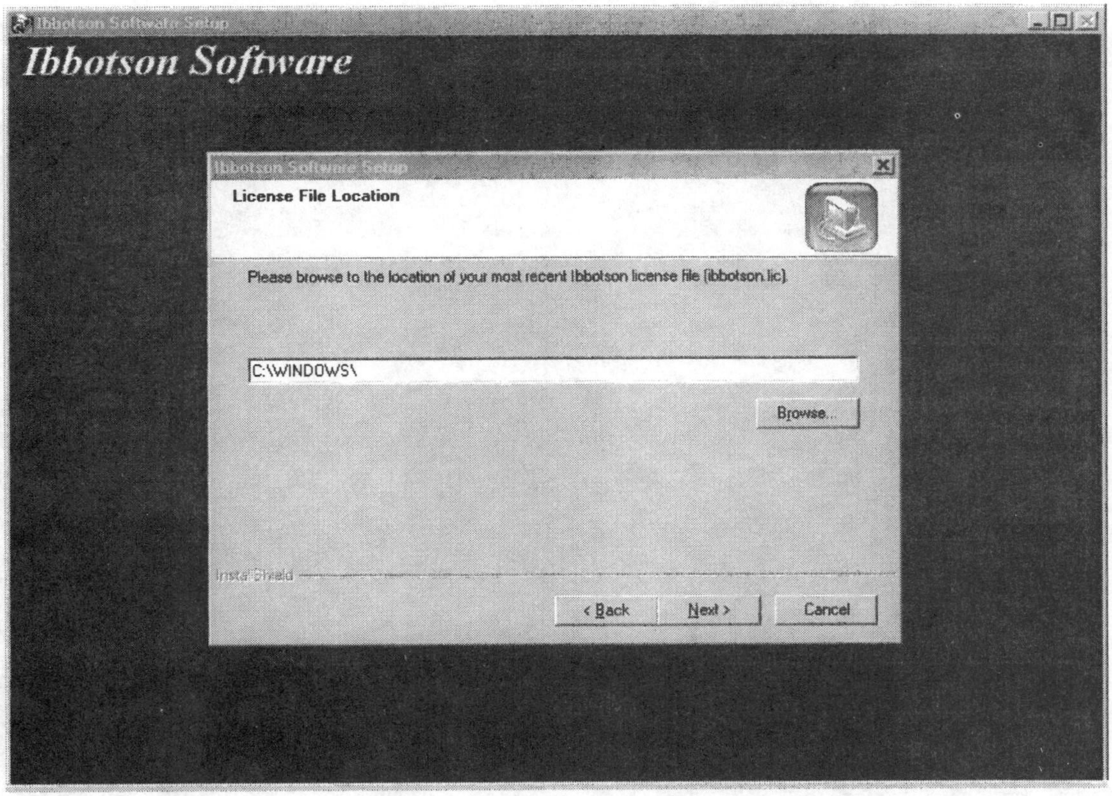

Figure 1.2 License File Location Dialog

- Your License File is located in a directory
  1. Select **Other directories**.
  2. **Browse** to the appropriate location of the License File.
  3. **Select** the file Ibbotson.lic, then click **Next.**

4. The Ibbotson Install dialog box appears (Figure 1.3). Check each component that you wish to install. **Please remember that the Borland Database Engine must be installed to view the data in the Ibbotson software.**

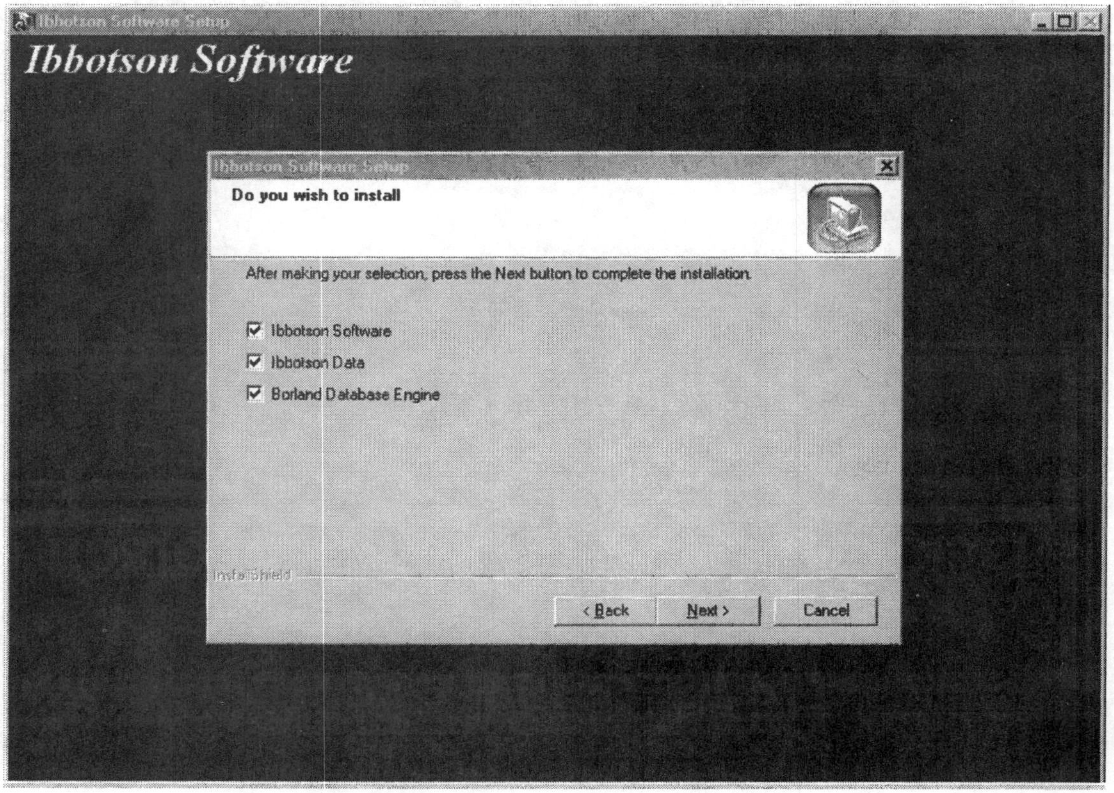

Figure 1.3 Ibbotson Install Dialog

- **Ibbotson Software:** Check the box to install Ibbotson software components.
- **Ibbotson Data:** Check the box to install data included in CD package.
- **Borland Database Engine (BDE):** Check this box to install BDE onto a system.
- Click **Next**.

5. The Software Destination Location box is displayed (Figure 1.4). Select a location for the software to reside on your system. For first-time installations, the default directory is . . . \program\ibbotson; for consecutive installations, the

default directory is the same as the directory of the existing software. You can create a different directory by clicking the **Browse** button. When you have finished creating the directory, click **Next**.

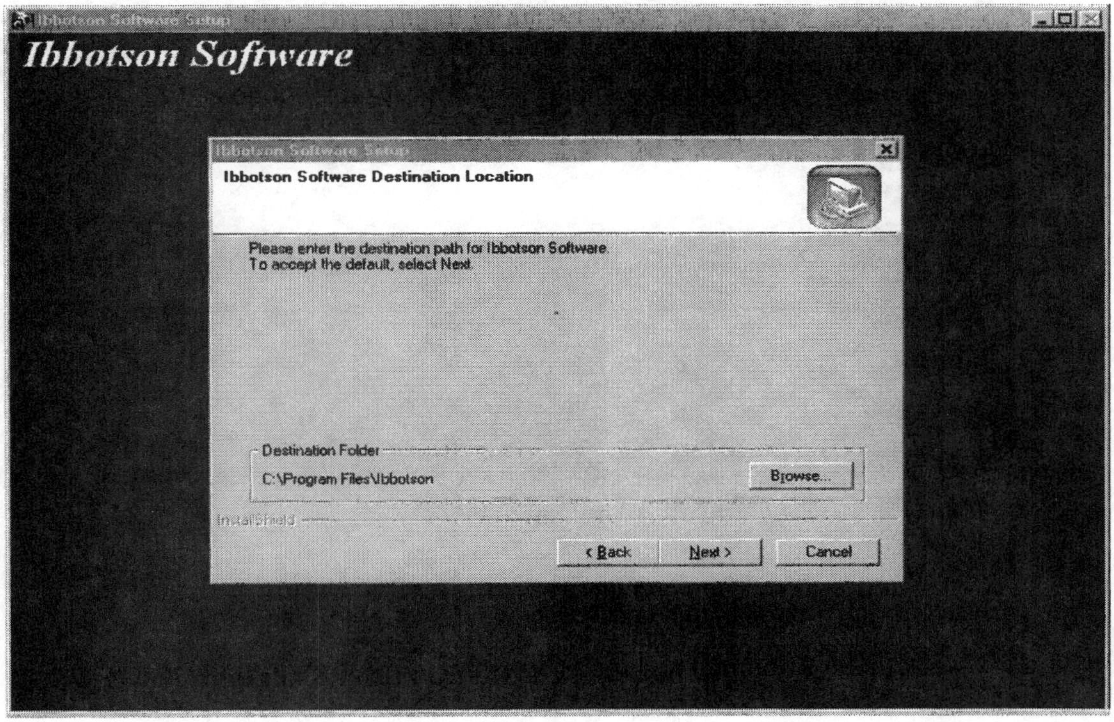

Figure 1.4 Software Destination Location Dialog

6. The Ibbotson Software 8.0 dialog box appears (Figure 1.5) with a list of the software components that you are licensed to use. Click **Next**.

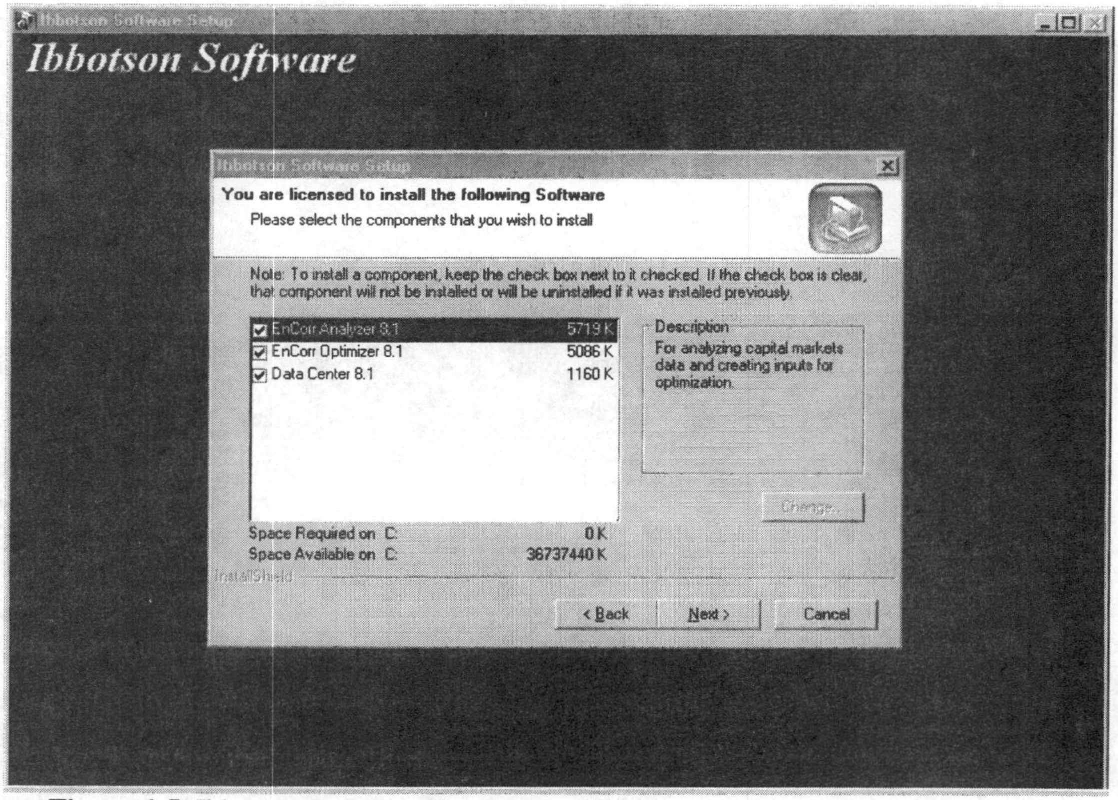

Ibbotson Software Setup

Ibbotson Software

Ibbotson Software Setup

You are licensed to install the following Software

Please select the components that you wish to install

Note: To install a component, keep the check box next to it checked. If the check box is clear, that component will not be installed or will be uninstalled if it was installed previously.

☑ EnCorr Analyzer 8.1	5719 K
☑ EnCorr Optimizer 8.1	5086 K
☑ Data Center 8.1	1160 K

Description

For analyzing capital markets data and creating inputs for optimization.

Change...

Space Required on C: 0 K

Space Available on C: 36737440 K

InstallShield

< Back | Next > | Cancel

Figure 1.5 Ibbotson Software Components Dialog

7. The Ibbotson Software 8.0 Data Modules dialog box is displayed with a list of the data modules that you are licensed to use. (Figure 1.6). Click **Next**.

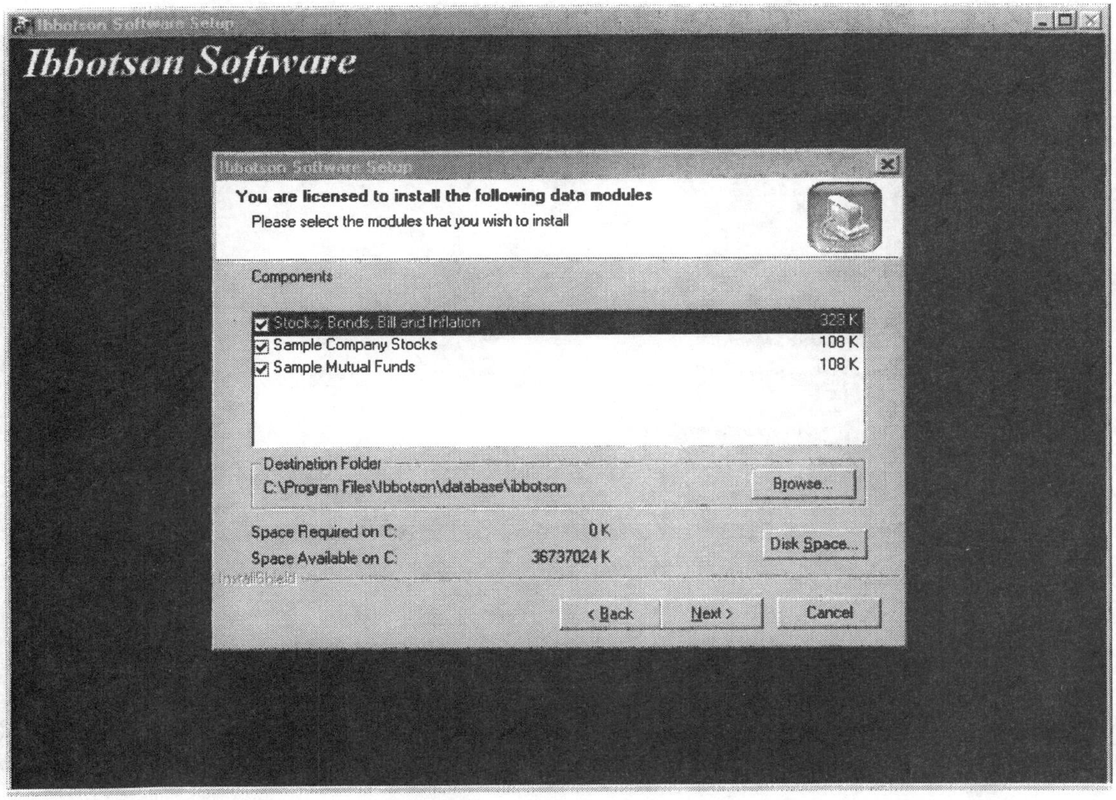

Figure 1.6 Ibbotson Data Modules Dialog

8. The Ibbotson Software 8.1 Icons dialog box is displayed (Figure 1.7). Setup will crete Icons in a Program Folder. The default folder is Ibbotson Software 8.1, but you can select a different folder from the **Existing Folders** list. Click **Next**.

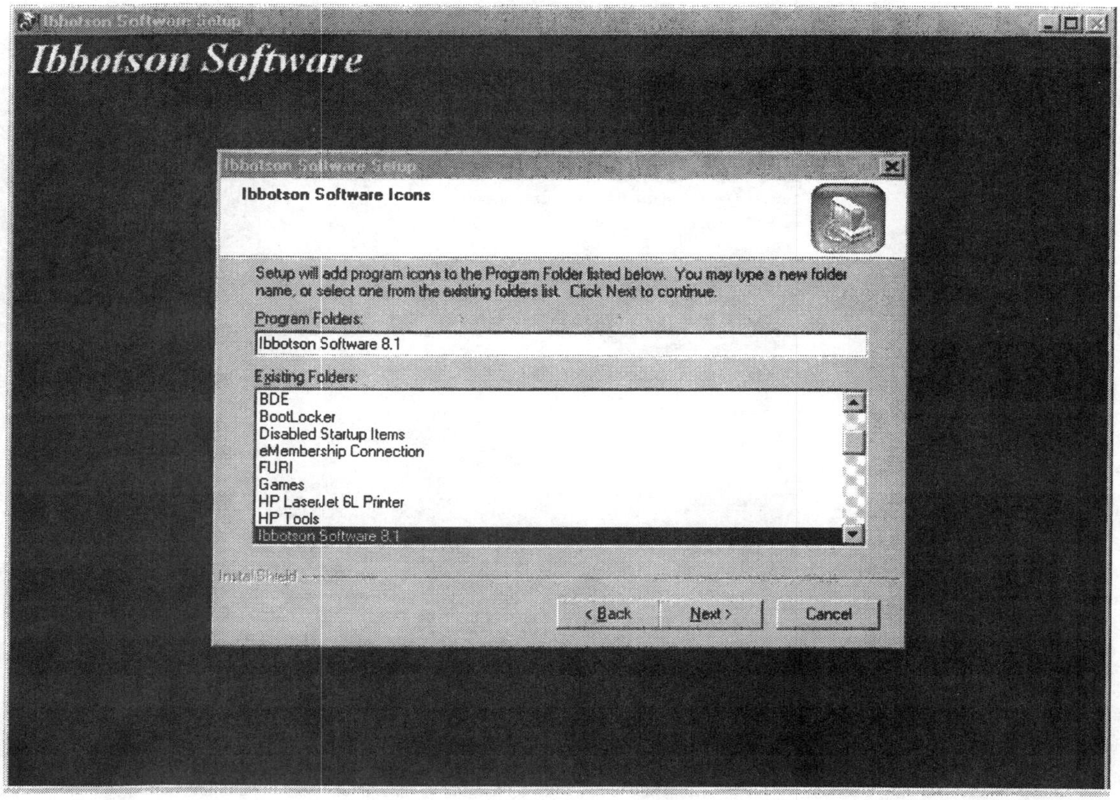

Figure 1.7 Ibbotson Software Icons Dialog

9. When the setup is complete, the Setup Complete box appears (Figure 1.8). Click **Finish.**

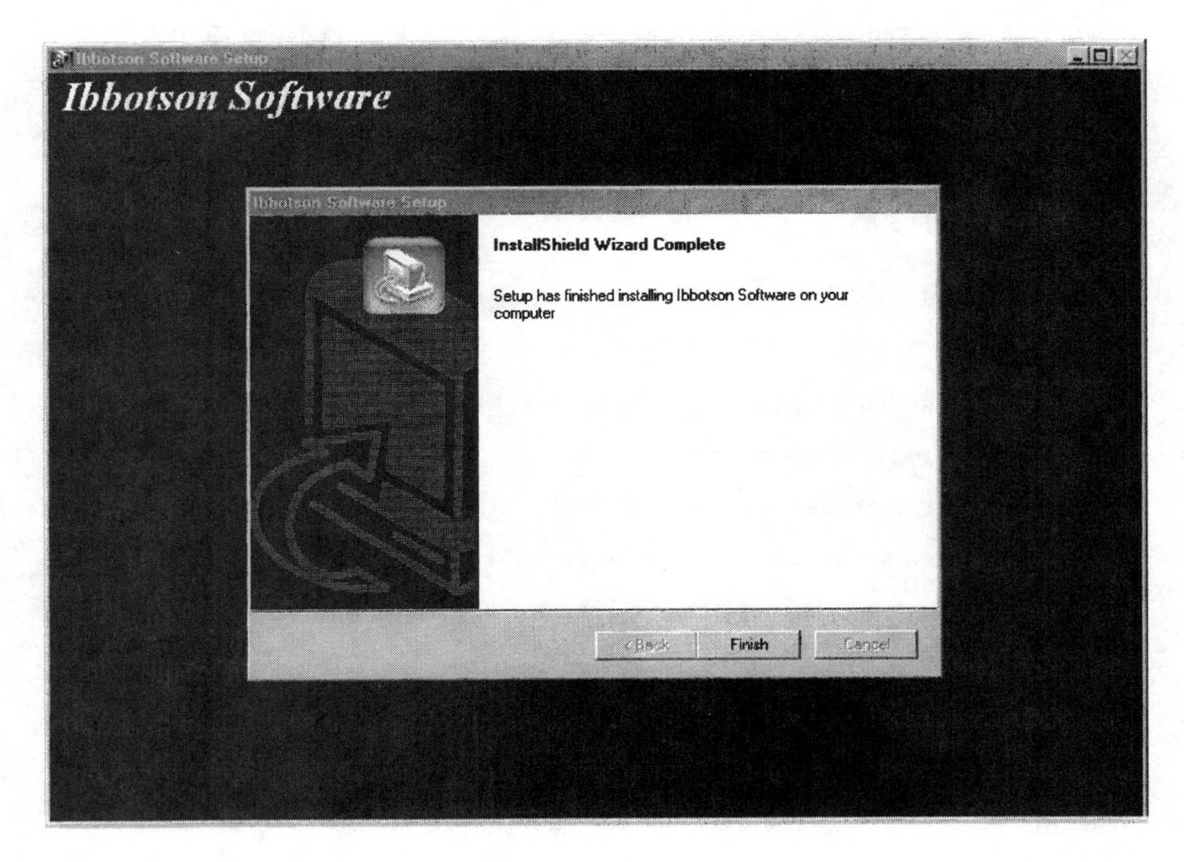

Figure 1.8 Setup Complete Dialog

EnCorr Analyzer

The EnCorr Analyzer enables you to perform historical data analysis and create historical inputs files. You can examine the historical performance of data series from as early as 1926 and create graphs, charts, and tables of statistical data. Historical analysis can be performed with data supplied by Ibbotson Associates and other series from the authors of your textbook.

Navigating Analyzer Menus

With the EnCorr Analyzer software program, you can:

- Perform in-depth data analysis on historical time series
- Analyze and backtest investment strategies
- View and graph data series
- Construct asset allocation inputs for portfolio optimization
- Create portfolios and performance benchmarks
- Adjust data for inflation

Main Folder Window

When you start up EnCorr Analyzer, the Main Folder Window opens (Figure 1.9).

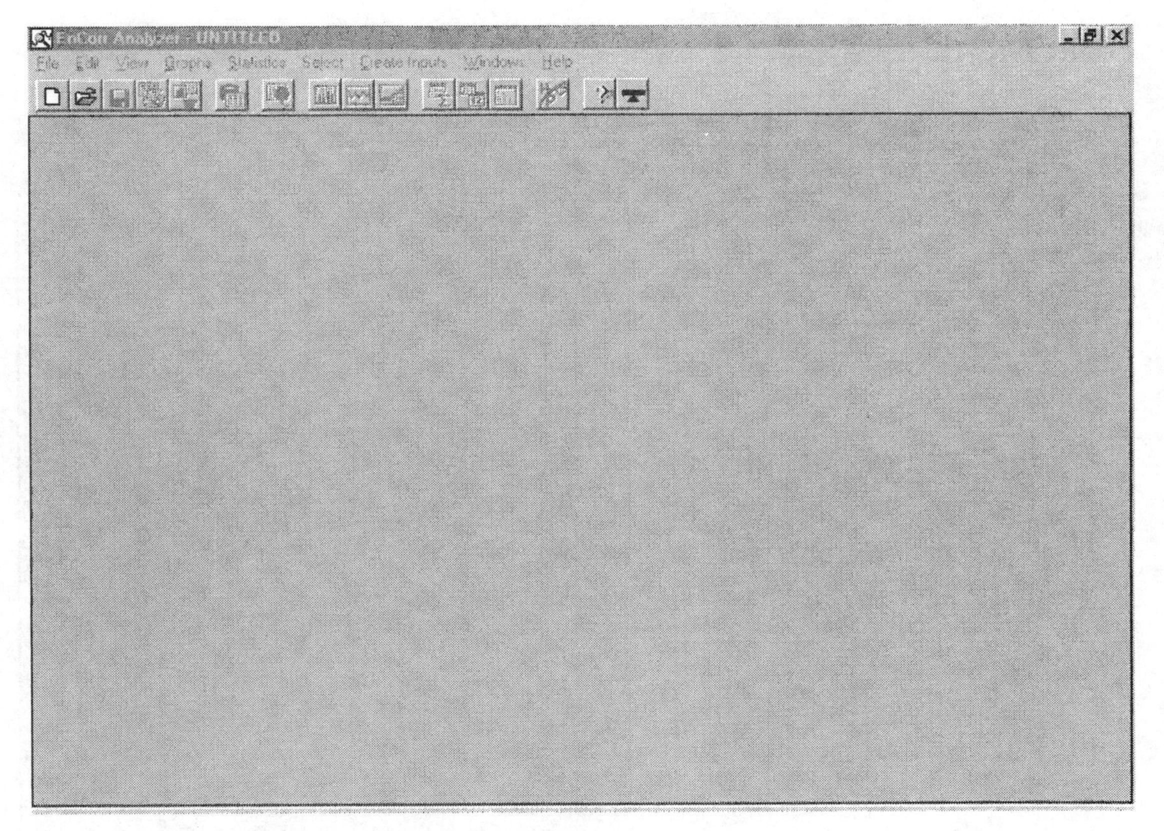

Figure 1.9 EnCorr Analyzer Main Folder Window

Menu Map

The commands available from the menu bar in the EnCorr Analyzer Main Folder Window are described in this section.

File Menu

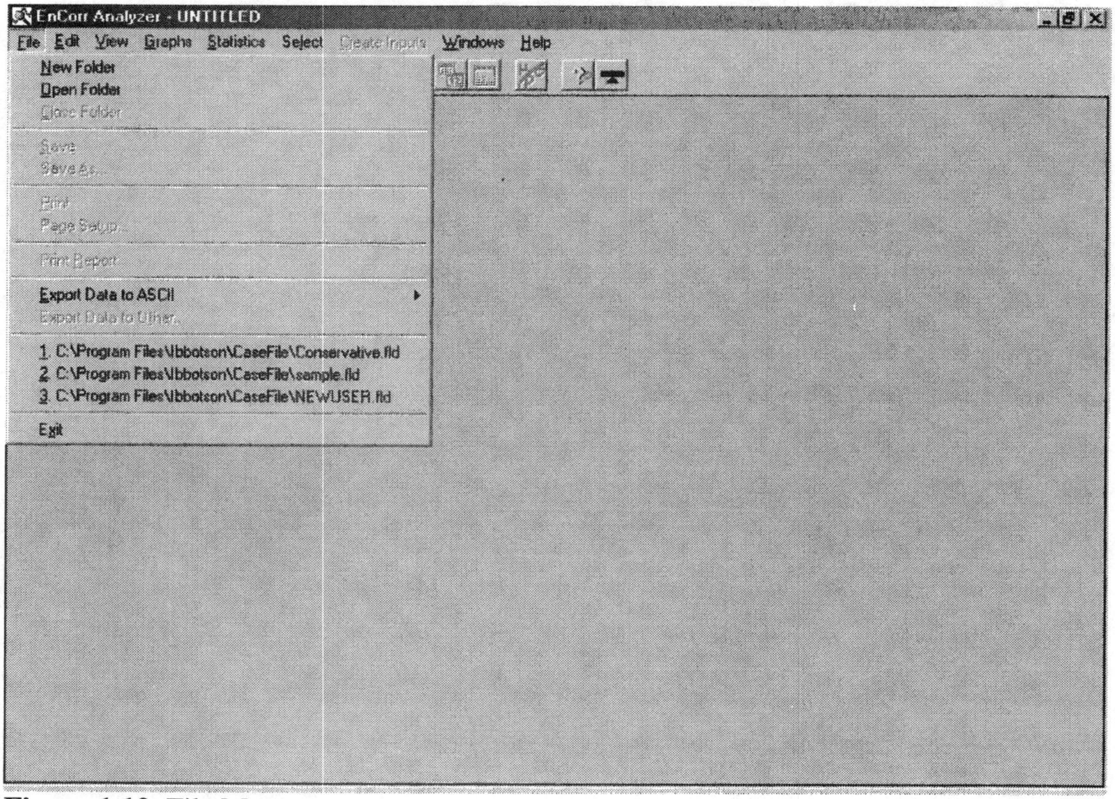

Figure 1.10 File Menu

New Folder enables you to create a new Analyzer case file (.fld), while keeping other case files open.

OpenFolder opens an existing case file (.fld) from the default directory. The default location is /ibbotson/case file. To change the default directory, click the **Databases** button from the Select Series window.

Save, Save As: Save saves the currently active folder under its existing name. **Save As** saves the active folder under a new name, creating a new folder while keeping the original folder intact under its own name.

Print prints all the data within the date range specified in t he date settings.

Page Setup specifies print parameters before printing tables. You can adjust text height, change margins, include time stamp, and add footers. These settings are not saved after you exit the software.

Print Report creates and prints a customized report with a title page and your choice of graphs and tables. This feature also allows you to insert your own text.

Export to ASCII and **Export to Other** exports the data series table to a file.

Exit closes the Analyzer.

Edit Menu

Copy copies an entire table to the Windows Clipboard. To copy a section of the table, highlight the desired rows in the table and click **Edit, Copy.** You can then paste the information into another software application.

Paste Portfolio pastes a portfolio that has been copied to the Windows Clipboard from the other Ibbotson software programs into the Analyzer. This option allows you to use all Analyzer analytics to backtest Efficient Frontier portfolios created in the EnCorr Optimizer.

Notes allows you to enter notes on the current Analyzer case file (.fld).

Copy Portfolio copies a selected portfolio so that you can use it in another EnCorr application.

View Menu

Returns displays returns in the folder window based on t he data type and t he Date Settings frequency. The method for computing a return varies with the nature of the payment and the time period of measure. Use **Data Help** from the Help menu to resolve methodology and return calculation questions.

Index displays cumulative wealth values in t he folder window based on the data type. The Index Value and Index (Start) Date are determined by the date settings.

Both displays returns and index wealth values in the folder window, side by side.

Decimal Format displays data in decimal format.

Percent Format displays data in percent formula.

Preferences allows you to globally edit or turn on/off the following table options: button bar, fonts, column width, and number of decimal places.

Graphs Menu

Graphs Menu Options:

Return Bar Graph plots historical return data based on the frequency and time period in your folder's date setting.

Return Line Graph – Analyzer allows you to create line graphs for return or index wealth values. The X-axis displays the data frequency of your folder: monthly, quarterly, semiannually, or annually. The Y-axis displays the returns.

Index Graph illustrates how one dollar invested in each asset grows over time. The index stating date defaults to the firs period before the common starting date of the chosen data. If you were to track the growth of $1 from 1926 through 1994, you would not invest on January 1, 1926 but immediately before the first day of trading in 1926. Therefore, the initial date would be set to the end of 1925, just before the beginning of 1926.

Rolling Period Bar Graph displays average returns over user-defined rolling periods in bar graph format.

Rolling Period Line Graph displays average returns over user-defined periods in line graph format.

Independent Period Bar Graph displays average returns over independent periods.

Pie Chart displays the holdings of a selected portfolio in pie chart format.

Graphs Menu Functions

From the menu bar on each type of graph, you can perform the following common graph functions:

Print prints the current graph.

Page Setup allows you to specify print parameters before printing graphs. You can change margins, include a time stamp, and add footers.

Note: You must click the Display Options Save button to set the current display settings as the default for that graph.

Copy to Clipboard copies the selected graph to the Windows Clipboard so that you can insert it to another software application.

Export to Metafile saves the current graph as a Windows Metafile so that you can insert it into another software application.

Display Options enables you to customize a graph to suit your needs b y changing common settings such as decimal places, fonts, and colors, or settings that are particular to a specific graph.

Note: You must click the Display Options Save button to set the current display settings as the default for that graph.

Zoom In rescales a graph. Click the mouse and drag over the area you wish to examine before using the command.

Zoom Out returns a magnified graph to its previous scale.

Summary Statistics calculates various summary statistics, such as arithmetic mean and standard deviation for your selected series.

Note: For Rolling Period and Independent Period graphs, the Summary Statistics tables can be misleading because the statistics represent averages of averages.

Correlation Statistics views the correlation matrix for your selected series.

Exit closes the graph.

Send to allows you to export a graph to Microsoft Excel or Microsoft PowerPoint.

Statistics Menu

Statistics Menu Options

Summary Statistics displays numerous historical summary statistics for all selected series in your current Analyzer case file (.fld) in a table. Statistics are calculated based on the frequency and time period specified in the Date Settings dialog box. Your current time period is displayed in the title bar of the Summary Statistics table.

Rolling Period Performance allows you to view, based on rolling periods, how often a series performed better or worse than a given percentage. You can also analyze the best and worst than a given percentage. You can also analyze the best and worst period over the time horizon.

Performance Periods allows you to view historical returns over multiple time periods and multiple frequencies. In the Performance Summary table, historical returns are always linked to the ending date in the date settings.

Correlation Matrix – A correlation coefficient measures the extent to which the two series are related. It examines the degree to which the returns of two data series, or portfolios, move in tandem. A correlation coefficient always falls between a range of –1 to 1 (-1 means it is not correlated; 1 means highly correlated). The Correlation Matrix calculates the correlation coefficients between all the assets and selected series in your Analyzer case file (.fld). A positive correlation coefficient means that asset returns move together. A negative correlation coefficient means that the asset returns move inversely.

Autoregression regresses each series in your Analyzer case file against its prior period return (1 period lag). An auto regression model measures how much serial correlation a series exhibits. (A series exhibits serial correlation if its value in one period can be used to predict its value in the following period.) The beta estimate in the autoregression is a measure of serial correlation. The closer the absolute value of the beta estimate is to 1, the greater the degree of serial correlation.

Linear Regression similar to the correlation coefficient, attempts to measure the relationship between one asset (dependent variable) and a group of assets (independent variable). Specifically, a linear regression determines how well the dependent variable can be explained b y the independent variable. The Analyzer uses the least squares regression technique. To calculate a linear regression, select your dependent and independent variables from the **Available Series** list box in the Linear Regression window. You can view the results of the linear regression in the Linear Regression window. You can perform regression analysis with multiple independent variables but not with multiple dependent variables.

Rolling Period Returns are obtained by rolling a data window of fixed length along each time series (asset). They are useful for examining the behavior of returns for holding periods similar to those experienced by investors and showing the effects of time diversification. For example, an investor with a five-year time horizon can use five-year rolling periods to see how an asset has performed over time.

Each Rolling Period Return represents the geometric average for a given holding period, based on your date setting's frequency and time period. For example, a five-year rolling period calculates an annual geometric average return over every five-year holding period available in your folder. If the beginning date is 1926, the first five-year annual holding period would be 1926 to 1930. The next five-year rolling period would be 1927 to 1931, then 1928 to 1932, and so on.

Independent Period Returns are obtained by looking at mutually exclusive windows of fixed length along each time series (asset). Each Independent Period Return represents the geometric average for a given holding period, based on your date setting's frequency and time period. For example, a five-year independent (holding) period calculates the annual geometric average return over every five-year period available in your Analyzer case file (.fld). If the beginning date is 1926, the first five-year annual independent period would be 1926 to 1930. Subsequently, the next five-year independent period would be 1926 to 1930. Subsequently, the next five-year independent period would be 1931 to 1935, then 1936 to 1940, an so on.

Statistics Menu Functions

You can perform the following common statistics functions from the options, or windows, accessible from the **Statistics** menu:

File allows you to print out the current window, adjust t he page setup, export to ASCII or another file format, and exit the open window.

Edit allows you to copy the data in the current window.

View enables you to choose the format in which you wish to view the data (i.e., decimal or percent) and to choose format settings such as column width and decimal places.

Help opens Analyzer help, help on the current window, and the help index.

Select Menu

Series

This menu option opens the Select Series window, which allows you to choose the data series to analyze as well as to create portfolios, exchange rates, and combined series.

- **Select Series Window**

  The **Available Series** list box displays the databases and modules available to you. To open a database, double-click the folder. You will see the modules the database contains. When you open a module, the bottom **Available Series** list box displays the names of the series in t he module, along with information on the series' frequency; and dates of availability.

- **Raw Data vs. Derived Data**

  The top **Available Series** list box contains three categories: **Raw Data, Derived Data, and Case Files**. **Raw Data** includes the Ibbotson Database and User Defined Database. **Derived Data** contains previously save portfolios, exchange rates, and combined series. **Case Files** displays the case files previously saved within the Ibbotson software and the series contained within those case files.

- **Selecting/Removing Data Series**

  To select an asset, highlight the series name(s) and click the **Add** button or double-click the series name. Click **Add All** to select all the series in a module. The series you selected now appear in the **Selected Series** list box. You can include up to 250 data series in an Analyzer case. To remove data series from the **Selected Series** list box, highlight the series name(s) and click the **Remove** or **Remove All** button.

- **Sorting Series**

  You can sort the data series listed in the **Available Series** and **Selected Series** list boxes by clicking on the column headings.

Date Settings

The date settings must be set for each new Analyzer case file (.fld). The Date Settings window allows you to specify the data frequency, beginning and ending dates, and the index variables used to create index values and the index (wealth) graph. You can analyze data on a monthly, quarterly, semi-annual, or annual basis, and on a calendar or non-calendar basis.

Create Inputs

The Create Inputs menu command links the Analyzer and Optimizer prog5rams. From this link, you can create an inputs file and move on to the Optimizer. The Analyzer creates a historical inputs file with all the data series selected in your Analyzer case file (.fld). An inputs file holds the summary statistics (expected return, standard deviation, correlation) needed to perform an optimization case. These statistics are based on the frequency and time period selected in the date settings. The expected return is calculated based on the summary statistics' arithmetic and geometric mean. See the "Inputs Generator" section of this manual for details on generating and modifying inputs.

Windows Menu

Cascade layers open windows on top of one another from left to right, with only one window fully visible.

Tile keeps a part of all windows visible, showing them from top to bottom on your screen.

Help Menu

Analyzer Help shows you a list of general topics specific to the Analyzer software. You can click the highlighted words, pop-ups, or jumps to navigate through the online help. Jumps lead you to another related section, while pop-ups provide definitions.

Help on Current Window jumps to the Help section containing information about the open tab. This help feature eliminates the need to search through the online help to solve a problem.

Search for Help on . . . sends you to the contents section of the Help file. From here you can browse through the table of contents or click on the Index tab to search for topics by keyword. In the Index section, you can type in the word you are looking for, or you can scroll to search for the list of keywords for the topic you want.

Data Help provides the methodology for all the data series Ibbotson Associates provides in your package. This feature is only available within the Ibbotson Database.

How to use Help provides information on using the Analyzer online help feature.

About Analyzer provides information about the specific Ibbotson software application you are using. There is also a support telephone number and address provided that allows the Company to respond to your issues and questions.

Selecting a Series

From the Select Series window you can choose data series or create portfolios for historical analysis. You can also perform many functions to manipulate series as well as look up the data methodology behind those series.

To access the Select Series window:

1. Click **File, New Folder** from the Main Folder Window to start a new case and select your series.
2. Click **Select, Series** from the Main Folder Window if you want to access the data series from within a case already opened.

You will see three options in the **Available Series** list box: Raw Data, Derived Data, and Case Files.

- **Raw Data** contains series distributed by Ibbotson Associates and any user-defined series you have generated or imported into the software.
- **Derived Data** contains previously save Portfolios, Exchange Rates, and Combined Series
- **Case Files** contains series in previously saved case files from the EnCorr **Case Files** directory

To select a data series:

1. Double-click the desired database from the top of the **Available Series** list box.
2. Choose the appropriate data module (e.g. **Stocks, Bonds, Bills, and Inflation**). A list of the available series appears in the bottom **Available Series** list box (Figure 1.11).

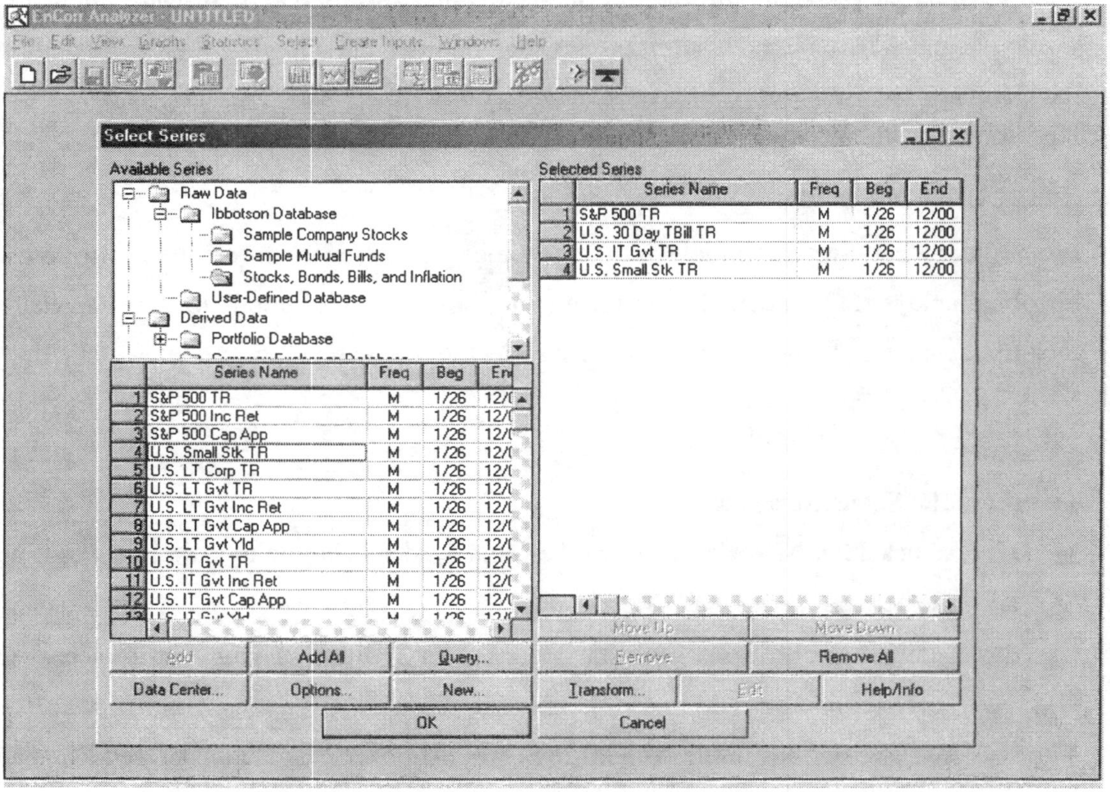

Figure 1.11 Selecting a Data Series

3. Double-click each series you wish to view, or highlight the series and click the **Add** button. The series you select appear in the **Selected Series** list box.

Data Help

Ibbotson Associates provides a helpful tool when it comes to discerning the different attributes between data series in the Data Help database. To access this database from the Select Series window, highlight a series in the **Available** or **Selected Series** list box and then click the **Help/Info** button, or click your right mouse button over a series and select **Series Information** (**Figure 1.12**)

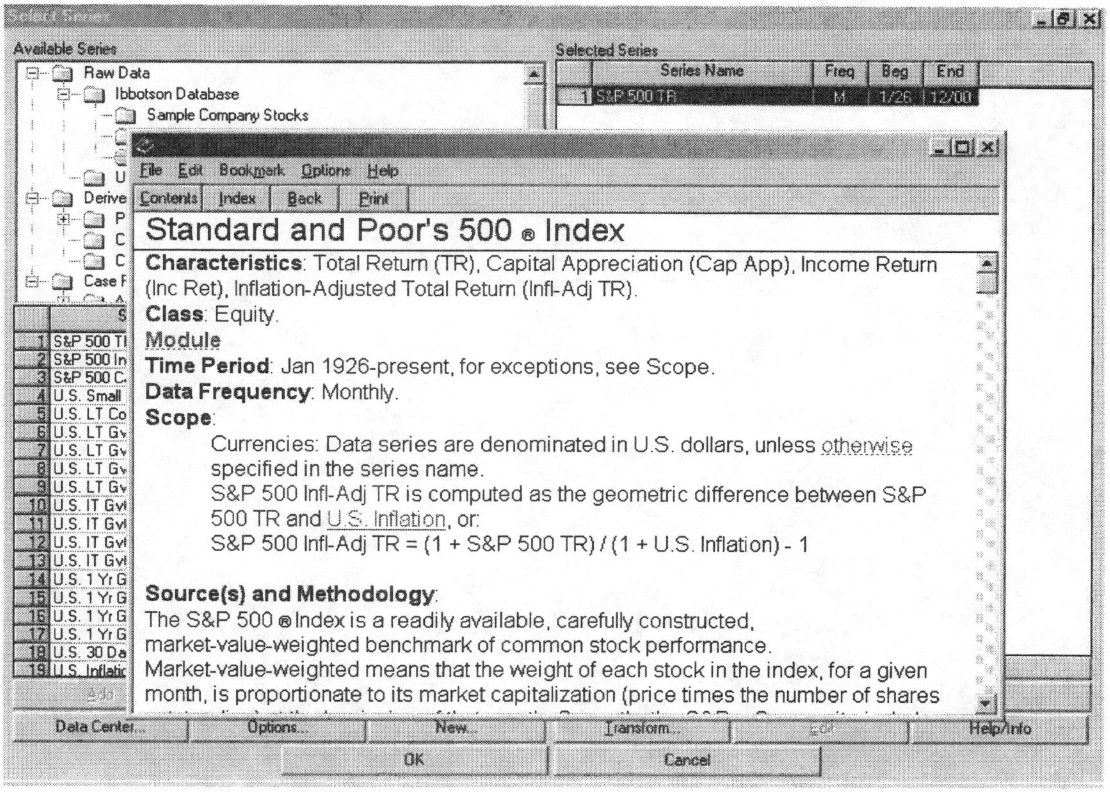

Figure 1.12 Using the Data Help Database

Date Settings

To access the date settings, click **Select, Date Settings** from the Main Folder Window. When you create a new case, the Date Settings window opens automatically when you click **OK** in the Select Series window, allowing you to set the date for the first time.

Date settings must be made for each new Analyzer case. The Date Settings dialog box (Figure 1.13) allows you to specify the data frequency, the beginning and ending dates, and the index variables (used to create index values and the Index [wealth] Graph).

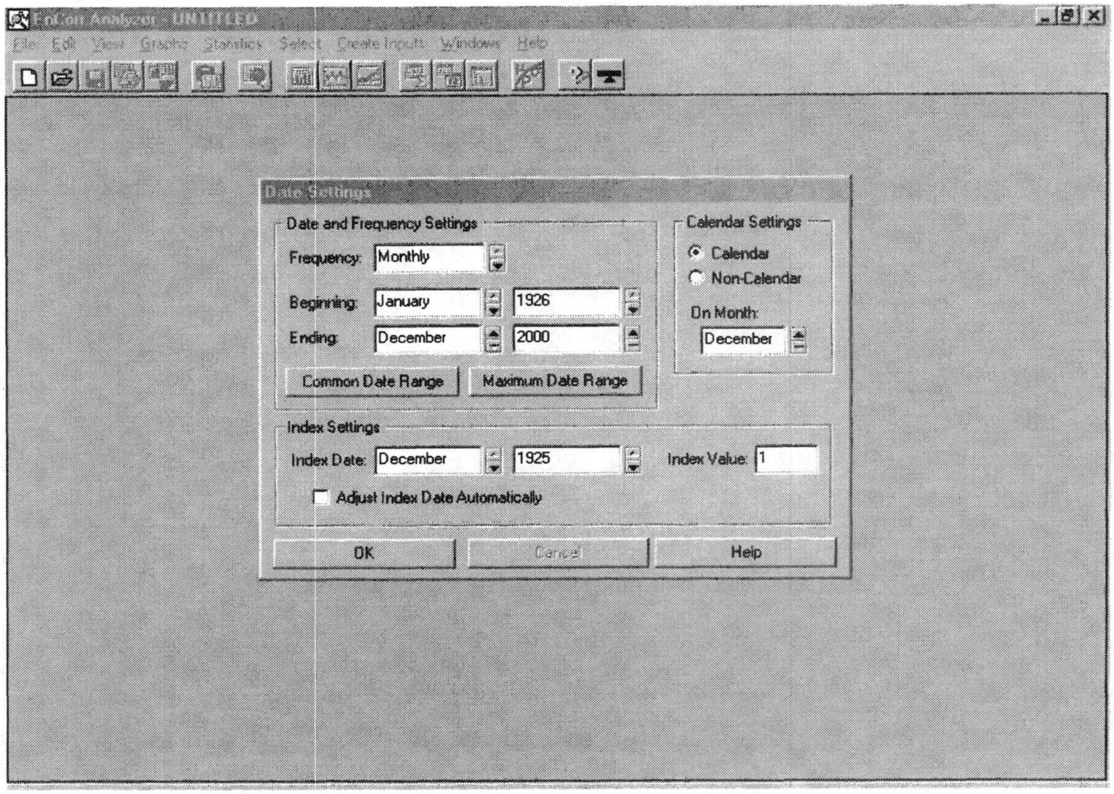

Figure 1.13 Setting Date for an Analyzer Case

Check **Adjust Index Date Automatically** to have the Index Date always set to one period before the beginning date. The Index Date is the first date from which an index or wealth value is created. To see the Growth of $1.00, enter 1 into the **Index Value** text box.

By default, annual dates represent the time period between January and December. If you want to define the annual time period as July and June, for example, you can use the **Calendar Settings** to specify the new setting. By clicking the **Common Date Range** button, you can set your analysis to look only at the dates on which all series selected have data. Choose **Maximum Date Range** to analyze data ranging from the earliest date available to the most current date for which your selected series have data.

Right-click the field you wish to change and select a setting from the list that appears. Or click the up and down arrows to move the settings one increment at a time. Click **OK** to view the data based on the date settings you selected.

Creating A Combined Series

Combined Series allows you to create a new series based on simple mathematical operations between two data series such as addition, subtraction, multiplication, division, geometric addition, and geometric subtraction. For example, you can quickly build historical risk premia or inflation-adjust with you inflation index.

Building a Combined Series

To create a combined series:

1. Open the Select Series window by clicking **Select, Series** from the Main Folder Window menu bar.
2. Click the **New** button and select **Combined Series** to display the Build/Edit Combined Series dialog box (Figure 1.14).
3. Select the first series in the **Selected Series** box.
4. Choose an Operator by clicking the down arrow to the **Operator** box.
5. Select the second series by clicking the down arrow in the **Series** box.
6. Enter a name for the Combined Series (up to 40 characters) in the **Name** box.
7. Choose the Type for the new series by clicking the down arrow in the **Type** box. Click **OK.**

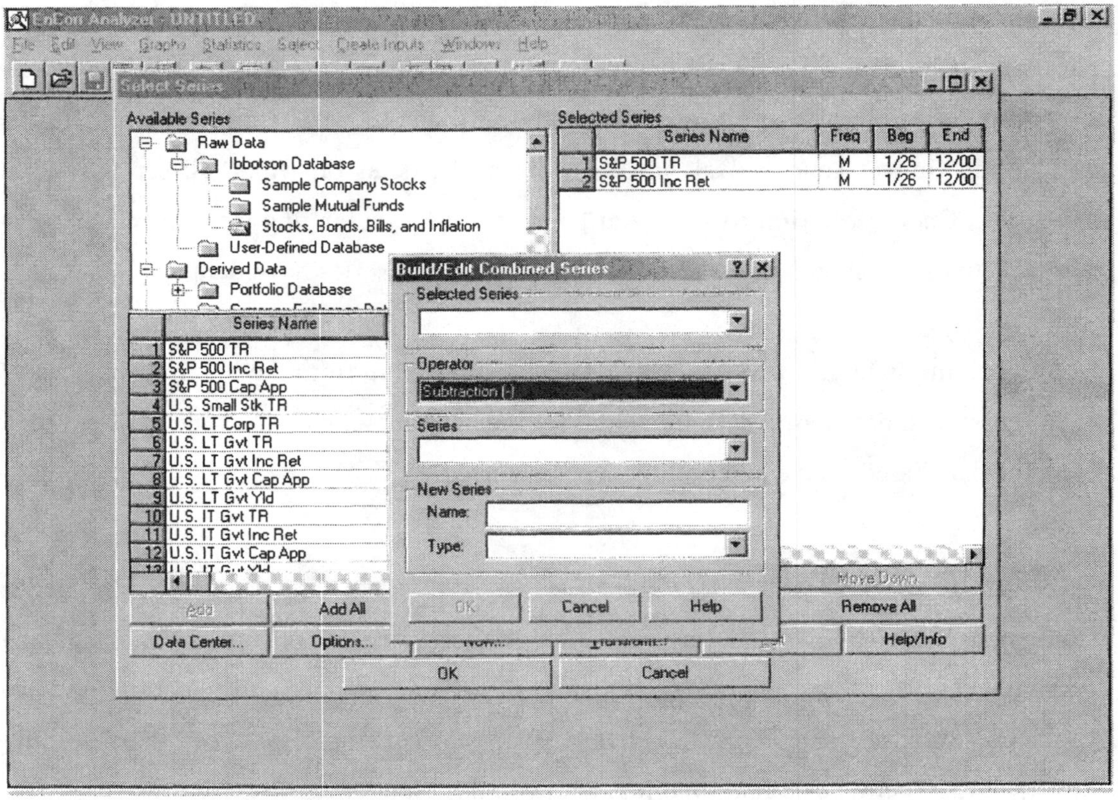

EnCorr Analyzer - UNTITLED
File Edit View Graphs Statistics Select Create Inputs Window Help

Select Series

Available Series
Raw Data
Ibbotson Database
Sample Company Stocks
Sample Mutual Funds
Stocks, Bonds, Bills, and Inflation
User-Defined Database
Derived Data
Portfolio Database

	Series Name
1	S&P 500 TR
2	S&P 500 Inc Ret
3	S&P 500 Cap App
4	U.S. Small Stk TR
5	U.S. LT Corp TR
6	U.S. LT Gvt TR
7	U.S. LT Gvt Inc Ret
8	U.S. LT Gvt Cap App
9	U.S. LT Gvt Yld
10	U.S. IT Gvt TR
11	U.S. IT Gvt Inc Ret
12	U.S. IT Gvt Cap App

Selected Series

	Series Name	Freq	Beg	End
1	S&P 500 TR	M	1/26	12/00
2	S&P 500 Inc Ret	M	1/26	12/00

Build/Edit Combined Series
Selected Series
Operator
Subtraction (-)
Series
New Series
Name:
Type:
OK Cancel Help

Add Add All Move Down Remove All
Data Center... Options... Help/Info
OK Cancel

Figure 1.14 Building a Combined Series

Editing an Existing Combined Series

To edit a combined series:

1. Open the Select Series window by clicking **Select, Series** from the Main Folder Window menu bar.
2. Highlight the Combined Series to be edited in the Selected Series window.
3. Click the **Edit Combined Series** button to access the Build/Edit Combined Series window (Figure 1.14).
4. Edit the appropriate cells and click **OK**.

Creating an Inputs File for Optimization

The **Create Inputs** menu command in the Main Folder Window links the EnCorr Analyzer and EnCorr Optimizer programs. The EnCorr Analyzer creates a historical inputs file with all the data series selected in your case.

An inputs file holds the summary statistics (expected return, standard deviation, correlation) needed to perform an optimization case. These statistics are based on the frequency and time period selected in t he Date Settings window. The expected return is calculated based on t he summary statistic's arithmetic mean or geometric mean.

From the Main Folder Window, click the **Create Inputs** menu command to open the EnCorr Input Generator. From the Inputs Generator, click **File, Save As** and save the file with an .inp extension (Figure 1.15).

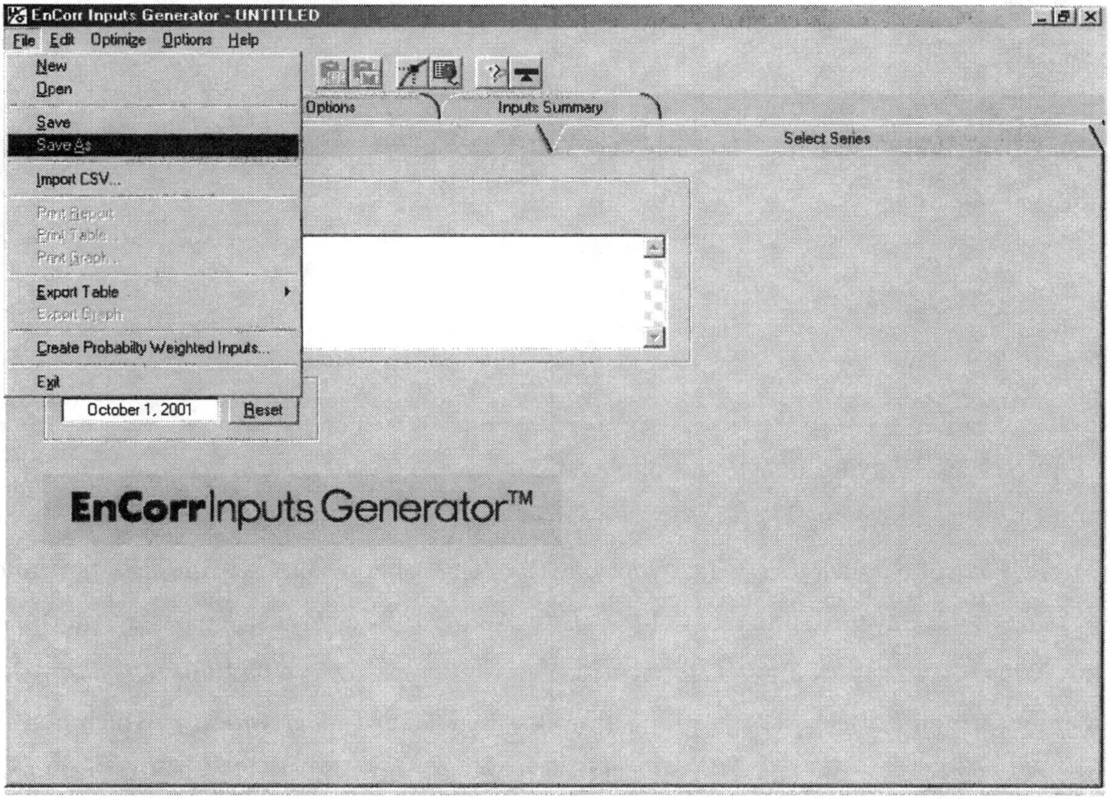

Figure 1.15 Saving an Inputs File

Main Folder Window

Edit Menu

The **Edit** menu allows you to copy the data series in the Main Folder Window to the clipboard. From the clipboard, the data can be pasted into other applications such as Microsoft Excel. Click **Edit, Copy** to copy the data to the Clipboard (**Figure 1.16**, below).

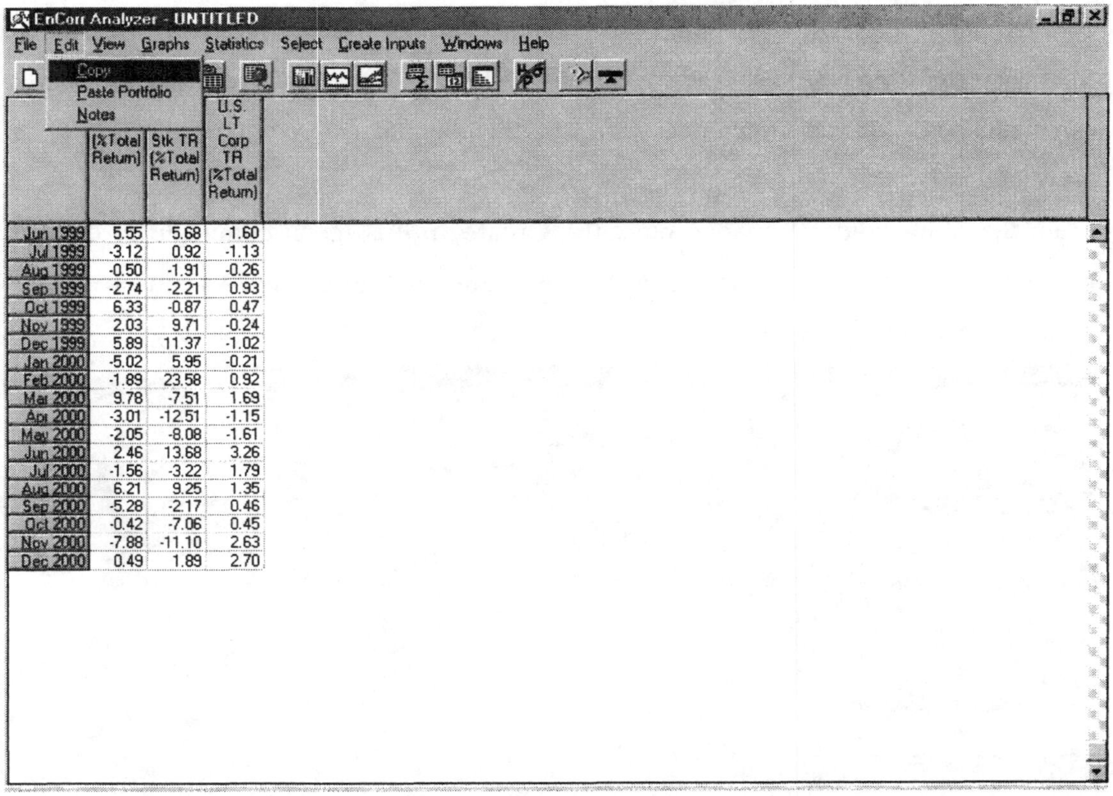

EnCorr Analyzer - UNTITLED
File Edit View Graphs Statistics Select Create Inputs Windows Help
Copy
Paste Portfolio
Notes
(%Total Return)
Stk TR (%Total Return)
U.S. LT Corp TR (%Total Return)
Jun 1999 5.55 5.68 -1.60
Jul 1999 -3.12 0.92 -1.13
Aug 1999 -0.50 -1.91 -0.26
Sep 1999 -2.74 -2.21 0.93
Oct 1999 6.33 -0.87 0.47
Nov 1999 2.03 9.71 -0.24
Dec 1999 5.89 11.37 -1.02
Jan 2000 -5.02 5.95 -0.21
Feb 2000 -1.89 23.58 0.92
Mar 2000 9.78 -7.51 1.69
Apr 2000 -3.01 -12.51 -1.15
May 2000 -2.05 -8.08 -1.61
Jun 2000 2.46 13.68 3.26
Jul 2000 -1.56 -3.22 1.79
Aug 2000 6.21 9.25 1.35
Sep 2000 -5.28 -2.17 0.46
Oct 2000 -0.42 -7.06 0.45
Nov 2000 -7.88 -11.10 2.63
Dec 2000 0.49 1.89 2.70

Figure 1.16 Copying Data to the Clipboard

Paste Portfolio is another **Edit** menu option. This option allows to paste a portfolio created in the EnCorr Optimizer to the EnCorr Analyzer for analysis. To paste a portfolio to Analyzer you must first have created a portfolio in EnCorr Optimizer. From the Optimizer you can copy the portfolio from the Efficient Frontier window, which places the portfolio on the clipboard. You can then move to Analyzer and click **Edit, Paste** and view the portfolio in Analyzer. See the "EnCorr Optimizer" section in this manual for instructions on manipulating portfolios within Optimizer.

The **Notes** option allows you to enter notes for your current Analyzer case file (.fld)

Statistics Menu

All the analytical tools in the EnCorr Analyzer can be found on the Statistics menu in the Main Folder Window (Figure 1.17). Eight options on the **Statistics** menu provide for a variety of statistical analyses.

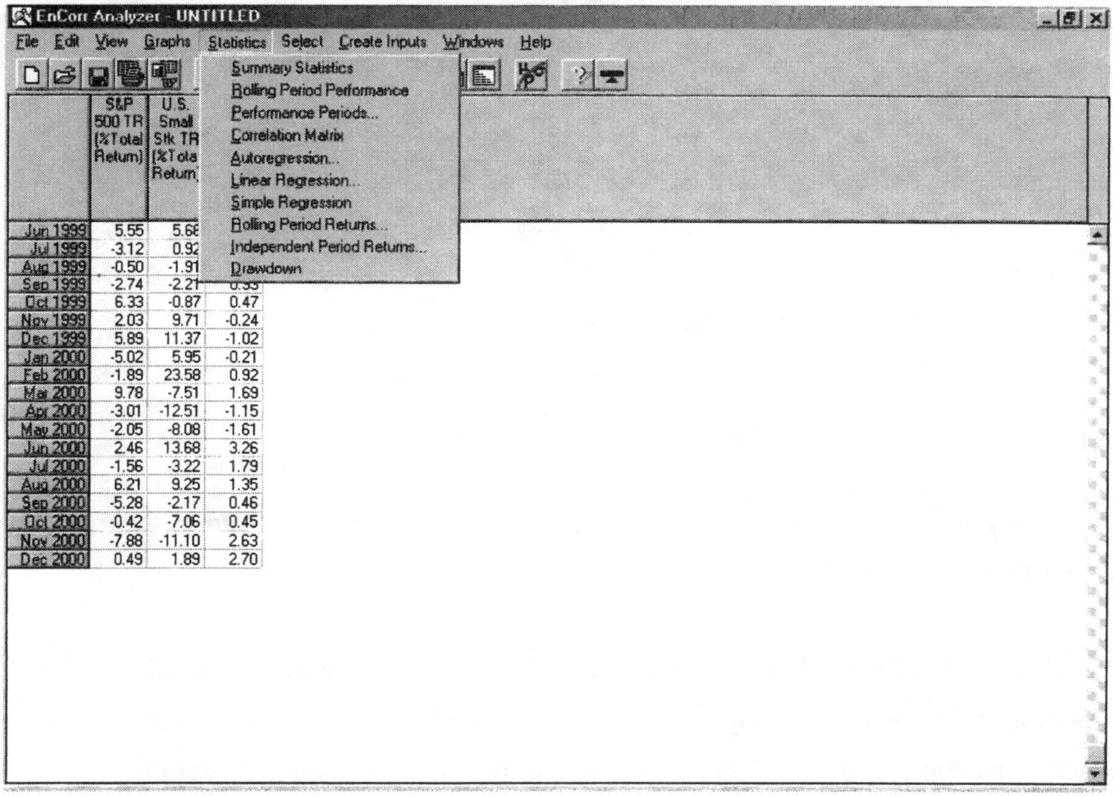

Figure 1.17 The Statistics Menu

Summary Statistics Table

The first option on the **Statistics** menu is **Summary Statistics**. The Summary Statistics table (Figure 1.18, below) displays numerous historical summary statistics for all selected series in your current EnCorr Analyzer case (.fld)

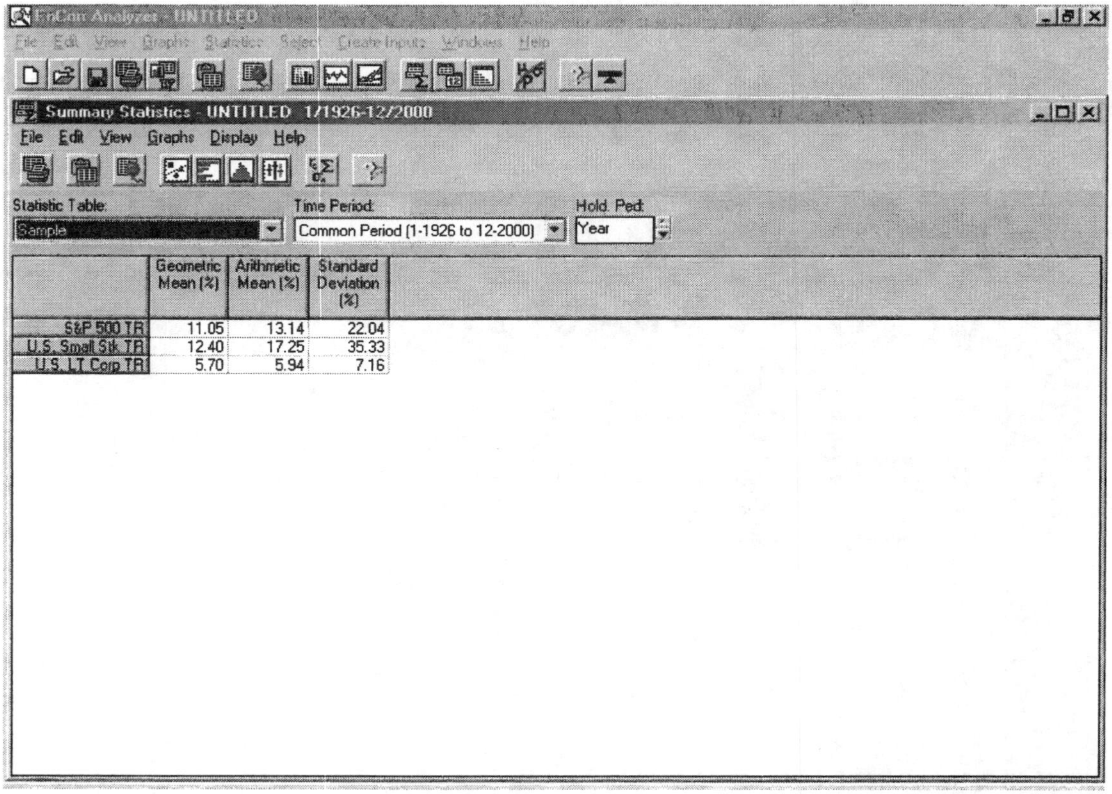
Summary Statistics - UNTITLED 1/1926-12/2000
File Edit View Graphs Display Help
Statistic Table:
Sample
Time Period:
Common Period (1-1926 to 12-2000)
Hold. Ped:
Year
Geometric Mean (%)
Arithmetic Mean (%)
Standard Deviation (%)
S&P 500 TR 11.05 13.14 22.04
U.S. Small Stk TR 12.40 17.25 35.33
U.S. LT Corp TR 5.70 5.94 7.16

Figure 1.18 Summary Statistics Table

Statistics are calculated based on the frequency and time period specified in the Date Settings window. Click **Display** to show additional statistics in the table and Graphs to graph statistics in three different forms: scatter plot, bar plot, and histogram.

Summary Statistics Display Options

To change the information displayed in the Summary Statistics table, click the **Display** menu command (Figure 1.19, below). Select or remove various statistics by checking the box next to their names. For Risk-Adjusted Return statistics, click **Define** to choose a risk-free rate and market series (necessary for calculating these ratios). See "Analyzer Formulas" in the online help for details on statistics and their calculations.

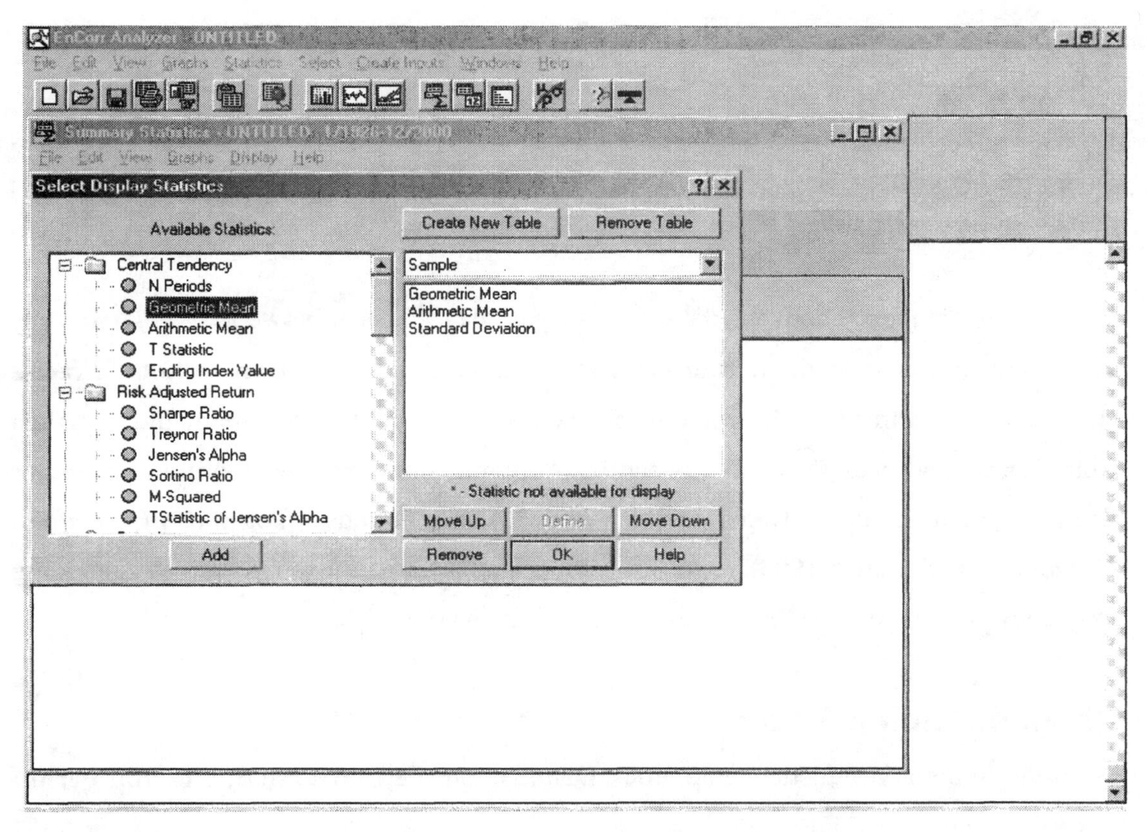

Figure 1.19 Select Display Statistics

Holding Period Frequency Conversion

By default, summary statistics are calculated using the data frequency specified in the Date Settings frequency field. In the Display window, you can change the summary statistics and the holding period to another frequency. A holding period frequency conversion does not change the frequency of data. Instead, it approximates the calculated statistics over a longer time period. Refer to "Analyzer Formulas" in the online help for the conversion formulas.

For example, let's say your folder has date settings set to monthly and a time period set from January 1980 to December 1989. As a result, the Summary Statistics table will calculated monthly statistics over 120 periods. You can now change the holding period to quarter, half year, and year. In this case, choose year. The converted summary statistics now compute year summary statistics based on the monthly data frequency. The data frequency has not changed, which can be confirmed by the N Period column still displaying 120.

Note: You should only select a holding period that is greater than or equal to your data frequency (as specified in the Date Settings dialog box). Converting annual data to a monthly holding period does not make sense statistically.

When you frequency-convert data series, you can choose between two frequency conversion formulas in the **Mean/Std. Dev. Conversion Convention** section: **Precise** (Default) and **Estimate.** The equation for converting using the Precise method is taken from Haim Levy and Deborah Gunthorpe, "optimal Investment Proportions in Senior Securities and Equities Under Alternative Holding Periods," *Journal of Portfolio Management*, Summer 1993, page 33. For more information on formulas, including frequency-conversion, see "Analyzer Formulas" in the online help.

Change Holding Period

From the Summary Statistics table, click **Display.** In the **Conversion, Holding Period** box, select the desired holding period.

Summary Statistics Graphs

From the summary statistics window, you can generate a risk vs. return scatter plot and bar plot, in addition to a histogram.

Scatter Plot

The Risk vs. Return scatter plot graphs assets or selected series based on the risk and return characteristics of their returns.(**Figure 1.20**, below) Risk is measured as the standard deviation of the returns, and return is either the arithmetic or geometric mean return.

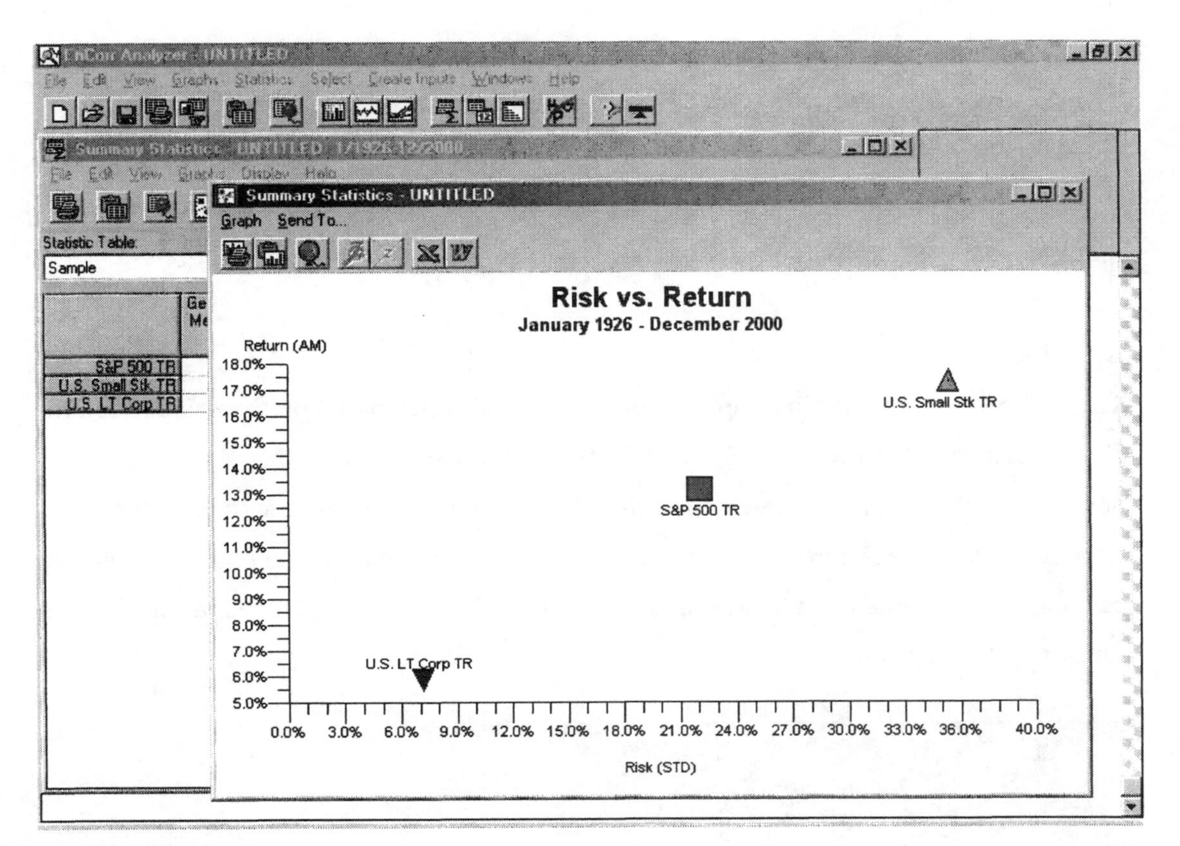

Figure 1.20 Scatter Plot

Available Options

Capital Market Line (CML)

You can draw the capital market line on the summary statistics scatter plot. The capital market line connects a market series and a risk-free series. By default, the S&P 500 TR and U.S. 30-day T Bill are used. In the Scatter plot window, click **Graph, Display Options** to choose whether to show the line and which two benchmarks to use. In the Scatter Graph Options dialog box, a check mark in the **Capital Market Line** check box indicates that the line will be plotted. To change the series that comprise the line, click the "..." button beside the **Capital Market Line** field, and use the **Select** buttons to reach the Select Series window, where you can choose the desired series.

Median Crosshairs

Median crosshairs are the two dotted lines that cross at the median asset in our folder. This indicates whether the selected asset's risk and return characteristics are above or below the median asset in your folder. Choose whether or not to show the lines by clicking **Graph, Display Options**. A check mark in the **Median Crosshairs** check box indicates that the lines will be plotted.

Bar Plot

The Risk vs. Return bar plot graphs assets or selected series based on the risk and return characteristics of their returns (Figure 1.21 below). Risk is measured as the standard deviation of the returns, and return is either the arithmetic or geometric mean return. Choose to calculate returns based on the arithmetic or geometric mean return. Choose to calculate returns based on the arithmetic or geometric mean by clicking **Graphs, Display Options, Display** tab.

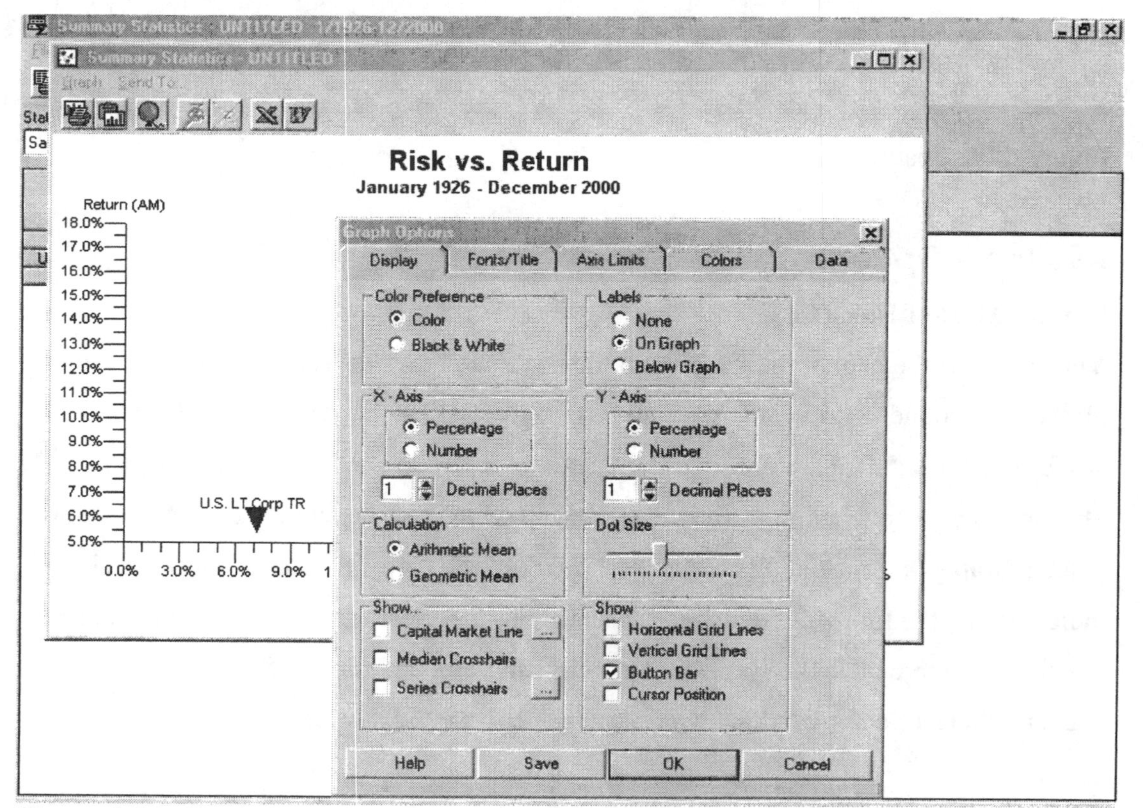

Figure 1.21 Graph, Display Options

Histogram

The histogram displays the range of returns for an index over time, where returns are grouped into bins (**Figure 1.22**, below). This graph shows the dispersion of returns and can display how many standard deviations away from the mean returns are. Click **Graph, Display Options** to show the standard deviations, normal or lognormal curve, and other display options.

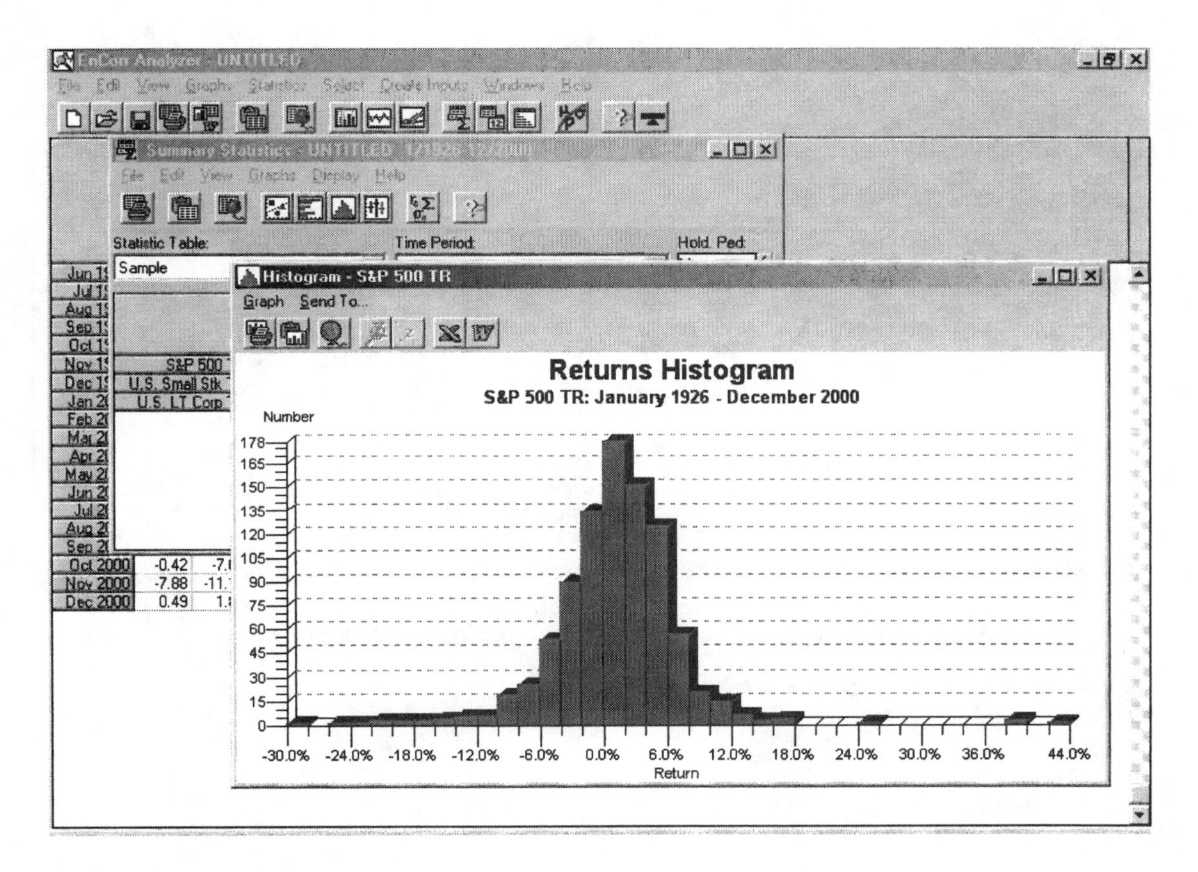

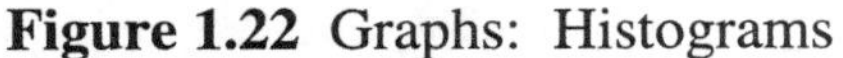

Figure 1.22 Graphs: Histograms

Rolling Period Performance

Click back to the Untitled window and the **Rolling Period Performance** option on the **Statistics** menu allows you to view, based on rolling periods, how often a series performed better or worse than a given percentage. You can also analyze the best and worst period over the time horizon (**Figure 1.23**, below).

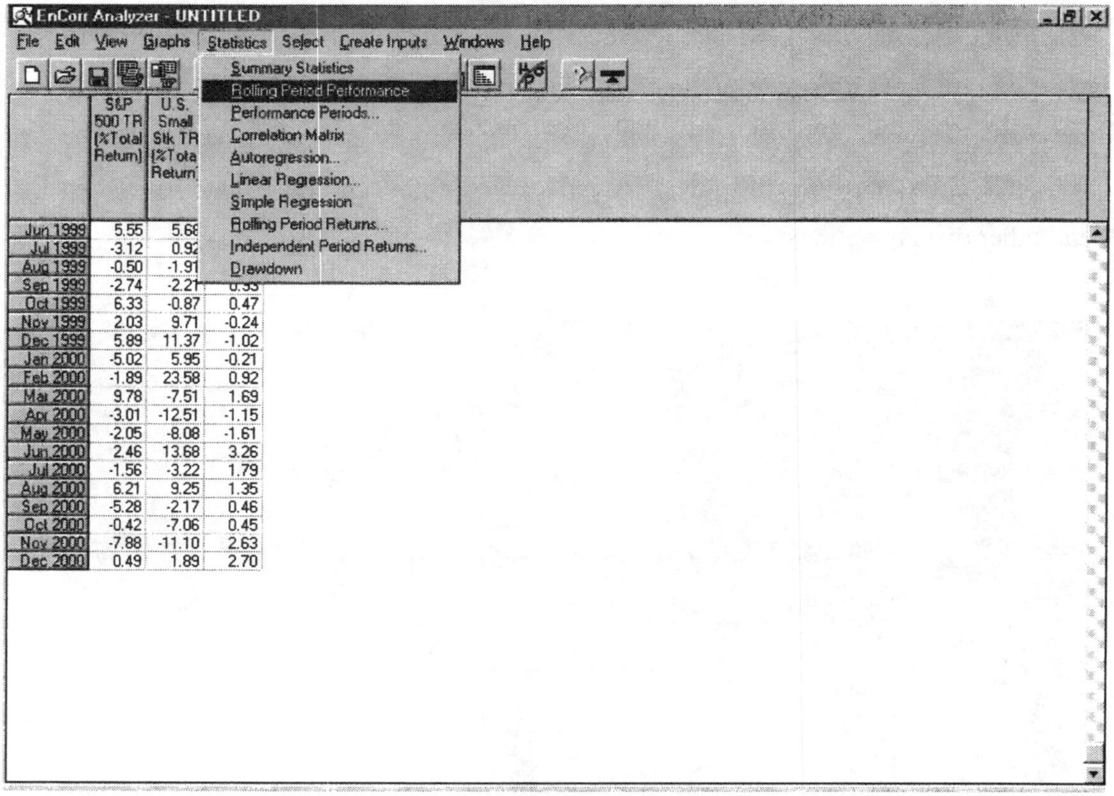

EnCorr Analyzer - UNTITLED

File Edit View Graphs Statistics Select Create Inputs Windows Help

Summary Statistics
Rolling Period Performance
Performance Periods...
Correlation Matrix
Autoregression...
Linear Regression...
Simple Regression
Rolling Period Returns...
Independent Period Returns...
Drawdown

	S&P 500 TR (%Total Return)	U.S. Small Stk TR (%Total Return)	
Jun 1999	5.55	5.68	
Jul 1999	-3.12	0.92	
Aug 1999	-0.50	-1.91	
Sep 1999	-2.74	-2.21	
Oct 1999	6.33	-0.87	0.47
Nov 1999	2.03	9.71	-0.24
Dec 1999	5.89	11.37	-1.02
Jan 2000	-5.02	5.95	-0.21
Feb 2000	-1.89	23.58	0.92
Mar 2000	9.78	-7.51	1.69
Apr 2000	-3.01	-12.51	-1.15
May 2000	-2.05	-8.08	-1.61
Jun 2000	2.46	13.68	3.26
Jul 2000	-1.56	-3.22	1.79
Aug 2000	6.21	9.25	1.35
Sep 2000	-5.28	-2.17	0.46
Oct 2000	-0.42	-7.06	0.45
Nov 2000	-7.88	-11.10	2.63
Dec 2000	0.49	1.89	2.70

Figure 1.23 Rolling Period Performance

Display allows you to change rolling performance periods. Click **Add** to create a new performance value (**Figure 1.24**, below).

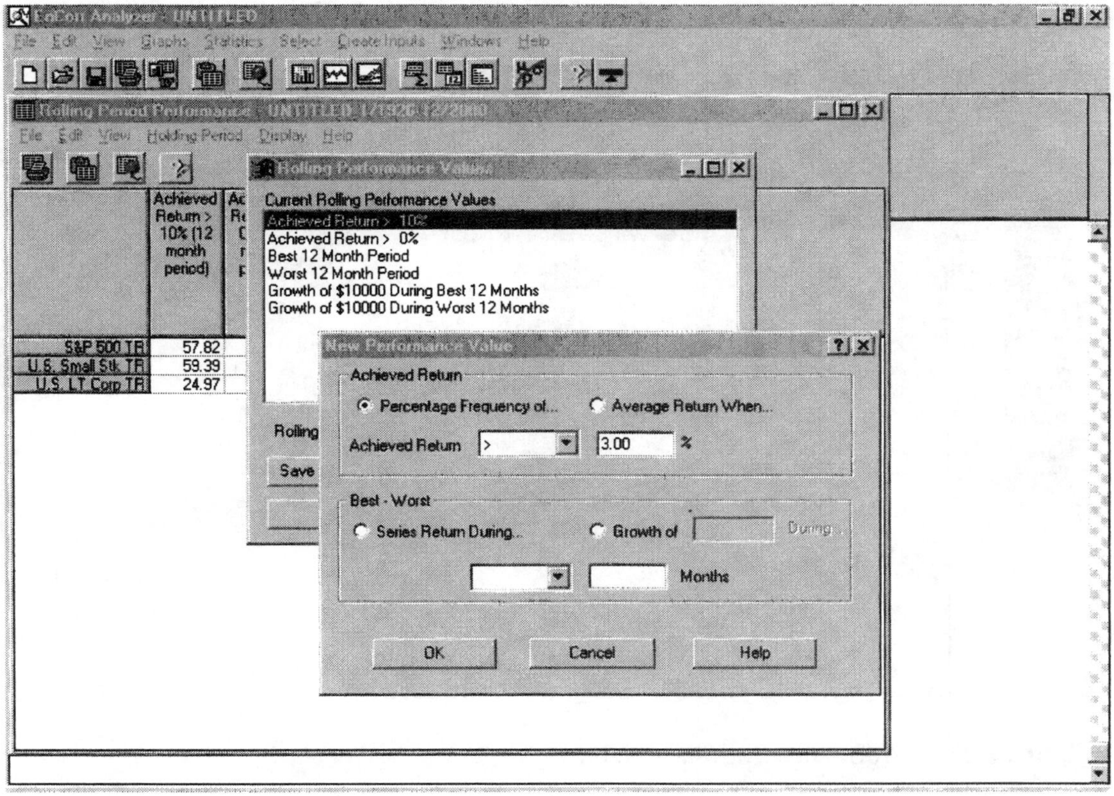

Figure 1.24 Changing Rolling Performance Periods

Performance Periods

The **Performance Periods** option on the **Statistics** menu allows you to view historical returns over multiple time periods and multiple frequencies. In the Performance Summary table (**Figure 1.25**, below), historical returns are calculated as geometric averages and cumulative total returns.

As of Dec 2000:	Last 3 Months (period) Return	Last 1 Year (annual) Return	Last 3 Years (annual) Return	Last 5 Years (annual) Return	Y-T-D (annual) Return
S&P 500 TR	-7.83	-9.11	12.26	18.35	-9.11
U.S. Small Stk TR	-15.81	-3.59	5.07	10.87	-3.59
U.S. LT Corp TR	5.87	12.87	4.98	5.79	12.87

Figure 1.25 Performance Summary Table

View allows you to view either the Return, the Standard Deviation, or both for the given period.

Graph allows you to pull up a Performance Graph (**Figure 1.26**). From here you can go to **Graph Options** and change colors, fonts, labels and more (Figure 1.27).

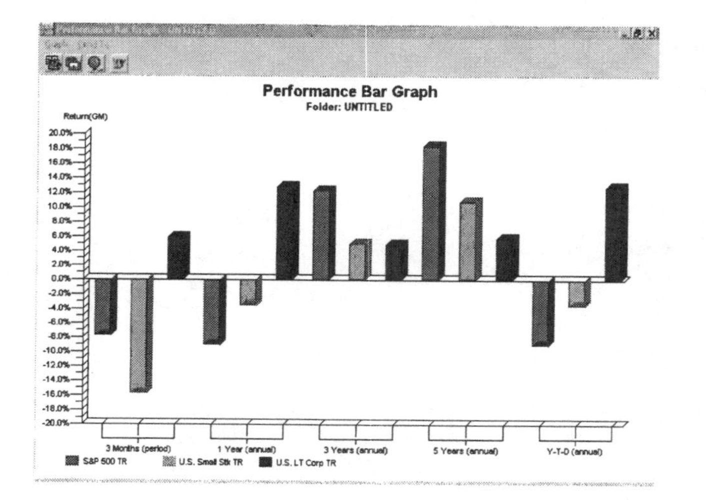

Figure 1.26 Performance Graph

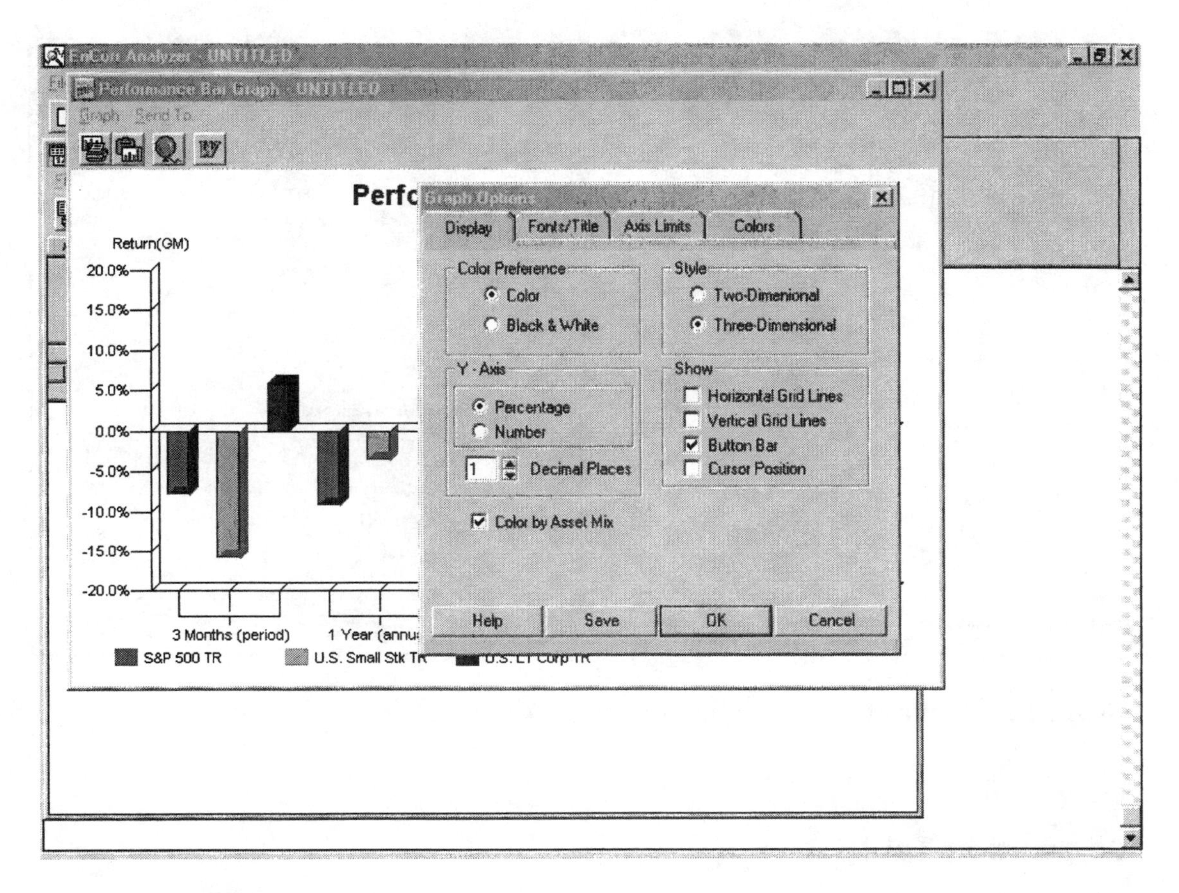

Figure 1.27 Graph Options

From the **Periods** menu, you can access the Performance Periods window (**Figure 1.28**). This window allows the user to add, edit, and remove performance periods (**Figure 1.29**)

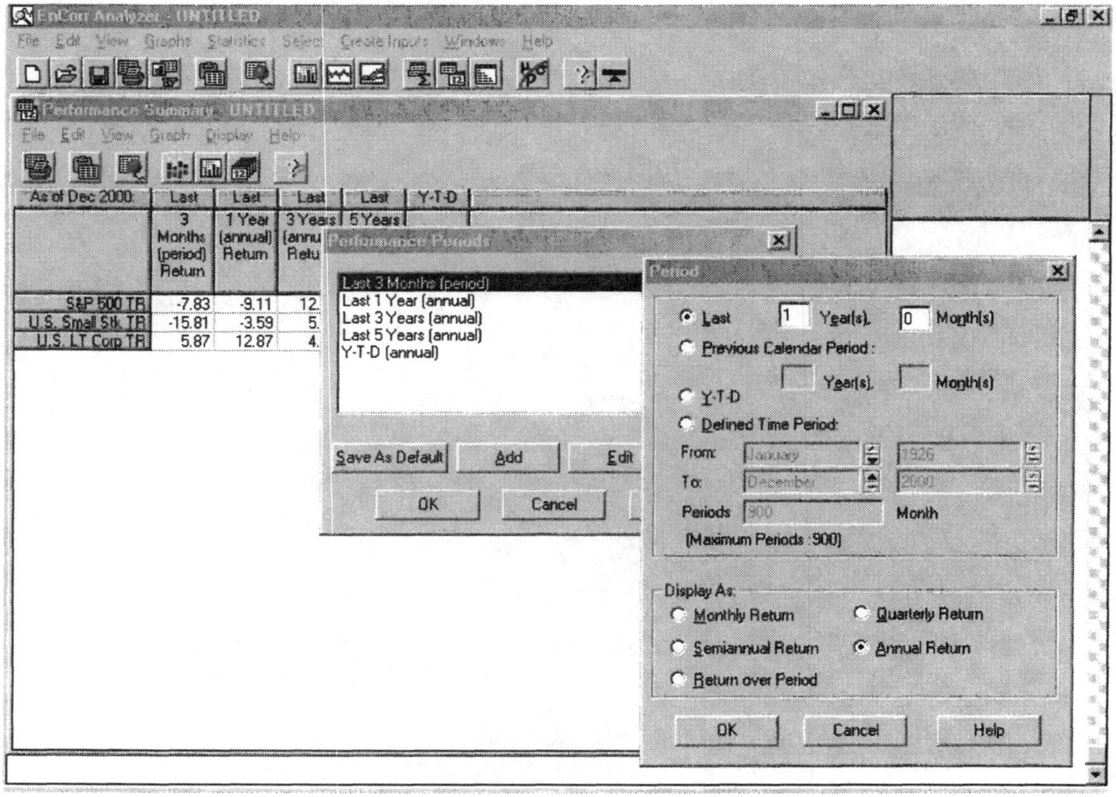

Figure 1.28/ Figure 1.29 Performance Periods/Adding a Period

Correlation Table

The **Correlation Matrix** option on the **Statistics** menu displays the degree of interaction (correlation) between every data series in your Analyzer folder (.fld). Correlations range between a value of –1 and 1. If two data series have different time periods, the correlation coefficient is calculated over the common time period, unless you select a shorter time period. For example, the correlation between the S&P 500 (January 1926-Present) and the Russell 2000 (January 1979-Present) is calculated over the time period January 1979-Present. (**Figure 1.30**)

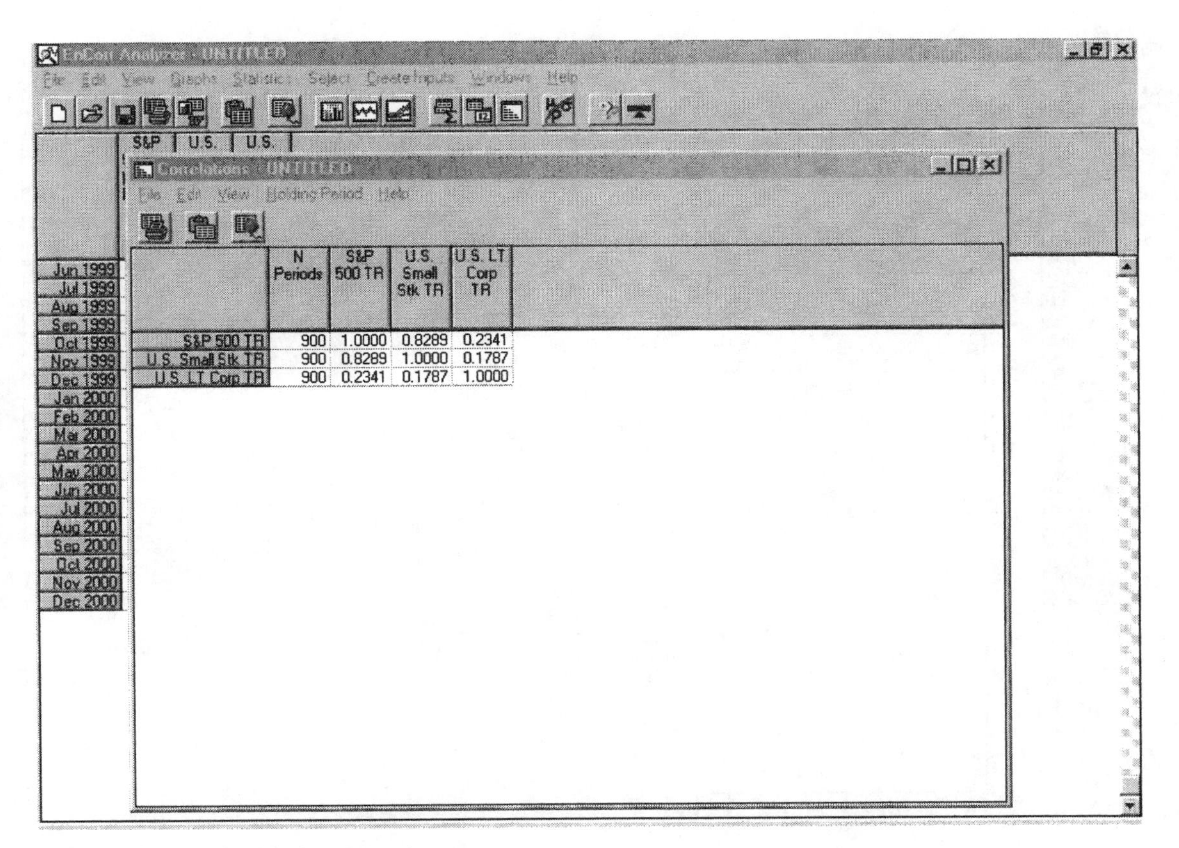

	N Periods	S&P 500 TR	U.S. Small Stk TR	U.S. LT Corp TR
S&P 500 TR	900	1.0000	0.8289	0.2341
U.S. Small Stk TR	900	0.8289	1.0000	0.1787
U.S. LT Corp TR	900	0.2341	0.1787	1.0000

Figure 1.30 Correlation Matrix

Autoregression

The **Autoregression** option on the **Statistics** menu regresses each series in your Analyzer case file against its prior period return (1 period lag). An Autoregression model measure how much serial correlation a series exhibits. (A series exhibits serial correlation if its value in one period can be used to predict its value in the following period.) The beta estimate in the Autoregression is a measure of serial correlation. The closer the absolute value of the beta estimate is to 1, the greater the degree of serial correlation.

(**Figure 1.31**)

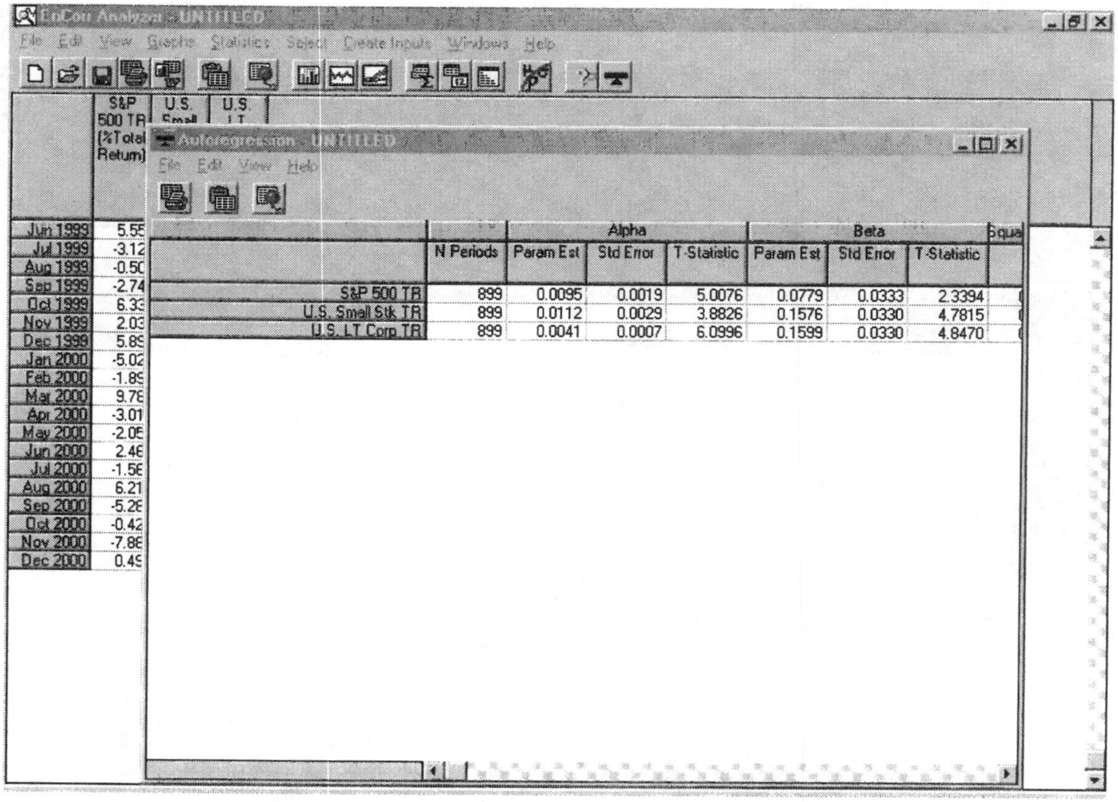

	N Periods	Alpha Param Est	Alpha Std Error	Alpha T-Statistic	Beta Param Est	Beta Std Error	Beta T-Statistic
S&P 500 TR	899	0.0095	0.0019	5.0076	0.0779	0.0333	2.3394
U.S. Small Stk TR	899	0.0112	0.0029	3.8826	0.1576	0.0330	4.7815
U.S. LT Corp TR	899	0.0041	0.0007	6.0996	0.1599	0.0330	4.8470

Figure 1.31 Autoregression

Linear Regression

The **Linear Regression** option on the **Statistics** menu allows you to calculate alphas and betas. Before you select this feature, you must select both the series you want to analyze and the benchmark you want to regress against. The alphas and betas in the linear regression are calculated based on the frequency and time period you selected in the Date Settings window.

To perform a linear regression:

1. Click **Statistics, Linear Regression** to display the Linear Regression dialog box. (**Figure 1.32**)

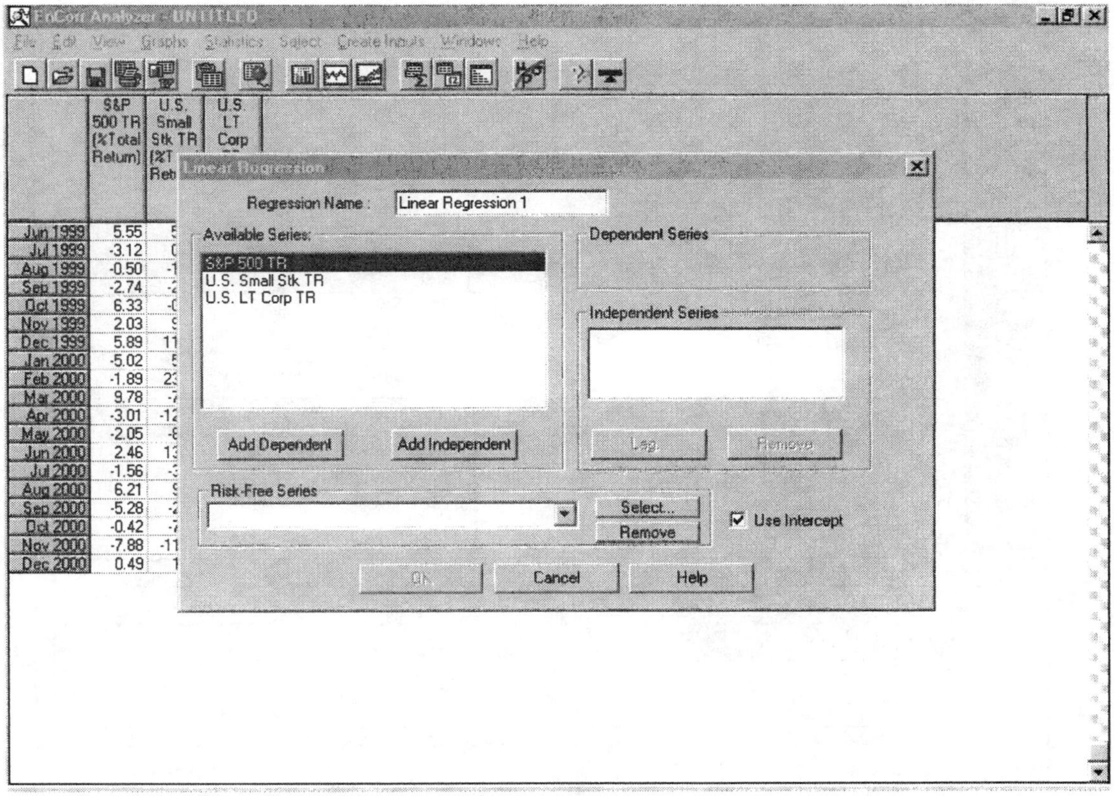

Figure 1.32 Performing a Linear Regression

2. Select the Dependent Series (data series to analyze, e.g. U.S. Small Stock TR).
3. Select the Independent Series (benchmark or series to regress against, e.g. S&P 500).
4. Click **OK** to open the Linear Regression table. (**Figure 1.33**)

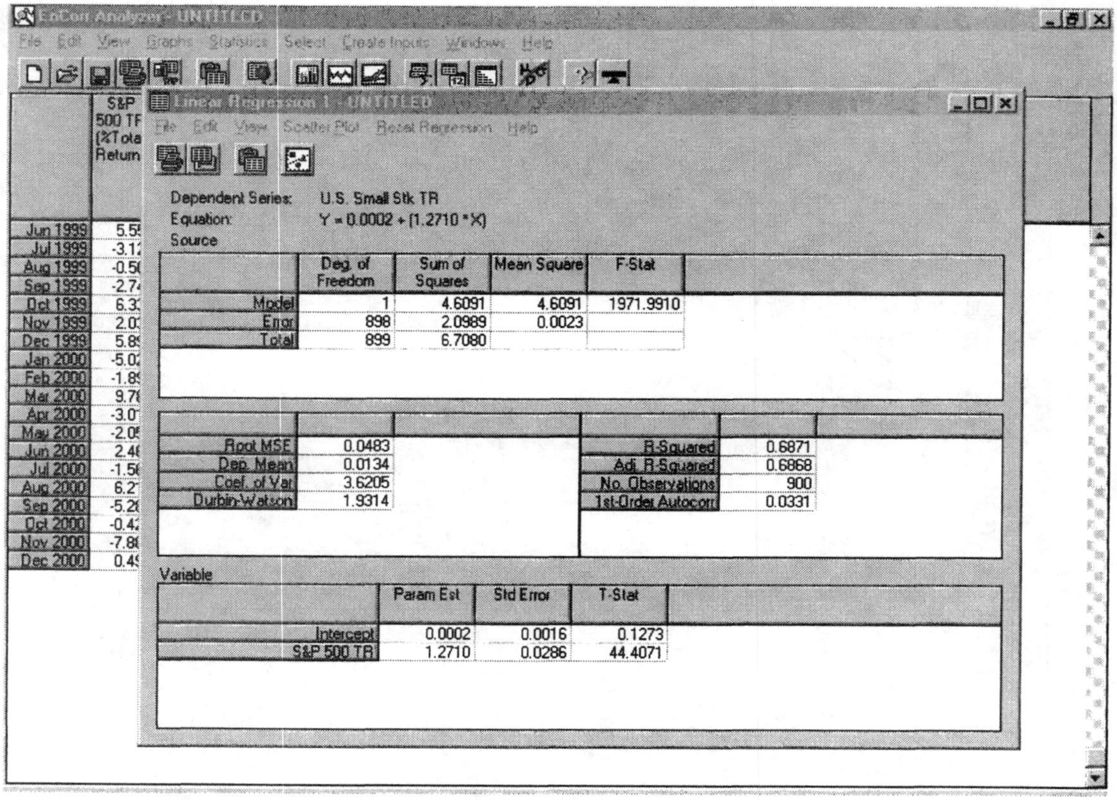

Dependent Series: U.S. Small Stk TR
Equation: Y = 0.0002 + (1.2710 * X)

Source	Deg. of Freedom	Sum of Squares	Mean Square	F-Stat
Model	1	4.6091	4.6091	1971.9910
Error	898	2.0989	0.0023	
Total	899	6.7080		

Root MSE	0.0483	R-Squared	0.6871
Dep. Mean	0.0134	Adj. R-Squared	0.6868
Coef. of Var	3.6205	No. Observations	900
Durbin-Watson	1.9314	1st-Order Autocorr	0.0331

Variable	Param Est	Std Error	T-Stat
Intercept	0.0002	0.0016	0.1273
S&P 500 TR	1.2710	0.0286	44.4071

Figure 1.33 Linear Regression Table

The top part of the window displays the regression results and various statistics to verify the validity of the regression. The bottom part displays the alpha and beta in the Parameter Estimate column, and their statistical significance in the Standard Error and T-Statistic columns. In the Parameter Estimate column, you can find the alpha in the Intercept row (.006131) and the beta in the benchmark (S&P 500) row (1.216462).

Scatter Plot

The **Scatter Plot** menu option displays the regression values in a scatter plot. In addition, the least squares regression line is drawn on the graph with the equation displayed in legend below. These options can be accessed through **Graph, Display Options.**

Rolling Period Returns

Each Rolling Period Return represents the geometric average for a given holding period, based on your Date Setting's frequency and time period. For example, a five-year rolling period calculates an annual geometric average return over every five-year holding period available in your folder. If the beginning date is 1926, the first five-year annual holding period would be 1926 to 1930. The next five-year rolling period would be 1927-1931, then 1928 to 1932, etc. (**Figure 1.34** below)

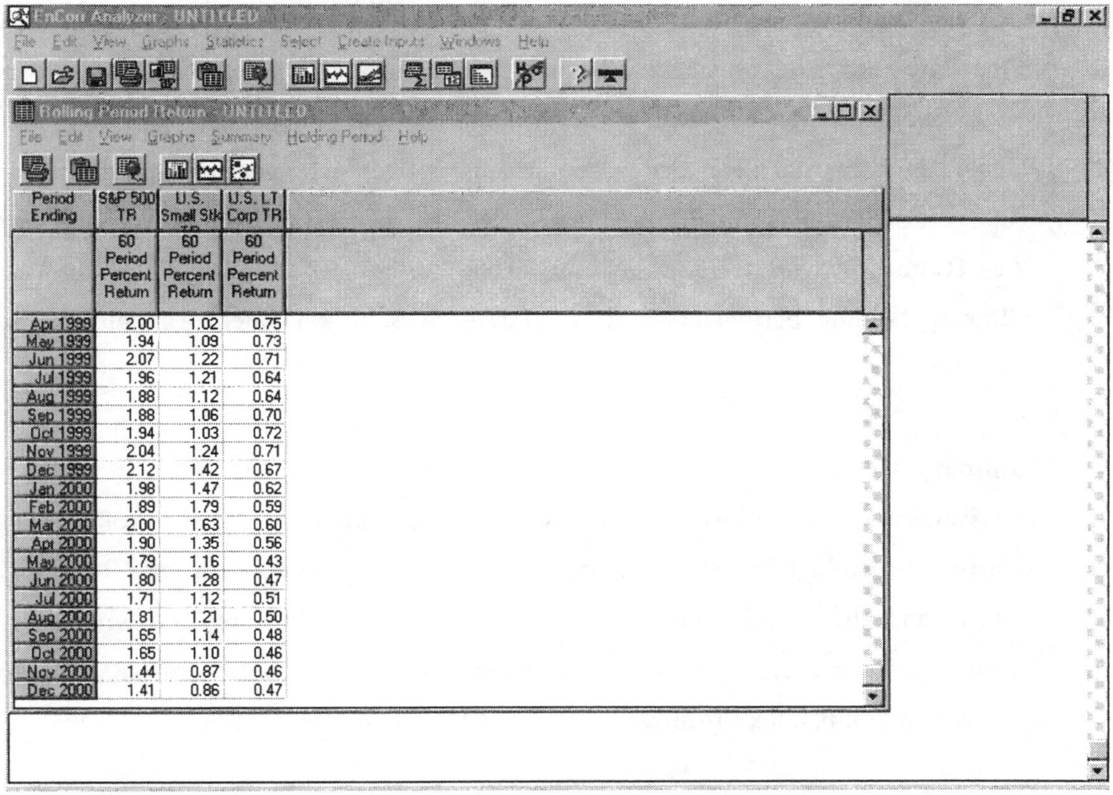

Period Ending	S&P 500 TR 60 Period Percent Return	U.S. Small Stk TR 60 Period Percent Return	U.S. LT Corp TR 60 Period Percent Return
Apr 1999	2.00	1.02	0.75
May 1999	1.94	1.09	0.73
Jun 1999	2.07	1.22	0.71
Jul 1999	1.96	1.21	0.64
Aug 1999	1.88	1.12	0.64
Sep 1999	1.88	1.06	0.70
Oct 1999	1.94	1.03	0.72
Nov 1999	2.04	1.24	0.71
Dec 1999	2.12	1.42	0.67
Jan 2000	1.98	1.47	0.62
Feb 2000	1.89	1.79	0.59
Mar 2000	2.00	1.63	0.60
Apr 2000	1.90	1.35	0.56
May 2000	1.79	1.16	0.43
Jun 2000	1.80	1.28	0.47
Jul 2000	1.71	1.12	0.51
Aug 2000	1.81	1.21	0.50
Sep 2000	1.65	1.14	0.48
Oct 2000	1.65	1.10	0.46
Nov 2000	1.44	0.87	0.46
Dec 2000	1.41	0.86	0.47

Figure 1.34 Rolling Period Returns

As with most Ibbotson tables, you can sort by clicking on the column heading. To frequency-convert the rolling periods (e.g., monthly to year), click **Holding Period** and then select a higher frequency (quarterly, semiannual, year, or return over the period).

Note: If you change the frequency, the rolling graph will not reflect this change.

Graphs

In addition to the statistic table, you can also review the Rolling Periods on a geographical basis by clicking **Graphs, Rolling Period Line, or Rolling Period Bar Graph** from the Rolling Period Returns table. These graphs can also be accessed from the Main Folder Window under the **Graphs** menu.

Rolling Period Frequency Conversion

Although you can calculate Rolling Period Returns using one data frequency (as specified in the Date Settings), you can change the holding period to another frequency. A holding period frequency conversion does not change the data frequency; instead, it used the calculated geometric mean and approximates it over a longer time period. Refers to "Analyzer's Formulas" in the online help for the geometric mean conversion formula. Click **Holding Period** to frequency-convert the Rolling Period Returns table to one of the following holding periods: Monthly, Quarterly, Semi-Annually, Annually, or Return over Period.

Summary Menu

The **Summary** menu allows you to view individual Summary Statistics for one or more rows of your Rolling Period. Begin by selecting one or more rows of your Rolling Period Returns and then click **Summary, Open.** To close all Summary windows, click **Summary, Close All**. If you would like to view summary statistics for all of the rolling periods as a group, click **Summary, Statistics.** (**Figure 1.35**)

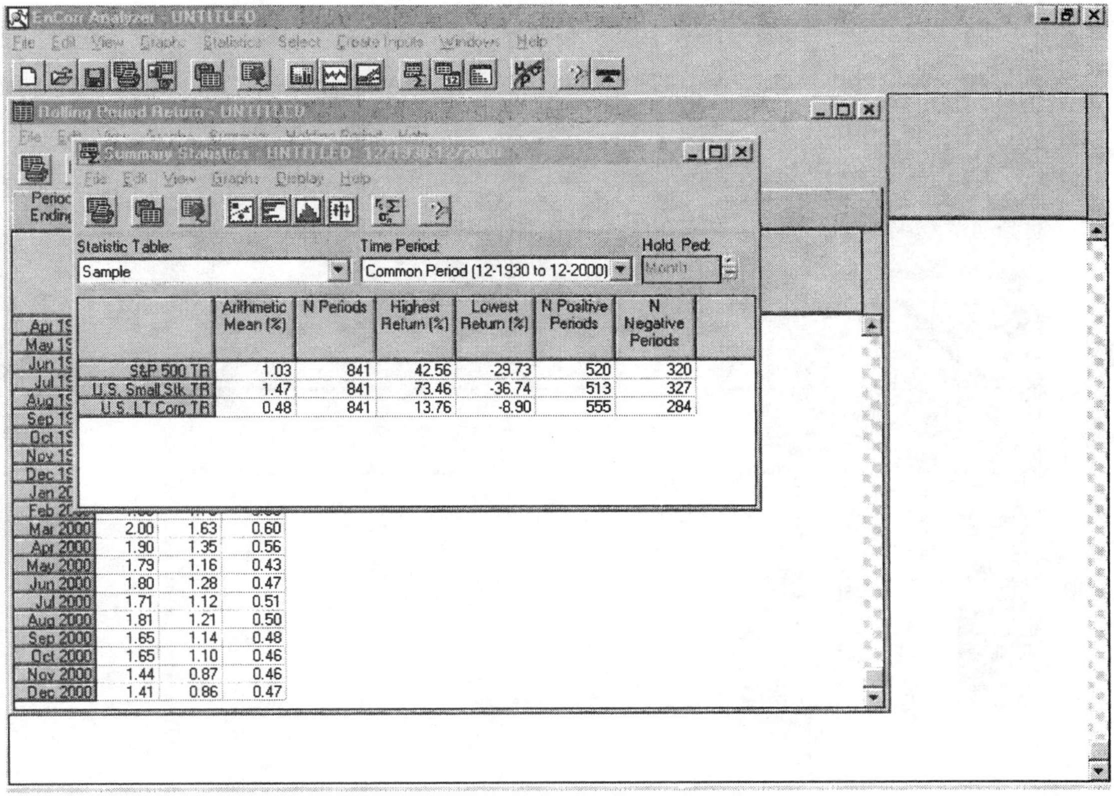

Figure 1.35 Rolling Period Summary Statistics Table

Graphs Menu (Summary Statistics Window)

You can open a scatter plot, bar plot, and histogram from the Summary Statistics window using Rolling Periods.

> **Note: Summary statistics are, by nature, an average of the complete distribution. Summary statistics generated from Rolling Periods can be misleading because the statistics represents averages of averages.**

Independent Period Returns

The another option on the **Statistics** menu is **Independent Period Returns.** These are obtained by looking at mutually exclusive windows of fixed length along each time series (asset). Each Independent Period Return represents the geometric average for a given holding period, based on your Date Setting's frequency and time period. For example, a five year independent (holding) period calculates the annual geometric average return over every five-year period available in your Analyzer case file (.fld). If the beginning date is 1926, the first five-year annual independent period would be 1926 to1930. Subsequently, the next five- year independent period would be 1931 to1935, then 1936 to 1940, etc. (**Figure 1.36**)

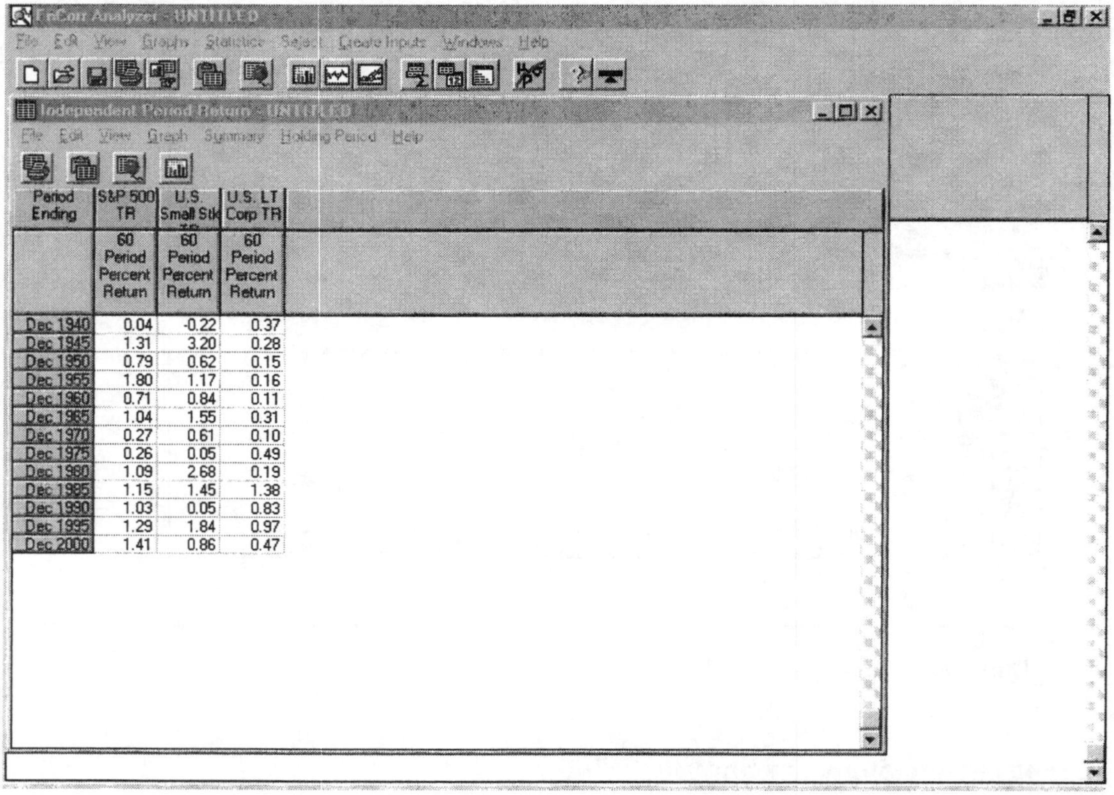

Period Ending	S&P 500 TR 60 Period Percent Return	U.S. Small Stk TR 60 Period Percent Return	U.S. LT Corp TR 60 Period Percent Return
Dec 1940	0.04	-0.22	0.37
Dec 1945	1.31	3.20	0.28
Dec 1950	0.79	0.62	0.15
Dec 1955	1.80	1.17	0.16
Dec 1960	0.71	0.84	0.11
Dec 1965	1.04	1.55	0.31
Dec 1970	0.27	0.61	0.10
Dec 1975	0.26	0.05	0.49
Dec 1980	1.09	2.68	0.19
Dec 1985	1.15	1.45	1.38
Dec 1990	1.03	0.05	0.83
Dec 1995	1.29	1.84	0.97
Dec 2000	1.41	0.86	0.47

Figure 1.36 Independent Period Return Table

Independent Period Returns can be calculated from the Main Folder Window by clicking **Statistics, Independent Period Returns.** Enter the desired independent period, and click **OK**.

Summary

The **Summary** menu allows you to view individual Summary Statistics for one or more rows of your Independent Period Returns. Begin by selecting one or more rows of your Independent Period Returns, and then click **Summary, Open**. (**Figure 1.37**)

Note: Summary statistics are an average of the complete distribution. Summary statistics generated from Independent Period Returns can be misleading because the statistics represent averages of averages.

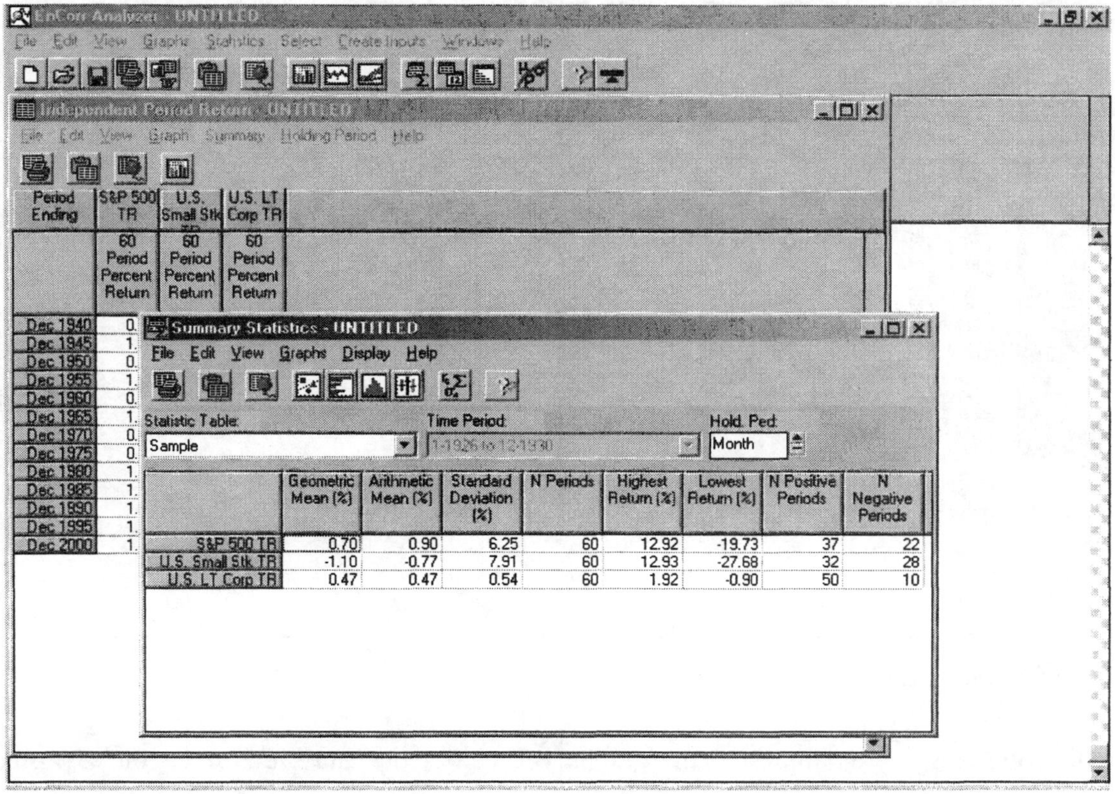

Summary Statistics - UNTITLED
File Edit View Graphs Display Help
Statistic Table:
Sample
Time Period:
Hold. Ped:
Month
Geometric Mean (%)
Arithmetic Mean (%)
Standard Deviation (%)
N Periods
Highest Return (%)
Lowest Return (%)
N Positive Periods
N Negative Periods
S&P 500 TR 0.70 0.90 6.25 60 12.92 -19.73 37 22
U.S. Small Stk TR -1.10 -0.77 7.91 60 12.93 -27.68 32 28
U.S. LT Corp TR 0.47 0.47 0.54 60 1.92 -0.90 50 10
Period Ending
S&P 500 TR
U.S. Small Stk TR
U.S. LT Corp TR
60 Period Percent Return
Dec 1940
Dec 1945
Dec 1950
Dec 1955
Dec 1960
Dec 1965
Dec 1970
Dec 1975
Dec 1980
Dec 1985
Dec 1990
Dec 1995
Dec 2000

Figure 1.37 Independent Period Summary Statistics Table

Graph

The summary window allows you to display a scatter plot, bar plot, and histogram using independent period summary statistics.

Graphs

The Graphs menu (**Figure 1.38**) allows you to create historical bar, line, and rolling interval graphs in your current case file. All graphs are based on the frequency set in the Date Settings window. You can zoom in on any line graph to view a section of the graph. You can also right-click a graph to change or display the options and print or copy a graph.

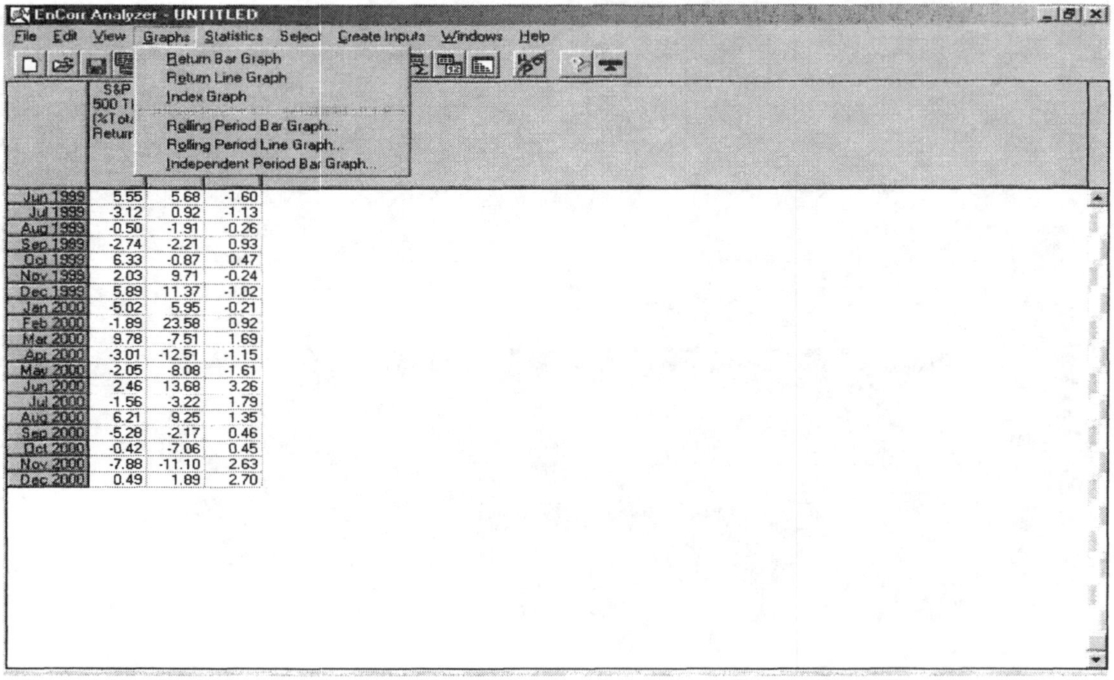

EnCorr Analyzer - UNTITLED

File Edit View Graphs Statistics Select Create Inputs Windows Help

Return Bar Graph
Return Line Graph
Index Graph
Rolling Period Bar Graph...
Rolling Period Line Graph...
Independent Period Bar Graph...

	S&P 500 T (%Tot Retur		
Jun 1999	5.55	5.68	-1.60
Jul 1999	-3.12	0.92	-1.13
Aug 1999	-0.50	-1.91	-0.26
Sep 1999	-2.74	-2.21	0.93
Oct 1999	6.33	-0.87	0.47
Nov 1999	2.03	9.71	-0.24
Dec 1999	5.89	11.37	-1.02
Jan 2000	-5.02	5.95	-0.21
Feb 2000	-1.89	23.58	0.92
Mar 2000	9.78	-7.51	1.69
Apr 2000	-3.01	-12.51	-1.15
May 2000	-2.05	-8.08	-1.61
Jun 2000	2.46	13.68	3.26
Jul 2000	-1.56	-3.22	1.79
Aug 2000	6.21	9.25	1.35
Sep 2000	-5.28	-2.17	0.46
Oct 2000	-0.42	-7.06	0.45
Nov 2000	-7.88	-11.10	2.63
Dec 2000	0.49	1.89	2.70

Figure 1.38 Graphs Menu

The following are examples of the graphs you can create and view under the **Graphs** menu:

Return Bar Graph

The Return Bar Graph (**Figure 1.39**) plots historical return data based on the frequency and time period in the Date Settings.

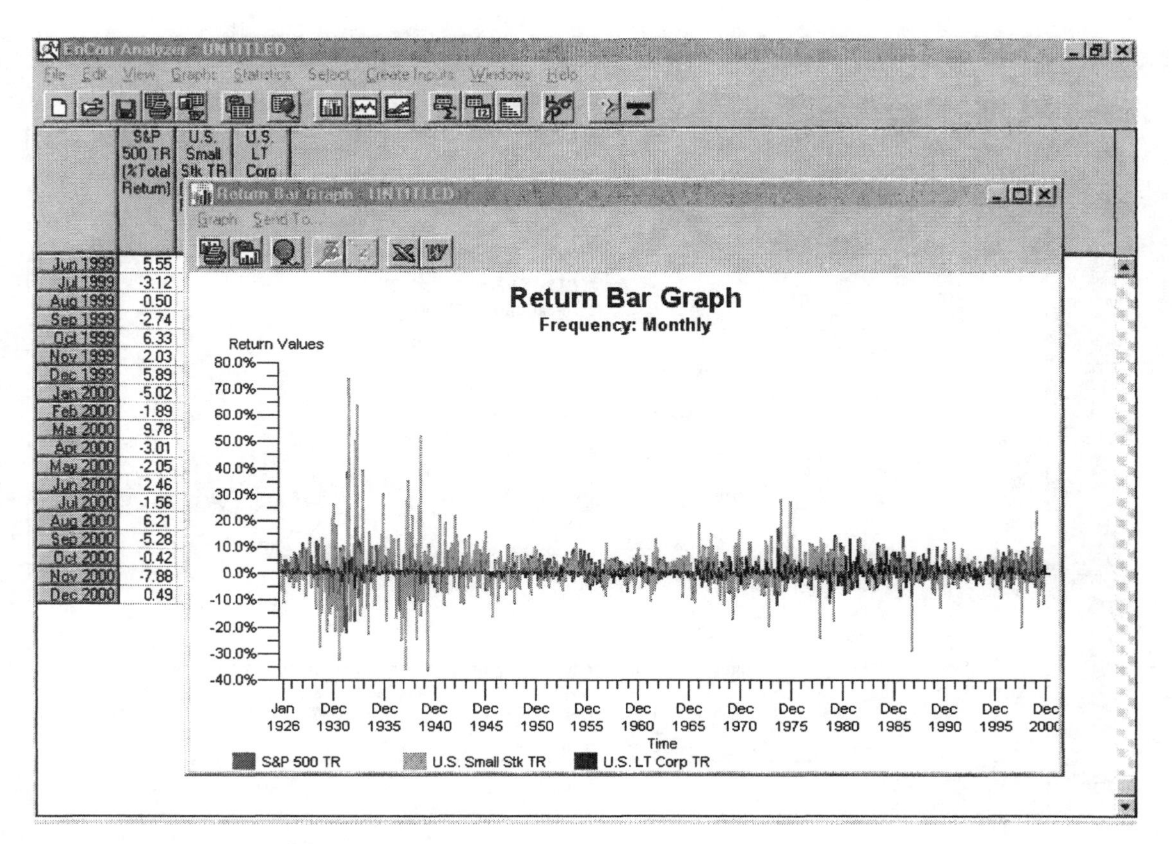

Figure 1.39 Return Bar Graph

Return Line Graph

Analyzer allows you to create line graphs for Return or Index wealth values. These line graphs are graphical representations of your folder's returns and index values. The X-axis displays the data frequency of your folder monthly, quarterly, semi-annually, or annually. The Y-axis displays the return. You can choose to display end labels as well. (**Figure 1.40**)

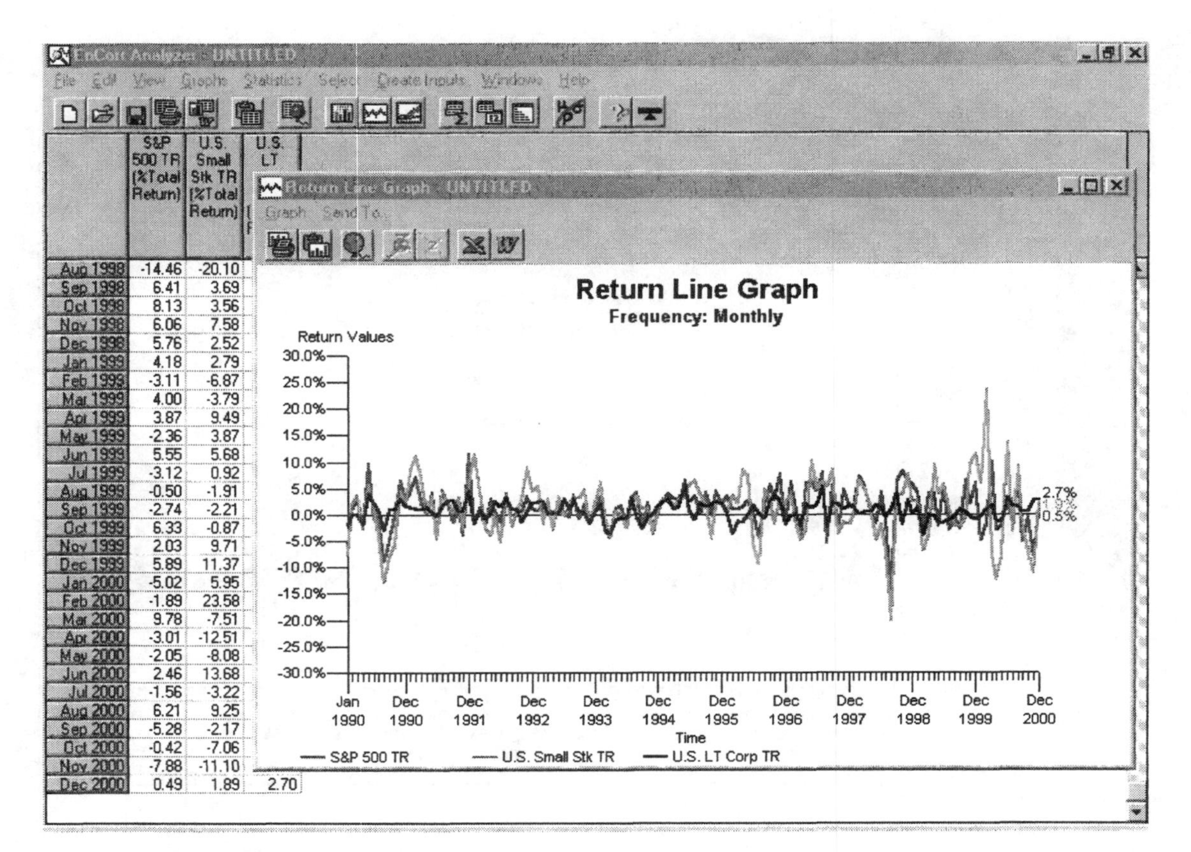

Figure 1.40 Return Line Graph

Index Graph

In the Graph menu, the Index (Wealth) Graph shows the growth over time of the investments in each asset class in your case file (**Figure 1.41**). The graph starts at the index date defined in the Date Settings window (**Series, Date Settings**). The Date Settings window is also where you set the Index Value, which determines the beginning dollar amount for the Index Graph. As with other graphs, end labels can be turned on or off.

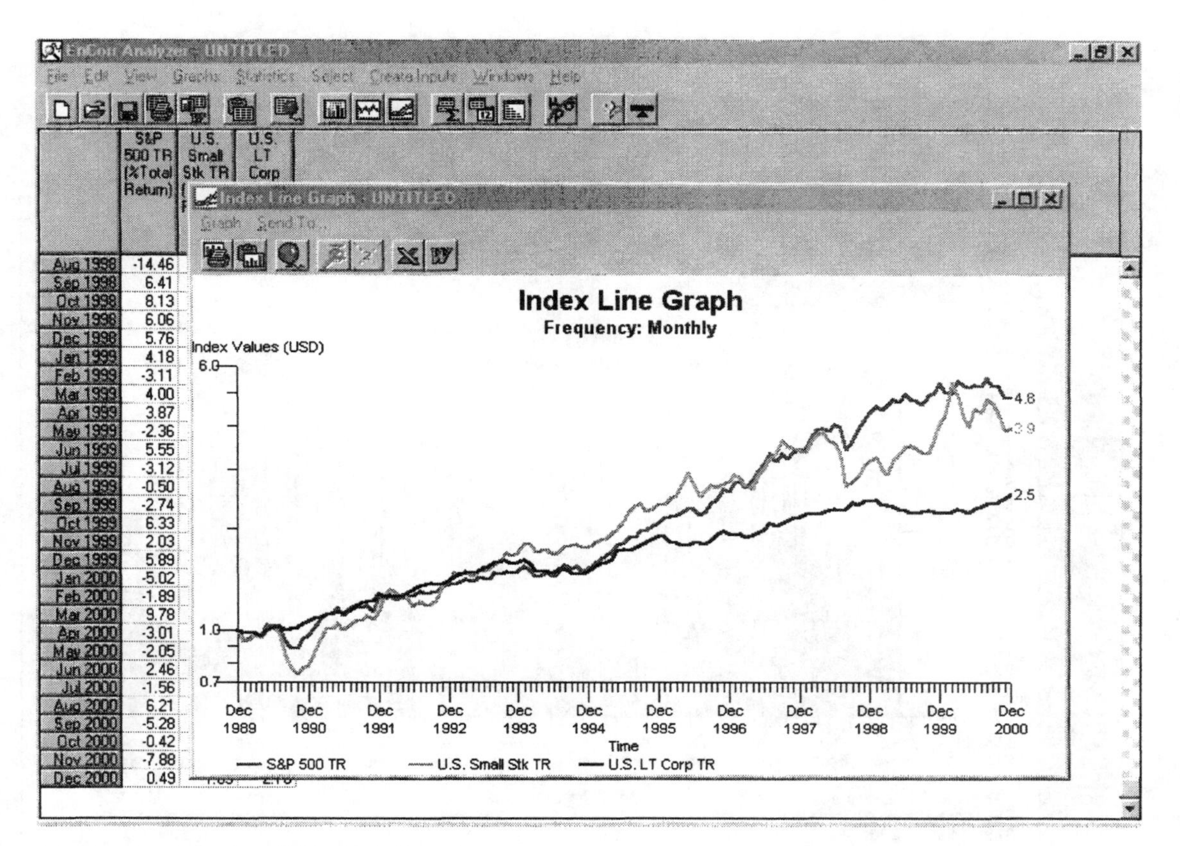

Figure 1.41 Index (Wealth) Graph

Index Graph Zooming Options

The Index Graph allows you to change the method in which you zoom. Right-click the graph and click **Options**. You can change the zooming method from **Constant** to **Adjust With Zoom** on the Display tab. The **Constant** option keeps the Index date at the original index date set in the Date Settings window. When you **Adjust with Zoom**, the graph resets the beginning index date to the beginning of the zoom period.

Rolling Period Bar Graph

The Rolling Period Bar Graph (**Figure 1.42**) allows you to view average returns over use-defined rolling periods in bar graph format. To view the numbers behind this graph, click **Statistics, Rolling Period Return.**

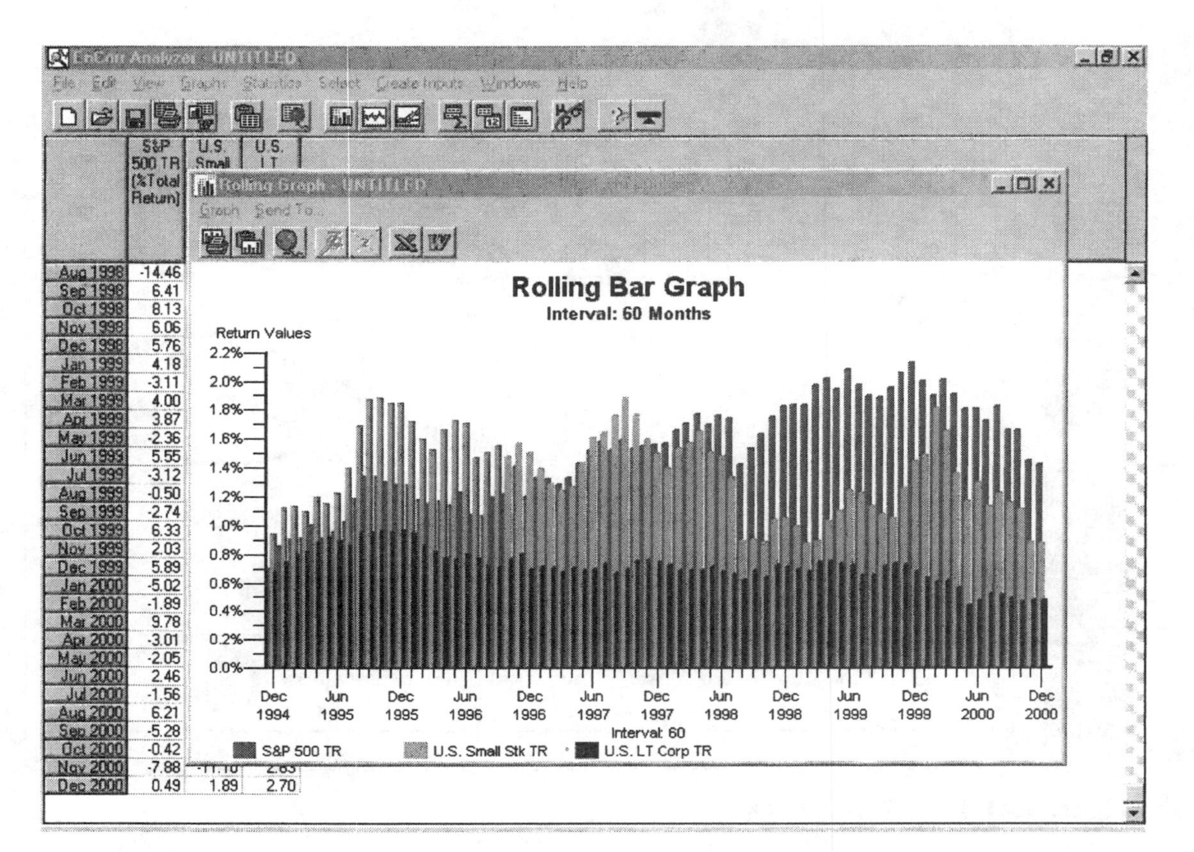

Figure 1.42 Rolling Period Bar Graph

Rolling Period Line Graph

The Rolling Period Line Graph (**Figure 1.43**) allows you to view average returns over user-defined rolling periods in line graph format. To view the numbers behind this graph, click **Statistics, Rolling Period Returns.**

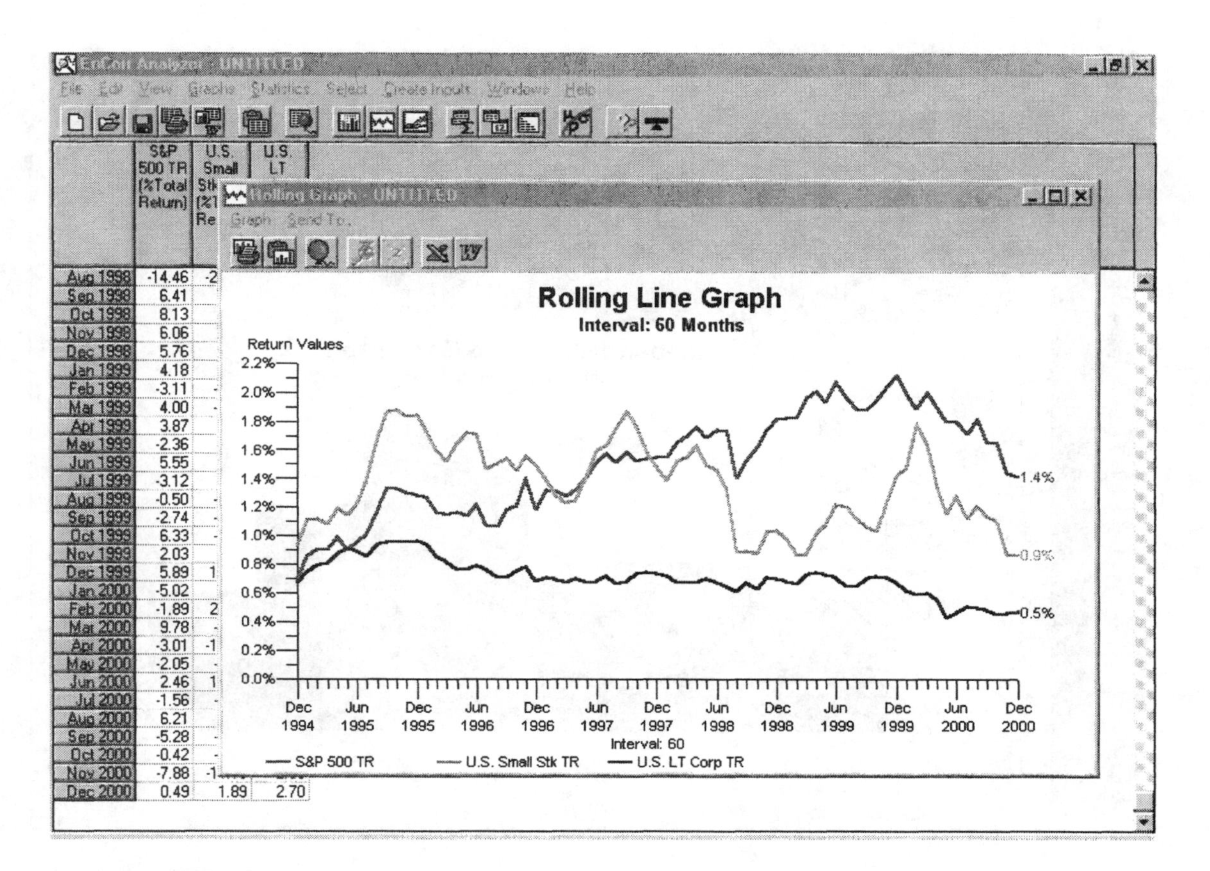

Figure 1.43 Rolling Period Line Graph

Independent Period Bar Graph

The Independent Period Bar Graph allows you to view average returns over independent periods. From the Main Folder Window, click **Statistics, Independent Period Returns**. (Figure 1.44)

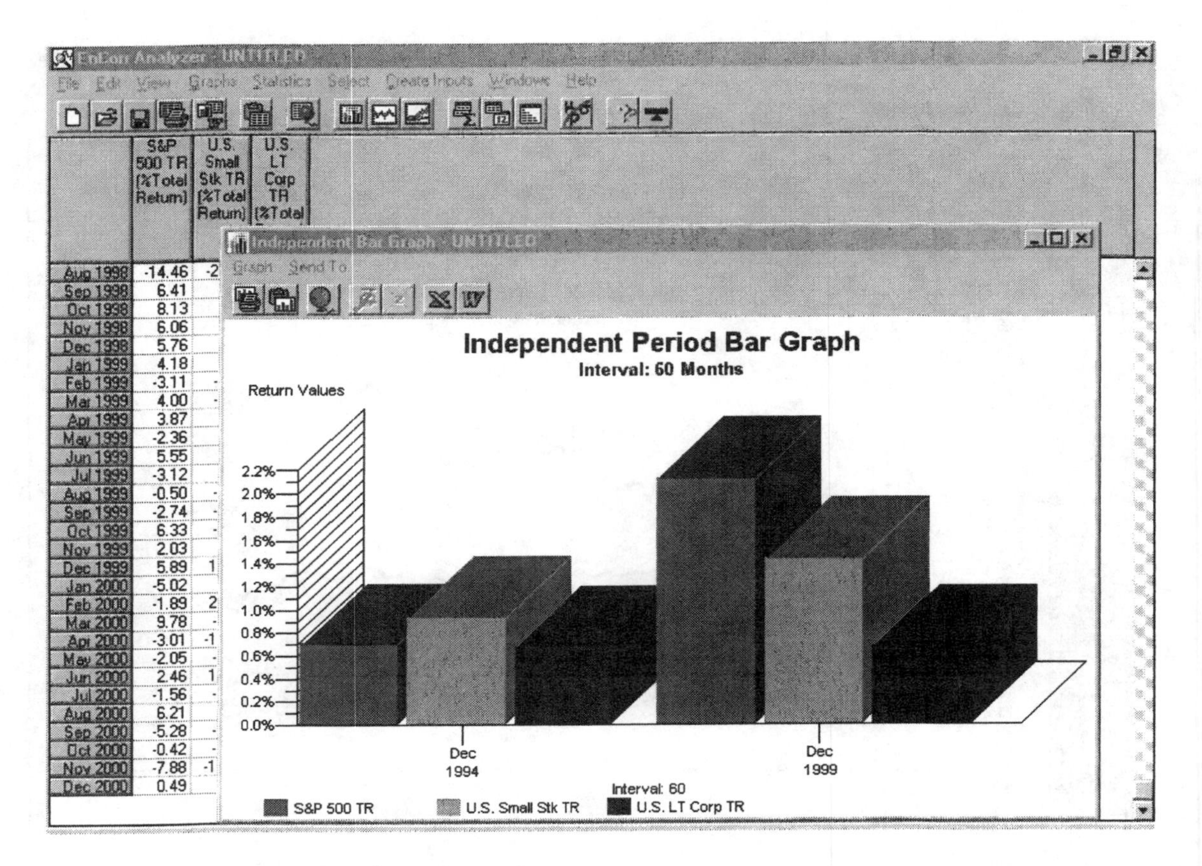

Figure 1.44 Independent Period Bar Graph

Graph Display Options

Graph Display Options enable you to customize your graph by changing common settings such as graph titles and fonts, or settings that are particular to a specific graph. Graph Display options can be accessed from any graph by clicking the **Graph, Display Options** menu command or by clicking your right mouse button on a graph, and selecting **Options.** Not all graphs have all tabs and all options.

Current Defaults

After specifying graph options, click **Ok** to set changes for the current graph only.

Global Defaults

After specifying graph options, click **Save** to set changes for the global defaults. Global defaults are saved by all future graphs and set in the Ibbotson ini.file

Display Tab

Display is the first tap for the Graph Display Options command. It enables you to customize graphs by changing common settings such as decimal places and fonts, or settings that are particular to a specific graph.

Calculation (Risk vs. Return Scatter and Bar Plots)

Switches between Arithmetic Mean and Geometric Mean return in Risk vs. Return scatter and bar plots.

Color Preference

Switches between color and black and white.

Distribution Curve

Overlays a normal or lognormal distribution line on a histogram graph.

Dot Size

Adjusts the size of dots in a scatter plot. Drag the scroll bar to the right for larger dots and to the left for smaller dots.

End Label

Shows or hides the end label of line graphs and changes the decimal places of these labels.

Interval Size

Adjusts the range of values or intervals for each bar on histogram graph. If you increase the interval size, you will have fewer bars in the histogram; if you decrease the interval size, you will have more bars.

Labels

Displays scatter plot labels on the graph beside the dot, below the graph as legends, or displays no labels.

Line Thickness

Adjusts the line thickness in a line graph. Drag the scroll bar to the right for thicker lines and to the left for thinner lines.

Shape (Pie Charts Only)

Makes a pie chart circular or oval.

Show

Chooses between showing and not showing features on specific scatter plots.

Show (Histogram)

Displays/hides the following items on a histogram:

- Bar Values—number of data points in an interval
- Horizontal Lines
- Mean
- Median
- Standard Deviations—displays standard deviation lines away from the mean.

Show Button Bar

Turns the Toolbars on or off when you check and uncheck the box.

Style

Displays bar graphs in two or three dimensions.

X-Axis or Y-Axis

Displays X- or Y-axis labels in either percentage or number (decimal) format and/or adjusts the decimal places on these labels.

Font/Title Tab

The Font/Title tab allows you to change the appearance of graph titles.

Change Fonts

To change fonts, click the **Change** button. You can change fonts for a graph's Title, Subtitle, and Label.

Graph Title

You can enter/edit the graph title in the **Show Title** box. To revert a title back to the Ibbotson default, click the **Default** button. A graph title can have up to 27 characters.

Hide the Graph Title

To hide the graph title, uncheck the **Show Title** box.

Hide the Graph Subtitle

To hide the graph subtitle, uncheck the **Show Subtitle** box. You cannot edit the subtitle of a graph.

Axis Limits Tab

Axis Limits defines the appearance of the X and Y axis for axis graphs.

Define Axis Limits

To define axis limits, click **User Defined Limits**. You can then enter the preferred lower and upper limits in the box(es).

Minimize Axis Limits

To minimize axis limits, click **Dynamic Axis Limits.** Dynamic Axis Limits minimizes the axis limits to maximize the graph space.

Colors Tab

Colors allows you to set the color schemes for your graphs.

Change Background Color

To change the background color, click the **Background** box.

Change Asset Color

To change the color for an asset, click the **Color** box. You can define the color for up to 12 assets. If your folder has more than 12 assets, more than one asset will have the same color.

Ibbotson Color Defaults

To display one of the three Ibbotson color schemes, click the **Default** button.

2

Summary Statistics and Graphing

INTRODUCTION

The investment industry uses a variety of statistics to analyze historical returns. We know from the text that Markowitz introduced modern portfolio theory based on expected returns and standard deviation statistics. In this chapter we will show how to generate a variety of tools such as the arithmetic as well as the geometric means, and the standard deviation displayed in the Summary Statistics table as well as the graphing function with related date settings and the zoom function.

STATISTICS MENU

Summary Statistics

Arithmetic Mean, Geometric Mean, and Standard Deviation

To create a customized Summary Statistics table, first go to the main EnCorr Analyzer – Untitled window, click on Select and choose the Ibbotson database. Click on the series Stocks, Bonds, Bills and Inflation. For this example we will choose the **U.S. LT Corp TR and the U.S. Small Stk TR series (Figure 2.1)**. Double click on each of these to add them to the selected series window on the left. Click OK to close the window.

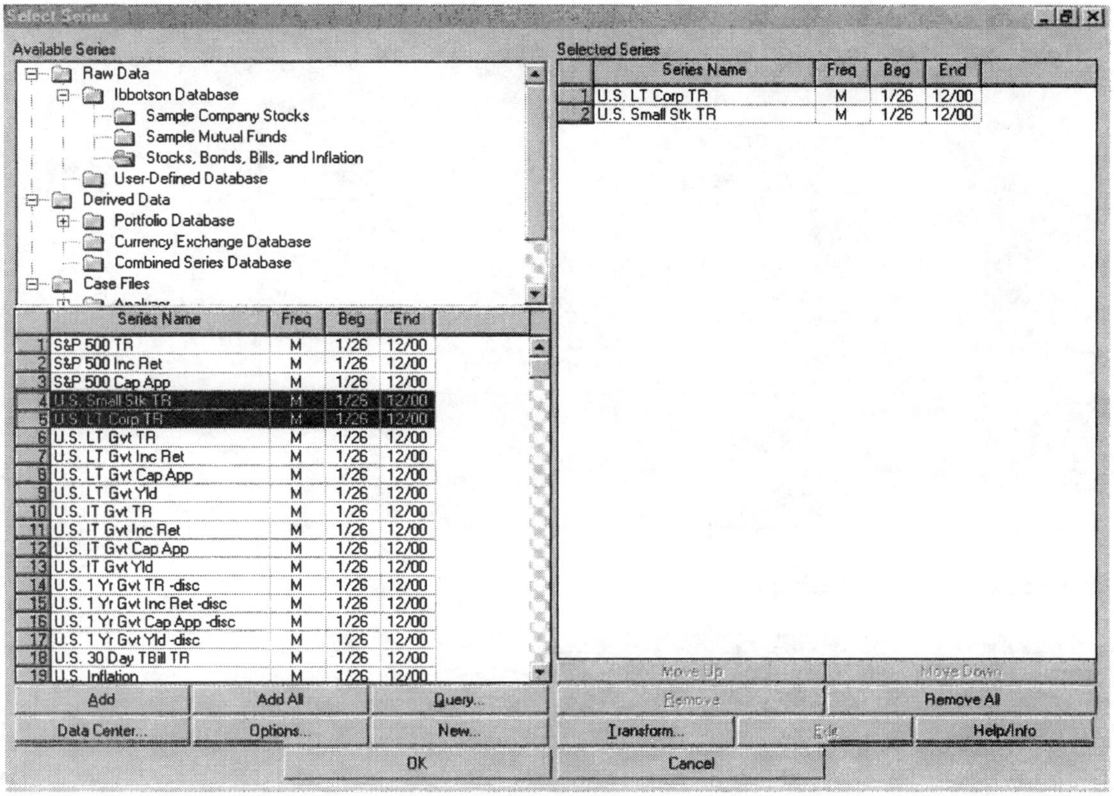

Figure 2.1 Select U.S. LT Corp TR and the U.S. Small Stk TR series

The Set Date window now appears (**Figure 2.2**). We will keep the date settings as indicated with the beginning date in January 1926 and the ending date of December 2000. Keep the remaining values as given. Click **OK**.

Date Settings
Date and Frequency Settings
Frequency: Monthly
Beginning: January 1926
Ending: December 2000
Common Date Range
Maximum Date Range
Calendar Settings
Calendar
Non-Calendar
On Month: December
Index Settings
Index Date: December 1925
Index Value: 1
Adjust Index Date Automatically
OK
Cancel
Help

Figure 2.2 Date Settings

	U.S. Small Stk TR (%Total Return)	U.S. LT Corp TR (%Total Return)
May 1998	-4.97	1.67
Jun 1998	-2.06	1.15
Jul 1998	-6.71	-0.56
Aug 1998	-20.10	0.89
Sep 1998	3.69	4.13
Oct 1998	3.56	-1.90
Nov 1998	7.58	2.70
Dec 1998	2.52	0.10
Jan 1999	2.79	1.23
Feb 1999	-6.87	-4.01
Mar 1999	-3.79	0.02
Apr 1999	9.49	-0.24
May 1999	3.87	-1.76
Jun 1999	5.68	-1.60
Jul 1999	0.92	-1.13
Aug 1999	-1.91	-0.26
Sep 1999	-2.21	0.93
Oct 1999	-0.87	0.47
Nov 1999	9.71	-0.24
Dec 1999	11.37	-1.02
Jan 2000	5.95	-0.21
Feb 2000	23.58	0.92
Mar 2000	-7.51	1.69
Apr 2000	-12.51	-1.15
May 2000	-8.08	-1.61
Jun 2000	13.68	3.26
Jul 2000	-3.22	1.79
Aug 2000	9.25	1.35
Sep 2000	-2.17	0.46
Oct 2000	-7.06	0.45
Nov 2000	-11.10	2.63

Figure 2.3 En Corr Analyzer: Main Page with Selected Series

You are back in the Main window of EnCorr Analyzer, but now you have the two series that we selected in columns down the left side of the window (**Figure 2.3**). Click on the **Statistics** dropdown window, and then click again on **Summary Statistics**. **Figure 2.4** will appear.

Click **Display, Create New Table,** type in a name for the table, and select the desired statistics. For this sample problem we will select geometric mean, arithmetic mean, and standard deviation. You can now view the table in the **Summary Statistics** window by selecting it from the Statistics Table dropdown box.

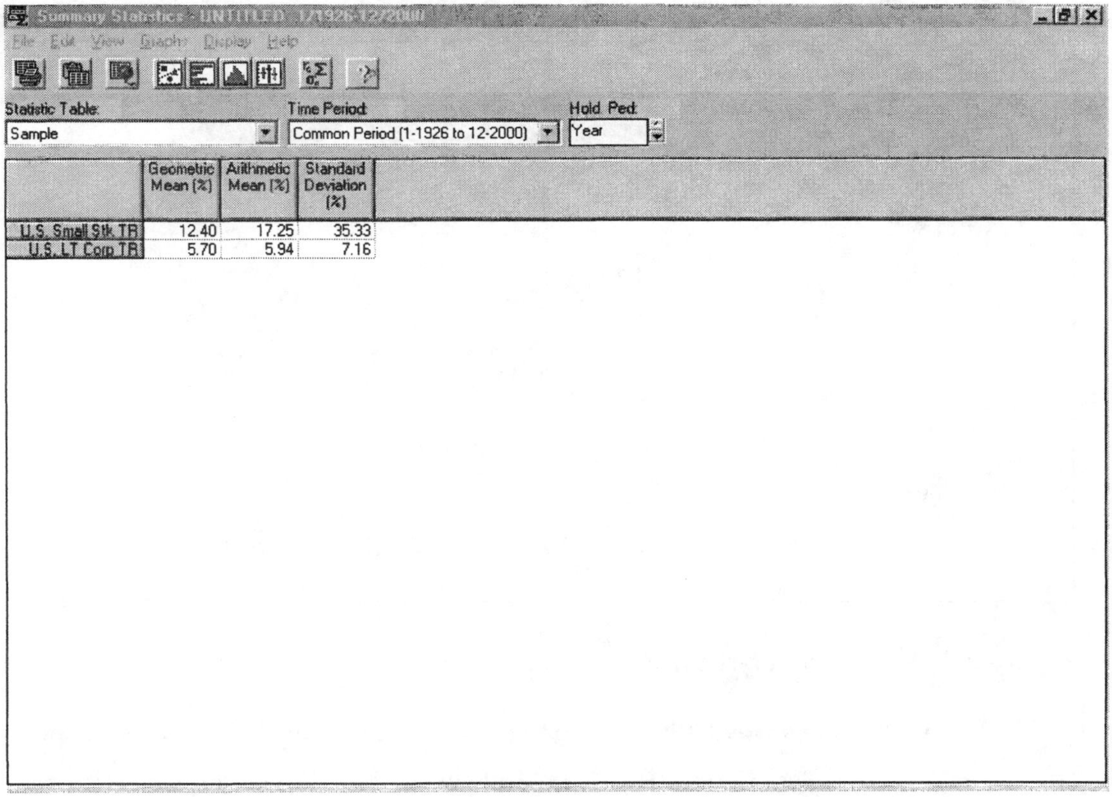

Summary Statistics - UNTITLED 1/1926-12/2000

Statistic Table: Sample | Time Period: Common Period (1-1926 to 12-2000) | Hold Pcd: Year

	Geometric Mean (%)	Arithmetic Mean (%)	Standard Deviation (%)
U.S. Small Stk TR	12.40	17.25	35.33
U.S. LT Corp TR	5.70	5.94	7.16

Figure 2.4 Summary Statistics

Time Periods

You can select specific periods for which to view the statistics. To define a new period, go to the Defined Series drop down box in the Summary Statistics page and click highlight **Edit Time Period.** The Time Period setup window opens (**Figure 2.5**).

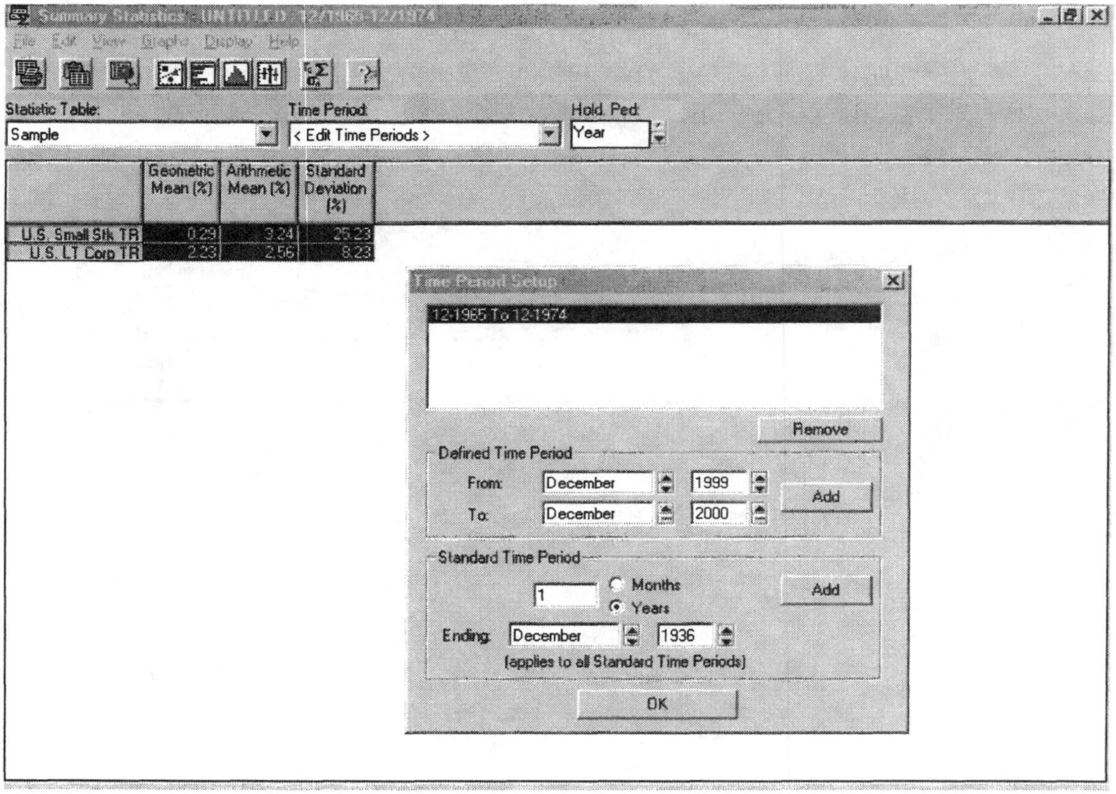

Summary Statistics - UNTITLED 12/1965-12/1974

File Edit View Graphs Display Help

Statistic Table: Sample

Time Period: < Edit Time Periods >

Hold. Ped: Year

	Geometric Mean (%)	Arithmetic Mean (%)	Standard Deviation (%)
U.S. Small Stk TR	0.29	3.24	25.23
U.S. LT Corp TR	2.23	2.56	8.23

Time Period Setup

12-1965 To 12-1974

Remove

Defined Time Period

From: December 1999

To: December 2000

Add

Standard Time Period

1 Months Years

Add

Ending: December 1936

(applies to all Standard Time Periods)

OK

Figure 2.5 Summary Statistics: Set the time period

- Select **Defined Time Period** and choose the month and year of the period you want to view. In this example we will use the period from January 1965 to December 1974. Click **Add.** You are now returned to the **Summary Statistics** where you will observe different values for a very volatile time period in market history.

EXERCISES

Use the data provided in the software by selecting **Ibbotson Database, Sample Company Stocks** in order to solve the following:

2.1 Select the 16 company series and compute the arithmetic and geometric means as well as the standard deviation for each time period of available returns.

2.2 In the **Ibbotson Database, Stocks Bonds Bills and Inflation**, select the **US Corporate LT TR** series and compute the arithmetic and geometric means and the standard deviation for the entire time period of available returns.

2.3 In the **Ibbotson Database, Stocks Bonds Bills and Inflation**, select the **S&P 500 TR** series and compute the arithmetic and geometric means and the standard deviation for the entire time period of available returns.

2.4 Compare the 16 company historical returns with the answers from exercises 2.2 and 2.3. Which companies outperformed the two aggregate series for the entire time period of available returns? Which ones underperformed the two aggregate indexes for the entire time period of available returns?

2.5 Compare the 16 company standard deviations with the answers from exercises 2.2 and 2.3. Which companies outperformed the two aggregate series for the entire time period of available returns? Which ones underperformed the two aggregate indexes for the entire time period of available returns?

2.6 We have been looking at a very long investment horizon, 1926 to 2000. Over the last two decades the story of who outperformed or underperformed the two aggregate series may be quite different. For this exercise separate the series into the decade of the 1980's and the 1990's. Perform the same tests as you did in 2.1-2.5 for each decade. Are the companies that outperformed and underperformed the two aggregate series still the same as in exercise 2.5?

Graphing

Types of Graphs

The Ibbotson software is capable of generating several types of graphs such as scatter plots, bar or line graphs. To create a new graph, select one or several series for the graph in the **Ibbotson Database, Stocks, Bonds, Bills and Inflation**. We have chosen the U.S. small stock TR series from 1926 to 2000. To create a new graph click **Graphs** and choose one of the graphs from the drop-down box. (**Figure 2.6**)

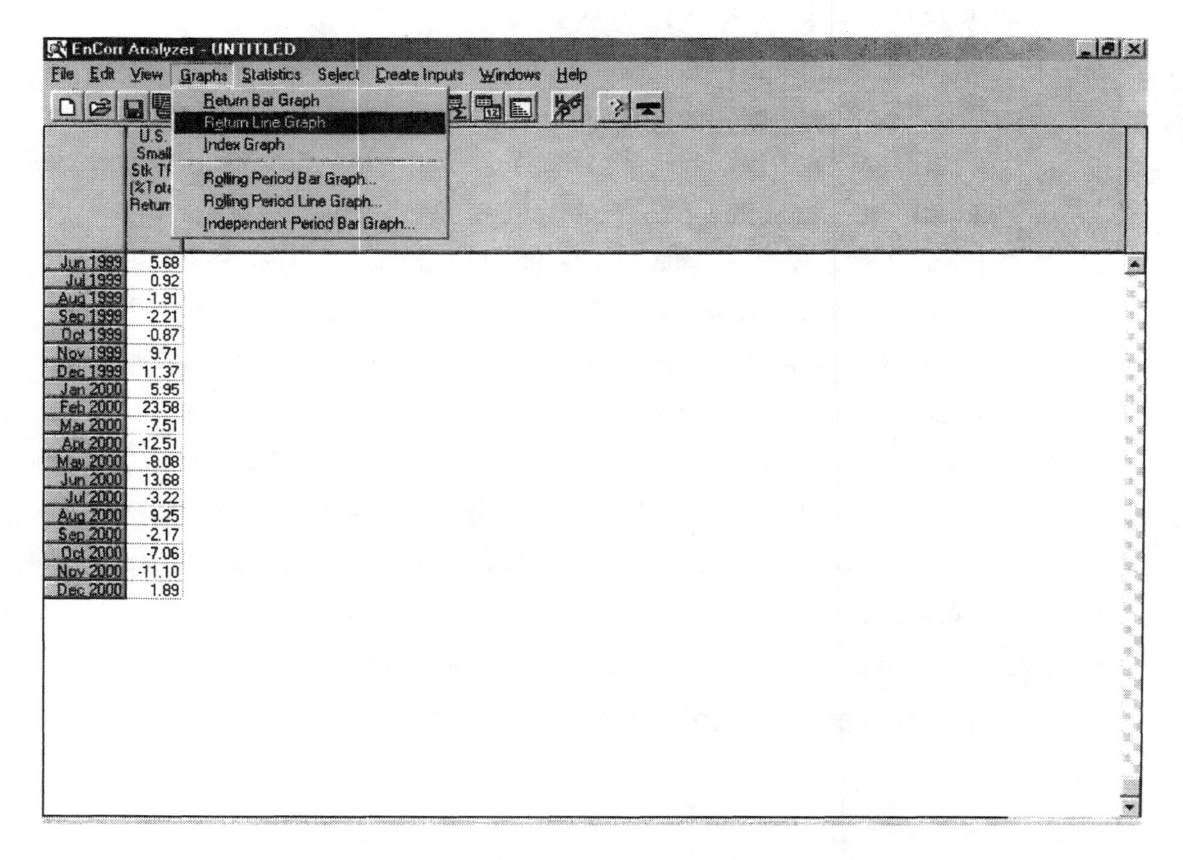

Figure 2.6 En Corr Analyzer: Main Page with Selected Graph

You are now presented with six choices of graph types. Select **Return Line Graph** and click on it. The graph shows the variability of returns for U.S. small companies between 1926 and 2000. (**Figure 2.7**)

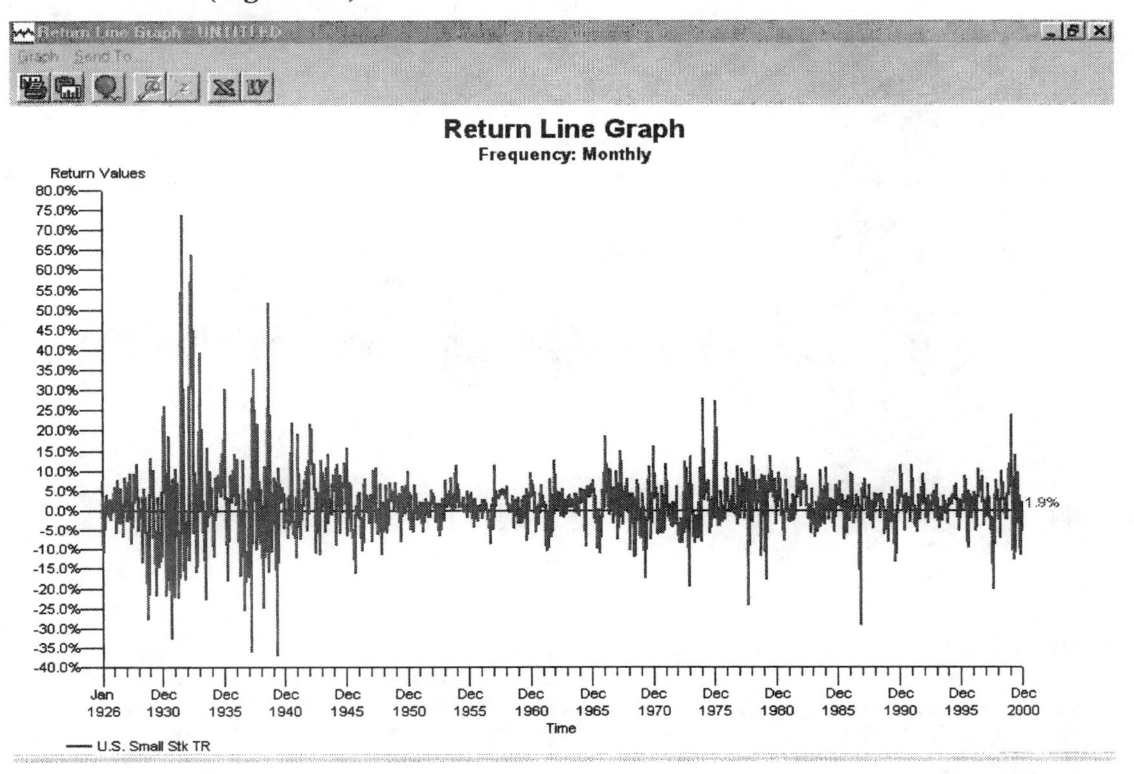

Figure 2.7 Graph of Monthly U.S Small Stock TR 1926-2000

To focus on a specific period such as a decade or an historical time period use the "hand" cursor labeled "ZOOM," hold down the left mouse button and drag the "hand" over the period you wish to view in more detail. Let's focus on the period 1929 to 1939, the Great Depression era. Drag the cursor over the time period. (**Figure 2.8**)

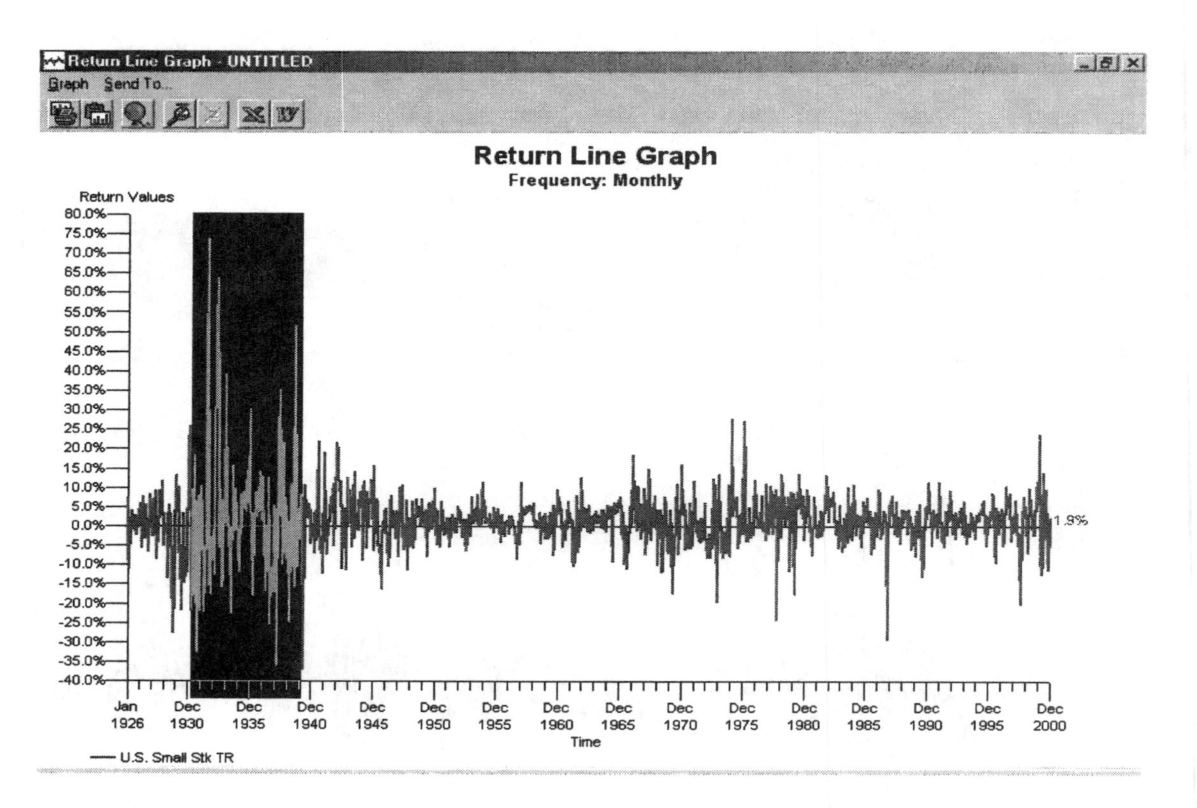

Figure 2.8 Highlighting a Specific Sub-period to Graph

Once it is highlighted, left click and the smaller time-series graph appears. **(Figure 2.9)**

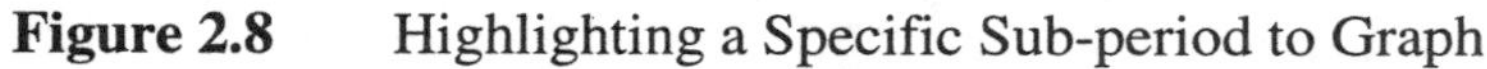

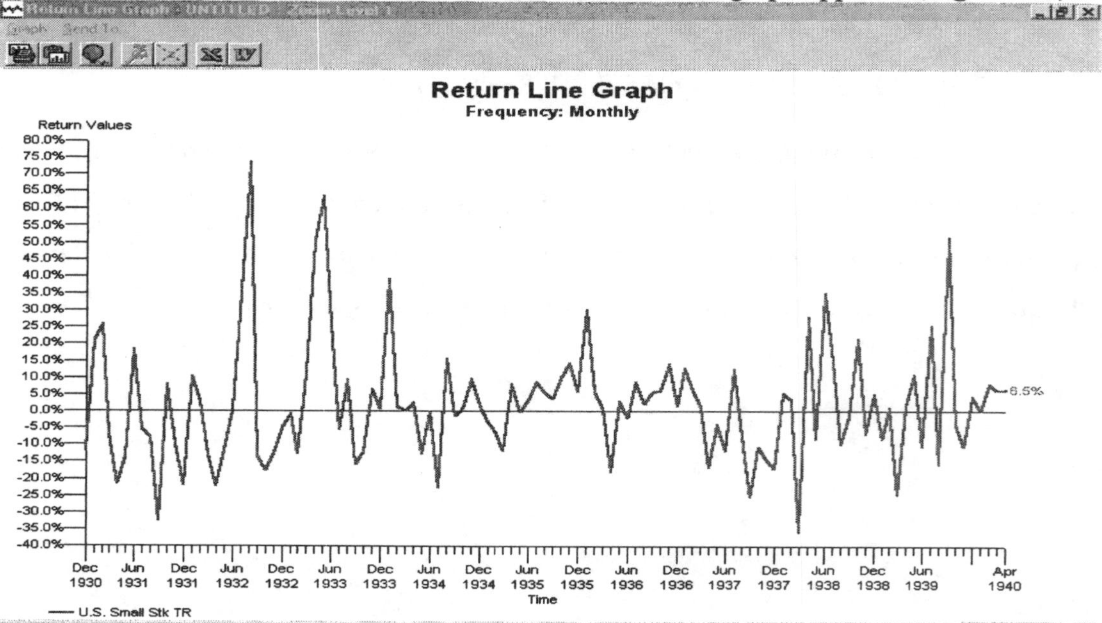

Figure 2.9 U.S. Small Stock TR 1929-1939

To return to the larger time series, simply right click the cursor and select **Zoom Out.** **(Figure 2.10)**

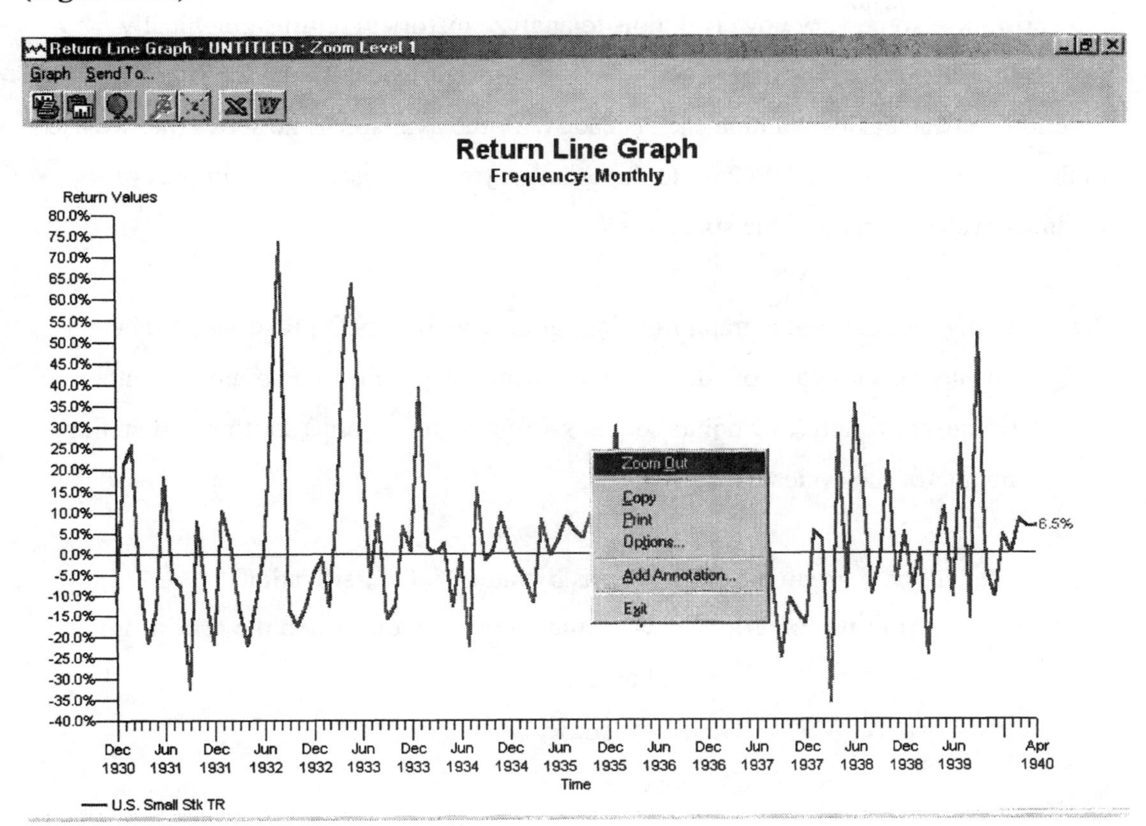

Figure 2.10 Zoom out

EXERCISES

You now have some very powerful tools to analyze historical returns graphically revealing some industry and company-specific characteristics. Using the graphing function you can easily examine each decade over the available time series that we used in the earlier exercises, 2.1 to 2.6. In the process, you will discover the impact of business cycles on each of the sixteen series.

2.7 Using the return line graph function, graph the S&P 500 TR series. What business cycles can you identify by viewing the graph? You many use either trough-to-trough (low points) or peak-to-peak (high point) starting and ending points for the cycles.

2.8 We will now group the stock returns by industrial classification.

a. **Manufacturers** Select and graph on one graph the following:

- General Motors
- General Electric
- Du Pont
- Boeing
- S&P 500 TR

b. **Consumer goods** Select and graph on one graph the following:

- Wal Mart
- Proctor and Gamble
- Pepsi Cola
- Nike
- Eastman Kodak
- Coca Cola
- S&P500 TR

c. Which one of the groups seems to be more sensitive (correlated) to the economic activity of the nation? Why?

Part II

Investment Analysis

3

Investment Indexes

INTRODUCTION TO INVESTMENT INDEXES

Seven basic indexes by Ibbotson Associates have been the foundation for the company's reputation in the investment industry. The indexes are important to investors because they provide answers to the basic questions about investing especially "How is the market doing today?" Indexes serve additional important functions. As we observed in Chapter 2 of this guide, an analysis of many series of historical stock returns may be time consuming. Graphing may speed up the process, but indexes help us to gain precise knowledge rapidly.

LONG-TERM RETURNS FOR MAJOR ASSET CLASSES

Investment indexes are useful because they accomplish the following:

- Gaining knowledge rapidly
- Combined indexes can build broader pictures that support or reject investment theories and strategies
- Investigating market interrelationships
- International indexes are useful to help further allocate and diversify your assets
- Indexes help us to observe overall economic relationships

In this chapter we will investigate some of the uses for indexes with the Ibbotson software with help from actual data from the domestic and international market indexes that are supplied. Solving the problems will focus on more detailed observations over shorter time periods and observe their different characteristics.

Gain knowledge rapidly

This section analyzes the monthly time-series of the seven U.S. price indexes cited in Chapter 11, page 296. The basic indexes presented show the growth of $1 invested in four instruments and one hypothetical asset that had the same return as the rate of inflation. Remember that the graphs we generate represent total returns (TRs) and include two sources of income: unrealized price changes and cash flows. We will also assume immediate reinvestment of all interest payments from bonds as well as cash dividends from stocks. Brokerage commissions, income taxes and other transactions costs are ignored for simplicity.

The Ibbotson Indexes

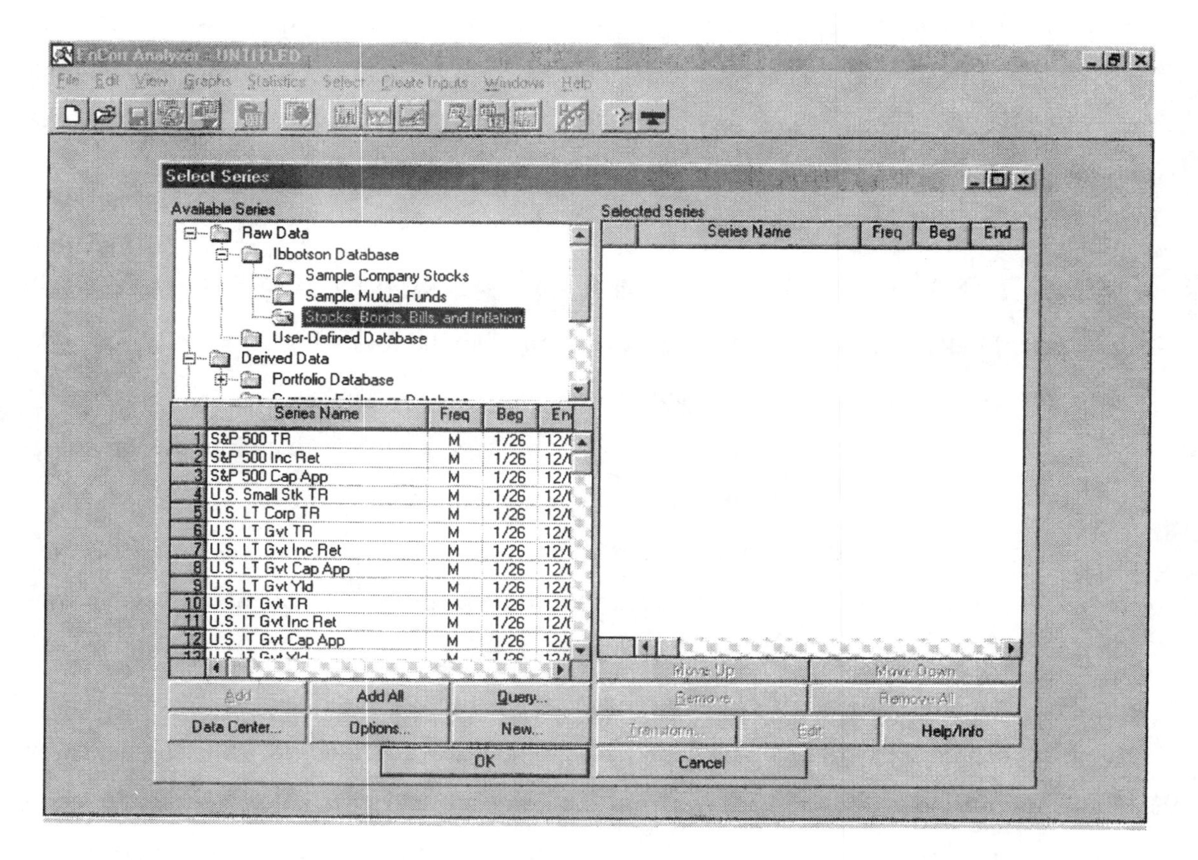

Figure 3.1 Select Series Window

The Large-Company Bond Index

The SBBI chart is an Index Graph that you can create with EnCorr Analyzer. After opening the Analyzer, from the **Select** drop down menu, click on **Series.** You now see the **Select Series** window as shown above in **Figure 3.1**

Select by highlighting the **Ibbotson Database**. Highlight and click on **SBBI** . In the lower left window of the Select Series, highlight series number 5, the **LT Corporate TR** series. Move down the window and click on the Add button (**Figure 3.2**). The series has now been selected and appears in the right window under the title Selected Series. In the lower left corner of the Select Series window, click **OK**.

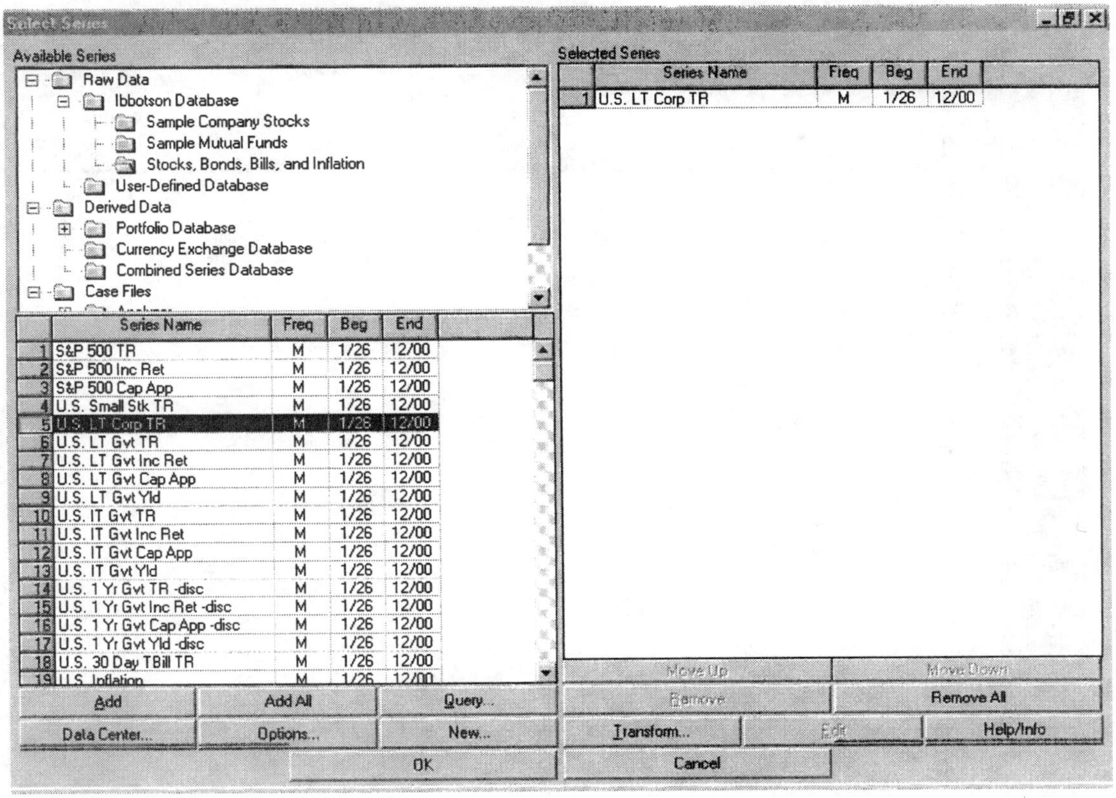

Select Series

Available Series

Raw Data
Ibbotson Database
Sample Company Stocks
Sample Mutual Funds
Stocks, Bonds, Bills, and Inflation
User-Defined Database
Derived Data
Portfolio Database
Currency Exchange Database
Combined Series Database
Case Files

	Series Name	Freq	Beg	End
1	S&P 500 TR	M	1/26	12/00
2	S&P 500 Inc Ret	M	1/26	12/00
3	S&P 500 Cap App	M	1/26	12/00
4	U.S. Small Stk TR	M	1/26	12/00
5	U.S. LT Corp TR	M	1/26	12/00
6	U.S. LT Gvt TR	M	1/26	12/00
7	U.S. LT Gvt Inc Ret	M	1/26	12/00
8	U.S. LT Gvt Cap App	M	1/26	12/00
9	U.S. LT Gvt Yld	M	1/26	12/00
10	U.S. IT Gvt TR	M	1/26	12/00
11	U.S. IT Gvt Inc Ret	M	1/26	12/00
12	U.S. IT Gvt Cap App	M	1/26	12/00
13	U.S. IT Gvt Yld	M	1/26	12/00
14	U.S. 1 Yr Gvt TR -disc	M	1/26	12/00
15	U.S. 1 Yr Gvt Inc Ret -disc	M	1/26	12/00
16	U.S. 1 Yr Gvt Cap App -disc	M	1/26	12/00
17	U.S. 1 Yr Gvt Yld -disc	M	1/26	12/00
18	U.S. 30 Day TBill TR	M	1/26	12/00
19	U.S. Inflation	M	1/26	12/00

Selected Series

	Series Name	Freq	Beg	End
1	U.S. LT Corp TR	M	1/26	12/00

Add | Add All | Query... | Move Up | Move Down
Data Center... | Options... | New... | Remove | Remove All
Transform... | Edit | Help/Info
OK | Cancel

Figure 3.2 Adding to Selected Series Window

This brings you to the **Date Settings** window **(Figure 3.3)**.

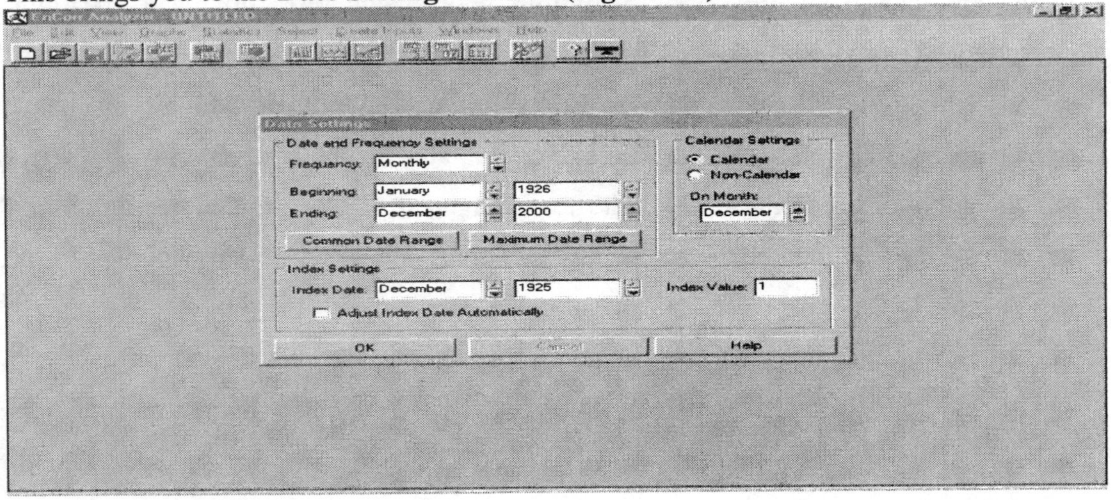

EnCorr Analyzer - [UNTITLED]

File Edit View Graphs Statistics Select Create Inputs Window Help

Date Settings

Date and Frequency Settings
Frequency: Monthly
Beginning: January 1926
Ending: December 2000
Common Date Range | Maximum Date Range

Calendar Settings
Calendar
Non-Calendar
On Month: December

Index Settings
Index Date: December 1925
Index Value: 1
Adjust Index Date Automatically

OK | Cancel | Help

Figure 3.3 Date Settings Window

EnCorr Analyzer - UNTITLED

File Edit View Graphs Statistics Select Create Inputs Windows Help

	U.S. LT Corp TR (%Total Return)
Apr 1998	0.53
May 1998	1.67
Jun 1998	1.15
Jul 1998	-0.56
Aug 1998	0.89
Sep 1998	4.13
Oct 1998	-1.90
Nov 1998	2.70
Dec 1998	0.10
Jan 1999	1.23
Feb 1999	-4.01
Mar 1999	0.02
Apr 1999	-0.24
May 1999	-1.76
Jun 1999	-1.60
Jul 1999	-1.13
Aug 1999	-0.26
Sep 1999	0.93
Oct 1999	0.47
Nov 1999	-0.24
Dec 1999	-1.02
Jan 2000	-0.21
Feb 2000	0.92
Mar 2000	1.69
Apr 2000	-1.15
May 2000	-1.61
Jun 2000	3.26
Jul 2000	1.79
Aug 2000	1.35
Sep 2000	0.46

Figure 3.4 EnCorr Analyzer – Untitled Window

We will now choose the time series we wish to analyze with the **Date Settings**. For Frequency, choose monthly. For Beginning, choose January. Moving to the right of Beginning, choose1926. This is the first year Ibbotson Associates collected data for the series. Moving down the window to Ending, choose December. Moving again to the right, choose 2000. This is the latest data available in the software. Make sure the remaining buttons have the values indicated in Figure 2.2. Click **OK** at the bottom of the window. You will now see the **Figure 3.4** EnCorr Analyzer – Untitled window.

The **EnCorr Analyzer – Untitled** window displays the data series selected in the first and second columns on the left side of the window. We are now ready to create a graph showing monthly rates of return from 1926 to 2000. To create the graphs, go to the drop down **Graphs menu** in the window and choose **Index Graph**. What appears is an index of large company bond returns over time. (**Figure 3.5**)

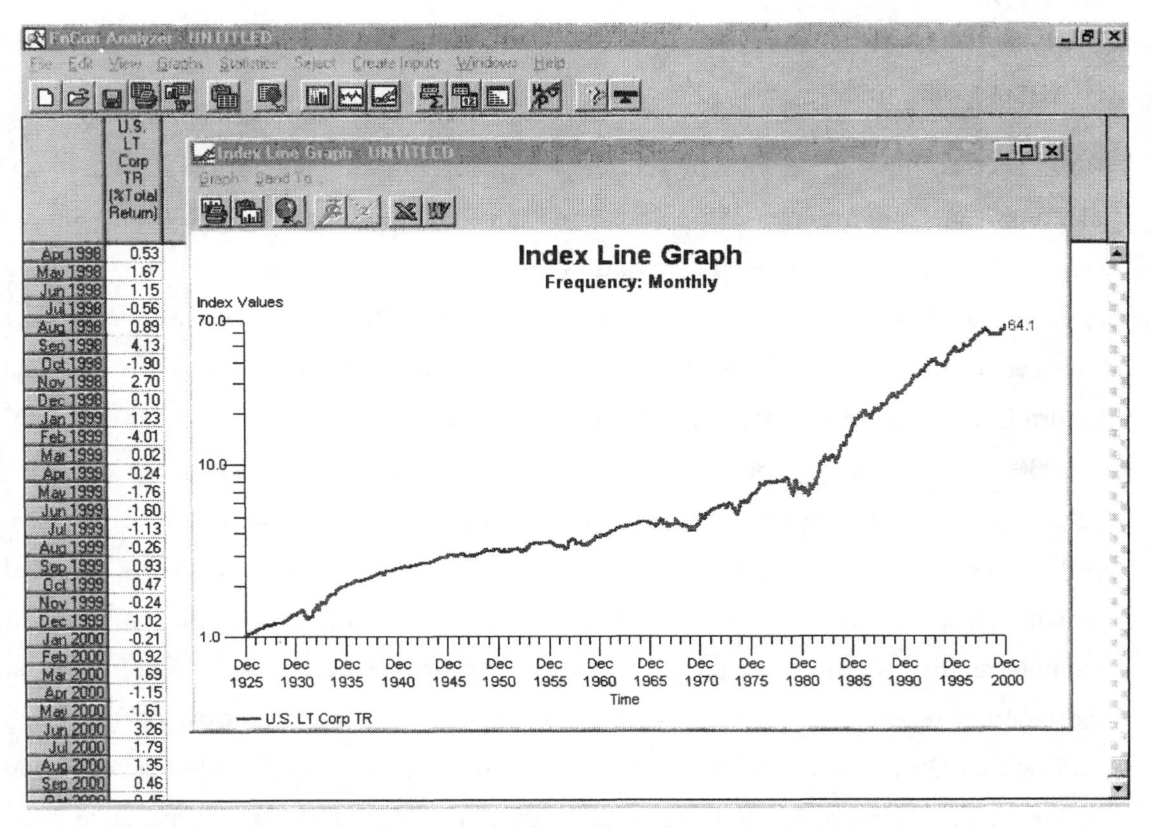

Figure 3.5 Index Graph, U.S. LT Corp TR, 1926-2000 by month

What distinctive features does the index show?

Much of the time series in the earlier years shows a steady growth in index values until 1980 when the growth rate accelerated significantly and stayed that way until the end of the series in the year 2000. The zoom feature allows us to focus in on specific time periods or decades. To observe the change in growth rate, place the cursor "hand" at its point on the graph line from the period 1979 hold the left button of your mouse down and drag it to 1989. You will have highlighted an area to zoom in. Left click your mouse. You will now see a more focused graph on the decade between 1979 and 1989. You will be able to see the start of the period of accelerated growth during the last quarter of 1979. To zoom out, place the point of the cursor "hand" on the graph, right click, choose zoom out, and you will be returned to the original graph from 1926 to 2000.

Combined Indexes

Return and Risk

What accompanied the period of accelerated large-company corporate returns?
The answer to this question can be accessed rather quickly with the software. Simply grab the top bar in blue of the graph window, hold down your left mouse button, and drag the graph to the right side of your computer screen. You will now see the EnCorr Analyzer-Untitled window. Go to the Graphs drop down menu, click on it and select Return Line Graph and click again. What you now observe is the same time period (1926 to 2000) as the original graph but with the monthly rates of returns rather than the index values. If you move one graph to the top of your screen, and the other to the bottom, you will be able to visually observe the two graphs, especially the period of accelerated growth. The period was accompanied by a significant increase in the volatility of monthly returns. Zoom in on the same decade as we observed before, 1979 to 1989, on the monthly returns. To do that again place the cursor "hand" or arrow on the graph starting in 1979 and drag the cursor to 1989. Left click on the highlighted area and you will be shown the more focused time series. You will note that the returns began to grow especially volatile in the same period the growth in the index values began a significant accelerated trend.

Summary
The exercise gave us a good example of the use for an index. First, we gained knowledge very quickly over the period from 1926 to 2000. We also observed that using indexes in combination with other series such as monthly rates of return was also very helpful and allowed us to investigate the market interrelationships. The value of large-company corporate bond returns grew significantly beginning in the last quarter of 1979 and the growth was accompanied by a significant increase in the volatility (risk) of monthly returns. Finally, we were able to verify that the overall economic relationship between market return (reward) and volatility (risk) was direct.

Ibbotson Associates has provided a series of wealth indices for Average U.S. Investments in the different asset classes we used in earlier chapters. With the software included with the text, you have the ability to access data, known as the Wealth Indices, that show the historical paths of $1 invested on December 31, 1925 in several asset classes. For the sake of comparison, we will also examine the inflation rate in the U.S. Consumer Price Index (CPI). We will now show how Figure 2.1 in your text was created.

How To Graph the Ibbotson Wealth Indexes (SBBI)

From the EnCorr Analyzer main page, click **Select, Series** from the menu bar. Then click on the **Ibbotson Database** and **Stocks, Bonds, Bills, and Inflation** (SBBI). Double click on the following series to be graphed:

- S&P 500 TR (Large company)
- U.S. Small Stk TR
- U.S. LT Gvt TR
- U.S. 30 Day Tbill TR
- U.S. Inflation

The values in **Figure 3.6** should be displayed.

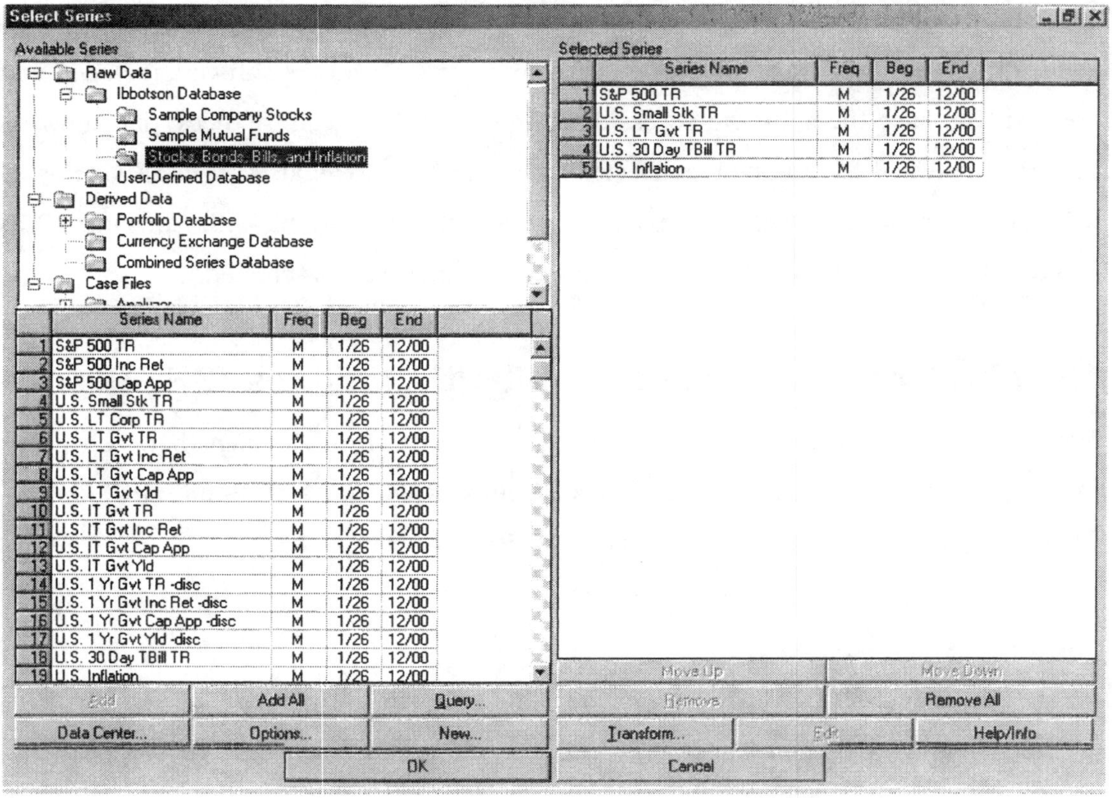

Figure 3.6 Selected Series for Stocks, Bonds, Bills and Inflation

Click **OK**, which brings up the **Date Settings** window. To reproduce Figure 2.1 in Chapter 2 of your text we will need to change the end date from December 2000 to December 1999. (**Figure 3.7**) Make the change in the Ending window, right-hand side. Click **OK**.

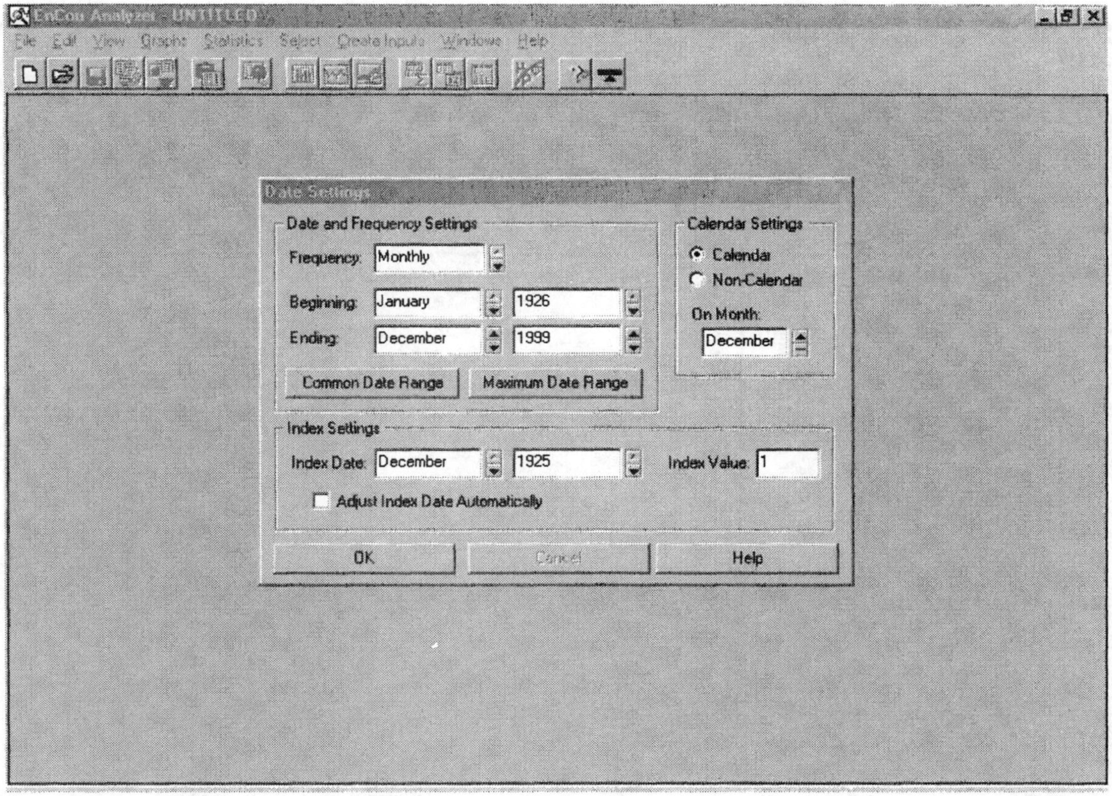

Figure 3.7 Adjusting Ending Year

The main window now appears with the selected series in columnar format. Select **Graph, Index Graph** to create the Wealth Indices Graph. (**Figure 3.8**)

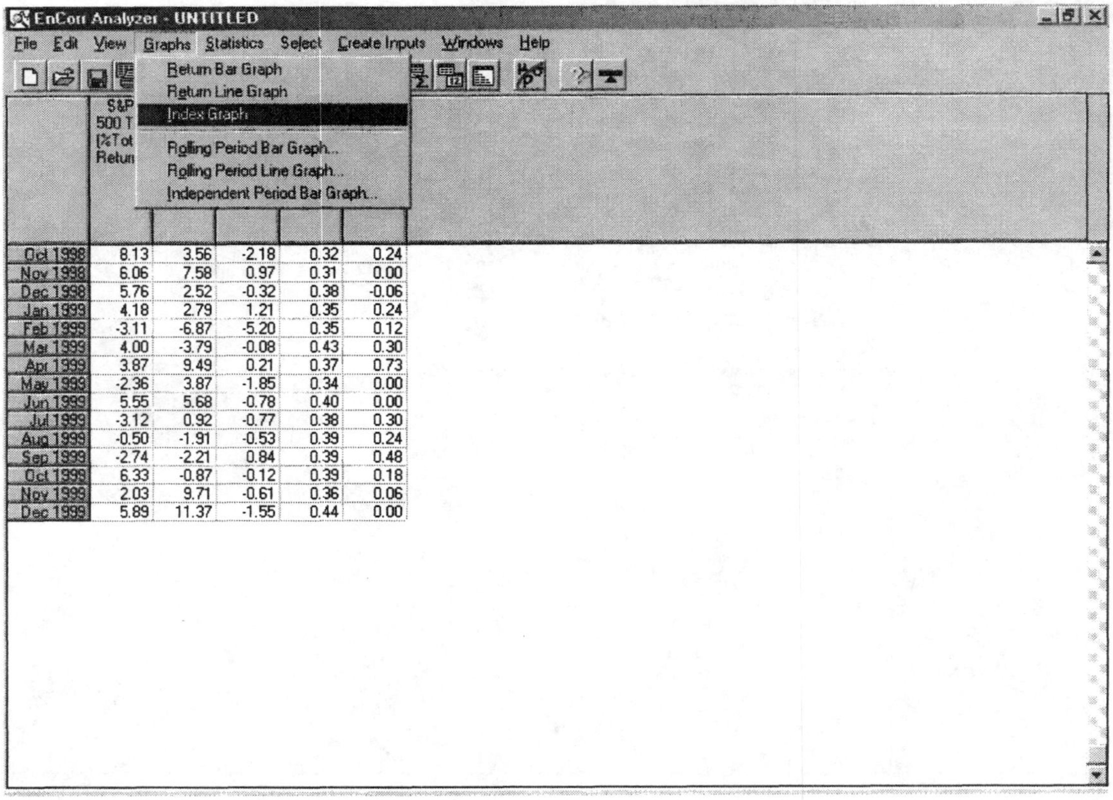

EnCorr Analyzer - UNTITLED

File Edit View Graphs Statistics Select Create Inputs Windows Help

Return Bar Graph
Return Line Graph
Index Graph
Rolling Period Bar Graph...
Rolling Period Line Graph...
Independent Period Bar Graph...

	S&P 500 T (%Tot Return				
Oct 1998	8.13	3.56	-2.18	0.32	0.24
Nov 1998	6.06	7.58	0.97	0.31	0.00
Dec 1998	5.76	2.52	-0.32	0.38	-0.06
Jan 1999	4.18	2.79	1.21	0.35	0.24
Feb 1999	-3.11	-6.87	-5.20	0.35	0.12
Mar 1999	4.00	-3.79	-0.08	0.43	0.30
Apr 1999	3.87	9.49	0.21	0.37	0.73
May 1999	-2.36	3.87	-1.85	0.34	0.00
Jun 1999	5.55	5.68	-0.78	0.40	0.00
Jul 1999	-3.12	0.92	-0.77	0.38	0.30
Aug 1999	-0.50	-1.91	-0.53	0.39	0.24
Sep 1999	-2.74	-2.21	0.84	0.39	0.48
Oct 1999	6.33	-0.87	-0.12	0.39	0.18
Nov 1999	2.03	9.71	-0.61	0.36	0.06
Dec 1999	5.89	11.37	-1.55	0.44	0.00

Figure 3.8 Main window

Click on Index Graph and **Figure 3.9** appears.

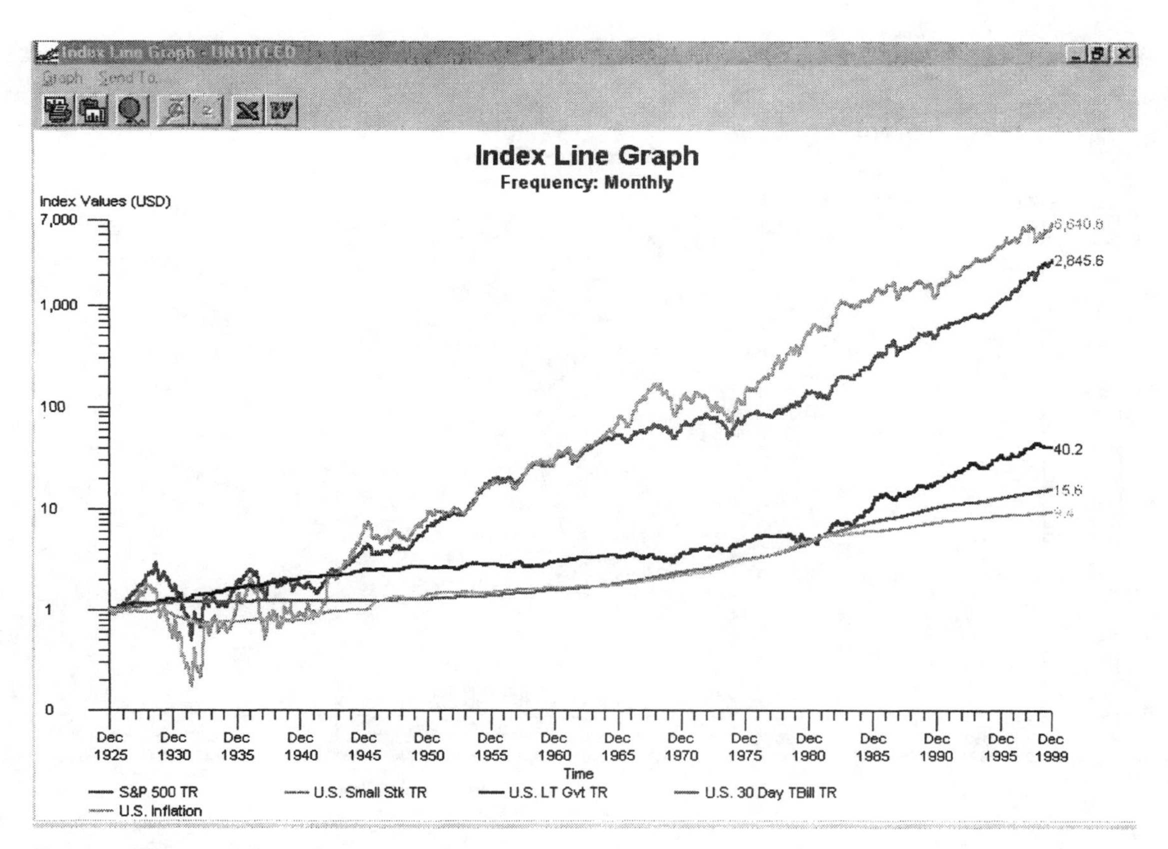

Figure 3.9 The Ibbotson Wealth Indexes

To format the ending values in dollars and cents, in the Graph window, click on the Graph dropdown and select **Display Options**. Change the value of the decimal places to 2. Click **OK**. (**Figure 3.10**)

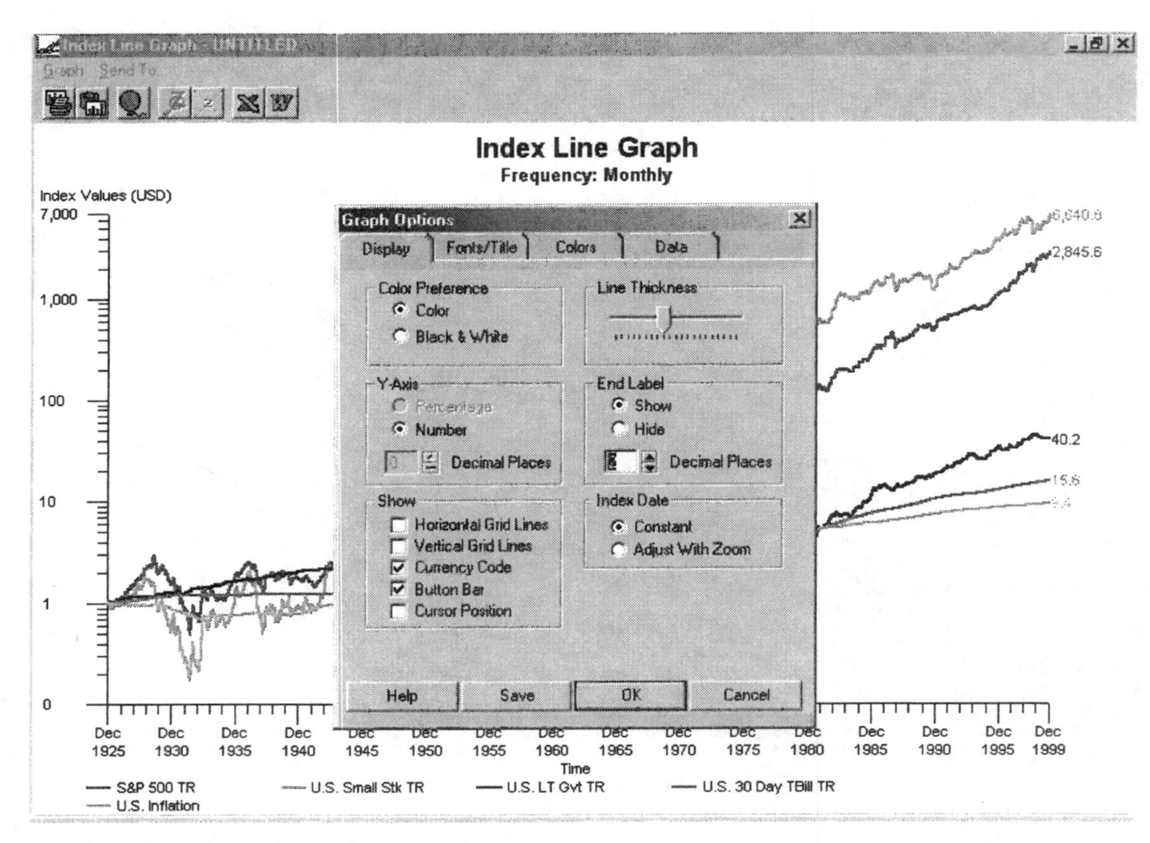

Figure 3.10 Changing the Decimal Places

You now have created the Ibbotson Wealth Indexes. You can get a much closer view of the individual decades between 1925 and 1999 using the highlight and Zoom function described in Chapter 2.

EXERCISES

General Series

3.1 Which one of the four asset classes was the least risky (erratic) over the time period, 1926 to 2000? What was the terminal value of the asset in 2000?

3.2 Which asset class outperformed the inflation rate the most? The Least? Compare the terminal values of the most and the least with the similar value for the inflation rate. What is the range from the least to the most?

3.3 In what years did inflation advance faster that T-bills? What was the effect on the investment in T-bills during these times?

3.4 Which one of the four asset classes was the most risky (erratic)? How does its terminal value rank along side the other asset classes?

3.5 What relationship can you observe using the Wealth Indices with respect to an investment's historical path?

Individual Decades (use the Zoom feature)

3.6 In the least risky asset, which decade was most volatile with respect to its returns? What reasons would you give to explain this variability?

3.7 In the most risky asset, which decade was most volatile with respect to its returns? What reasons would you give to explain this variability?

3.8 What asset proved the most rewarding during periods of high volatility? During what decades? Why?

4

Statistical Measures

Using Statistical Measures When Investing

When Harry Markowitz introduced us to Modern Portfolio Theory, certain statistical measures developed into commonly used terms in the investment industry such as expected rate of return, standard deviation, and the correlation coefficient. Each of the measures had a place in the Markowitz model.

The EnCorr Analyzer software creates the statistical measures above and much more for analyzing stocks and bonds. In this chapter we will show how the statistics are generated as well as prepare input files for the EnCorr Optimizer software that we will use to build portfolios in Chapter 7.

Rates of Return

In Chapter 2 we learn that two average rates of return are used in analyzing a return series, the arithmetic and the geometric means. Each type of mean has an appropriate role in the analysis.

The Arithmetic Mean

The arithmetic mean is a simple average of a series of returns that incorporates the volatility (the risk) into expectations for the future. Compared to the geometric mean, the arithmetic represents a better picture of a typical performance over single periods. The arithmetic means of historical annual returns should be measure over a representative sample period that might cover one complete business cycle from prosperity to recession to depression to recovery to prosperity (measured peak to peak) or from depression, recovery, prosperity, recession to depression (measured from trough to trough).

The Geometric Mean

The geometric mean, or t he compound rate of return, is a measure of the actual average performance of a series over a given time period. It is backward-looking since it relates the beginning and ending values of an investment. It is a rate of return, which if earned in every period would result in the ending wealth. A geometric mean is also sometimes referred to as the internal rate of return.

In general, the geometric mean for any time period is less than or equal to the arithmetic mean. The two means are equal only for a return series that is constant (i.e. the same return in every period). For a non-constant series, the difference between the two is positively related to the variability or standard deviation of the returns.

We will illustrate this with a sample exercise. From the Main Window of EnCorr Analyzer, click on **Select, Series.** Select the **Ibbotson Database**, **Stocks Bonds Bills and Inflation Series**. For this exercise double click on U.S. 30-day Treasury bills TR and U.S. Long Term Corporate TR. Click **OK**. The **Date Settings** window appears. To confine our analysis to one business cycle measured from peak to peak, select the beginning value of January 1929 and ending period of December 1941. Click **OK**. The two series now appear in the main window in columnar form. Choose **Statistics, Summary Statistics**. The **Summary Statistics** window appears providing the arithmetic and geometric mean of both series. (**Figure 4.1**)

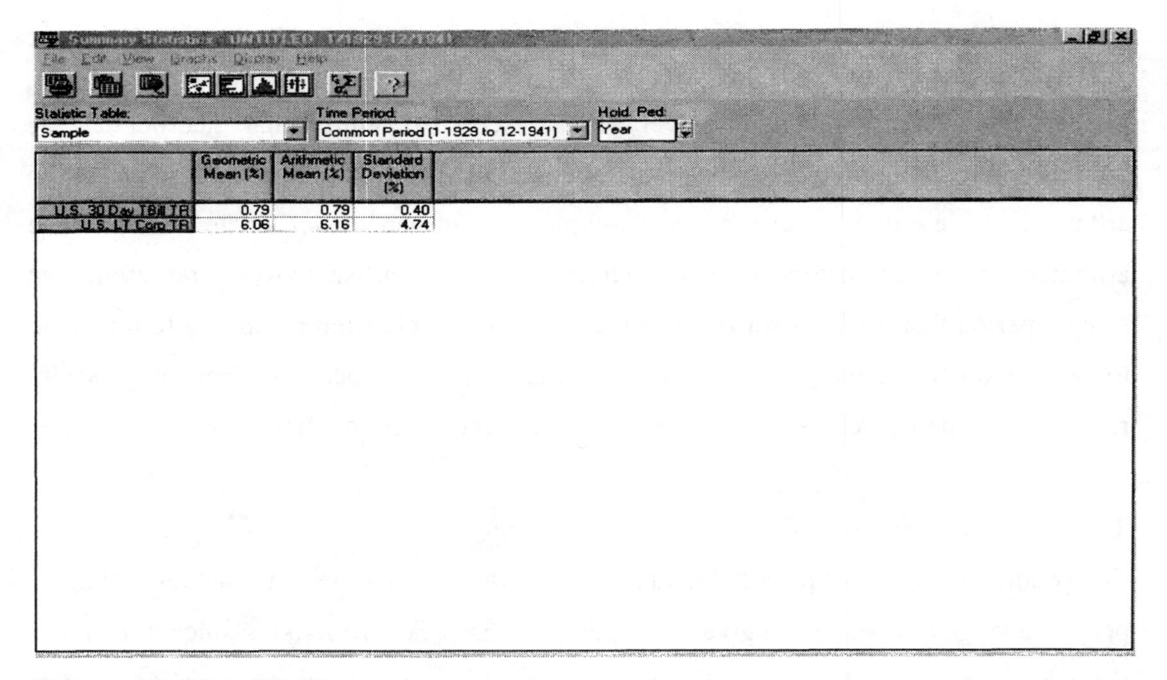

Figure 4.1 Main Window

As you can observe, the T-bill series contains the smaller standard deviation and the two means are identical. On the other hand, the U.S. Corporate series has a much larger value for standard deviation and the two means are not close. In both cases, we can observe that the geometric mean is less than or equal to the arithmetic but never greater.

To gain a better idea of the variability of the two series we can employ the graphing function. Click out of the Summary Statistics window and return to Main window that still has the two series in it. Select **Graph**, and click on **Return Line Graph.** The two series are now compared and the variability of the larger company bond returns becomes obvious. (Figure 4.2)

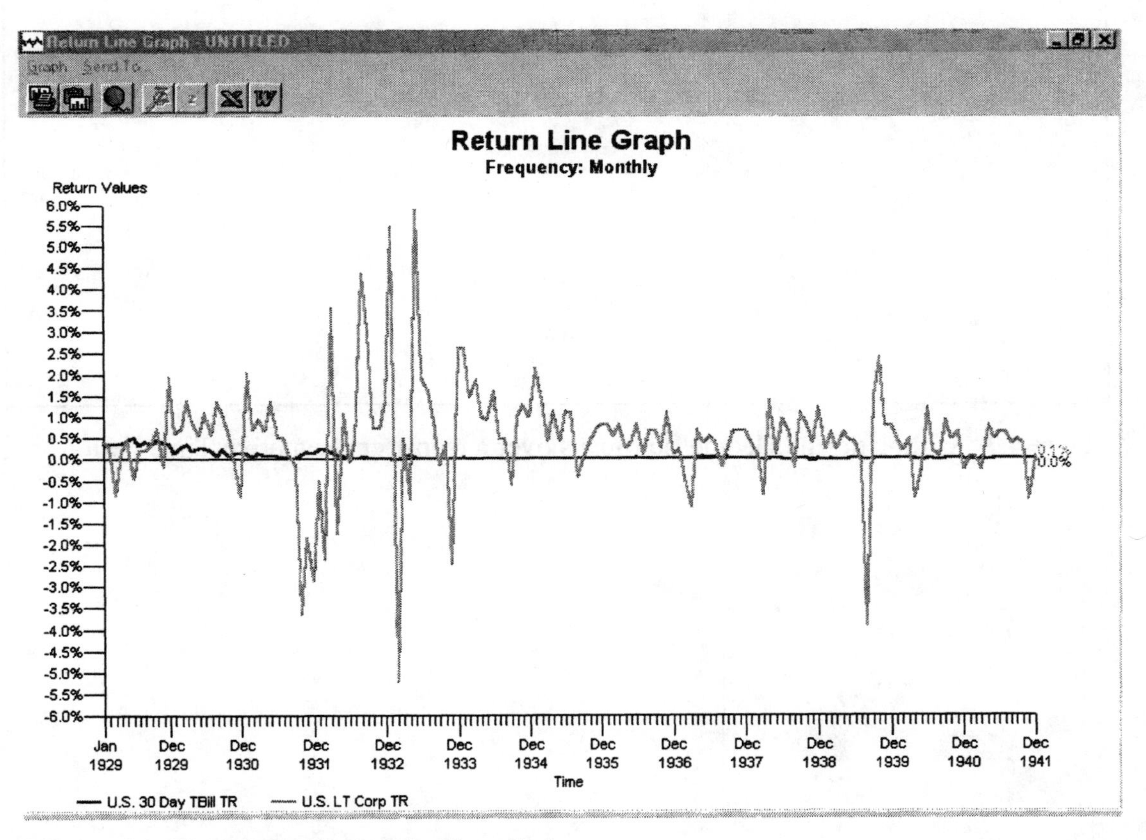

Figure 4.2 The Variability of the Two Series.

Now let's see what a non-representative sample does to the arithmetic mean. From the **Select** menu, click on **Date Settings**. Change the beginning value to January 1926 and the ending value to December 1950. Click OK. In the main window from the **Statistics** menu, click on **Summary Statistics**. A new window appears with very different arithmetic averages from the previous sample (Figure 4.3). The U.S. 30-day T-bill TR is not similar to the previous time period. For that matter neither is the U.S. LT Corp TR.

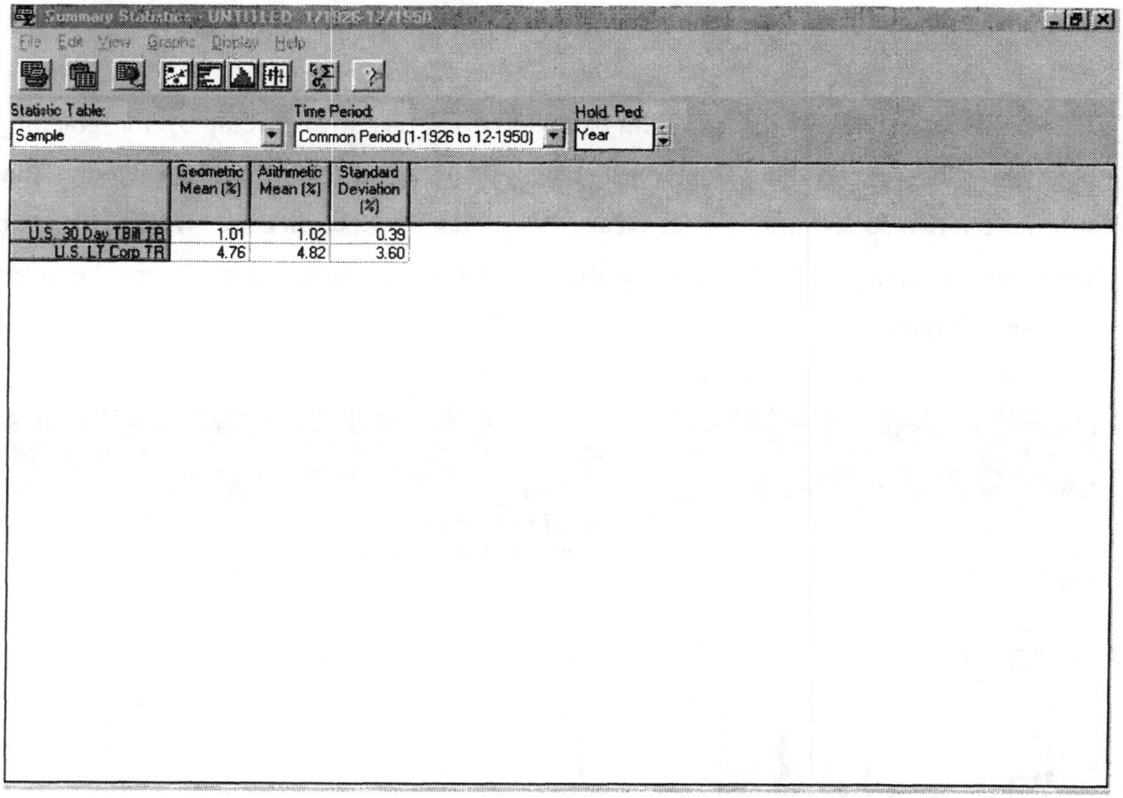

Summary Statistics - UNTITLED 1/1926-12/1950

File Edit View Graphs Display Help

Statistic Table: Sample | Time Period: Common Period (1-1926 to 12-1950) | Hold Ped: Year

	Geometric Mean (%)	Arithmetic Mean (%)	Standard Deviation (%)
U.S. 30 Day TBill TR	1.01	1.02	0.39
U.S. LT Corp TR	4.76	4.82	3.60

Figure 4.3 Arithmetic and Geometric Means over a Non-Representative Time Period

Exercises

4.1 The following exercises provide situations that allow for mean and risk analyses:

a. Table 2-1 in your text (p. 24) gives the geometric and arithmetic means for the assets in the Ibbotson Associates wealth indexes along with the inflation rates over the entire series, 1926 to 1999. This is definitely not a single business cycle nor a good sampling of the series. In the following series, use the business cycle we used in the example (1929-1941) to compare the differences in what the Table values are and what they were during the cycle.

   i. Small-company stocks total returns
   ii. Large-company total returns (S&P)
   iii. Long-term government bonds total returns
   iv. Intermediate-term government bonds returns

b. Plot the variance in returns for each series on a single graph.

c. Which one of the series displays the greatest volatility? The least volatility? How do the difference reflect in the arithmetic and geometric means?

4.2 Choose another complete business cycle from the overall time series (1926 to 1999 and repeat the steps you performed in Exercise 4.1. Compared to the 1929-1941 cycle, what assets displayed the highest returns? Lowest returns? Are these consistent with the volatility relationship that we observed in Exercise 4.1 and 4.2?

4.3 Of the two cycles you have analyzed which one was the riskier time for each asset class? Why? Use historical references in your explanation.

The Correlation Coefficient

The correlation coefficient is a standardized value that varies in the interval from +1 to –1. In modern portfolio theory, it measures how stock returns vary between two companies. If a stock's returns are *perfectly inversely correlated* with another stock's returns, the coefficient equals –1. If they are *perfectly positively correlated*, the value is +1. If the correlation coefficient equals 0, the two return series are *uncorrelated.*

The correlation coefficient serves as the engine for diversification in the Markowitz model. The closer the coefficient reaches –1 between assets in a portfolio, the greater the diversification benefits.

Calculating the Correlation Coefficient

To compute the correlation between the two stock series we used in the previous section of this chapter, click on **Select|Series|IbbotsonDatabase|Stocks,Bonds,Bills,andInflation.** Double click on the two series, **U.S. 30-dayTBill TR** and **U.S. LT Corp TR (Figure 4.4).**

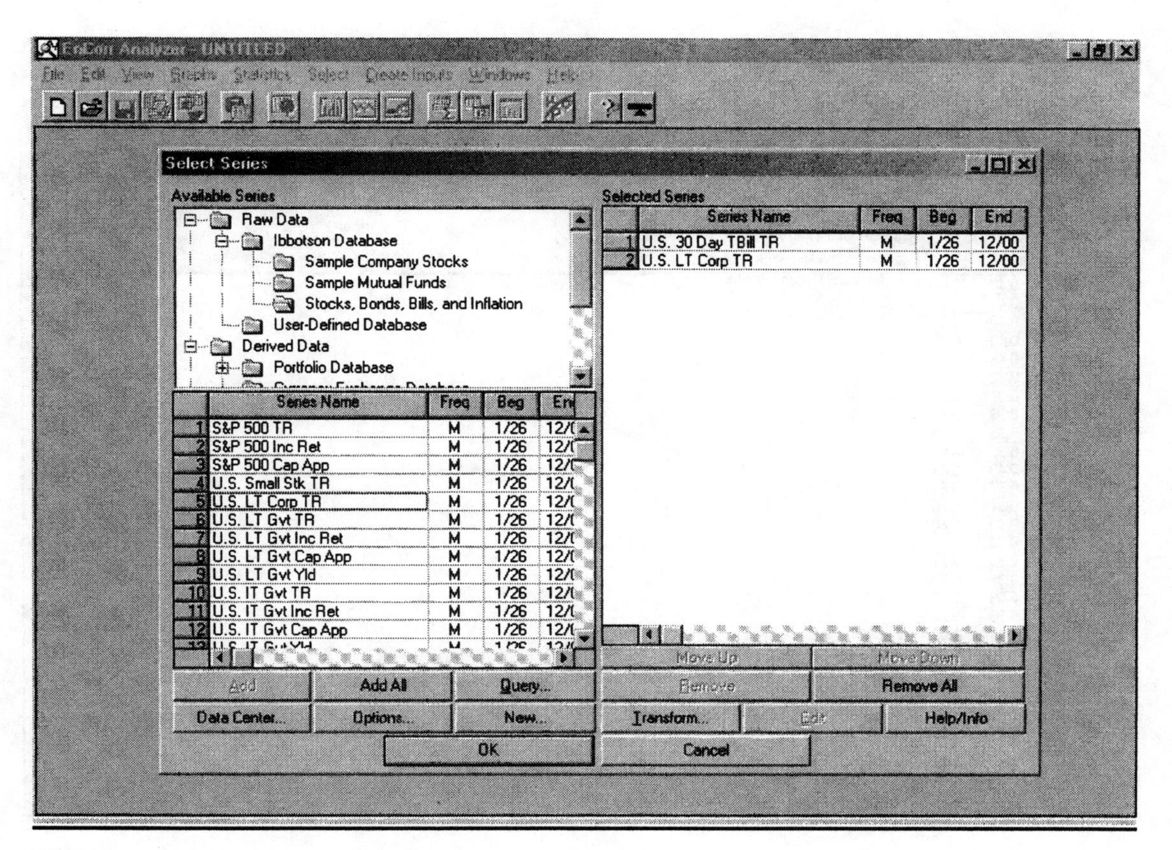

Figure 4.4 Selected Series

Click OK and the Date Setting Window appears. Let the series begin and end with the available data 1926-2000. Click OK. The two series appear in columnar form in the main window again. Click on the **Statistics|Correlation Matrix** (**Figure 4.5**).

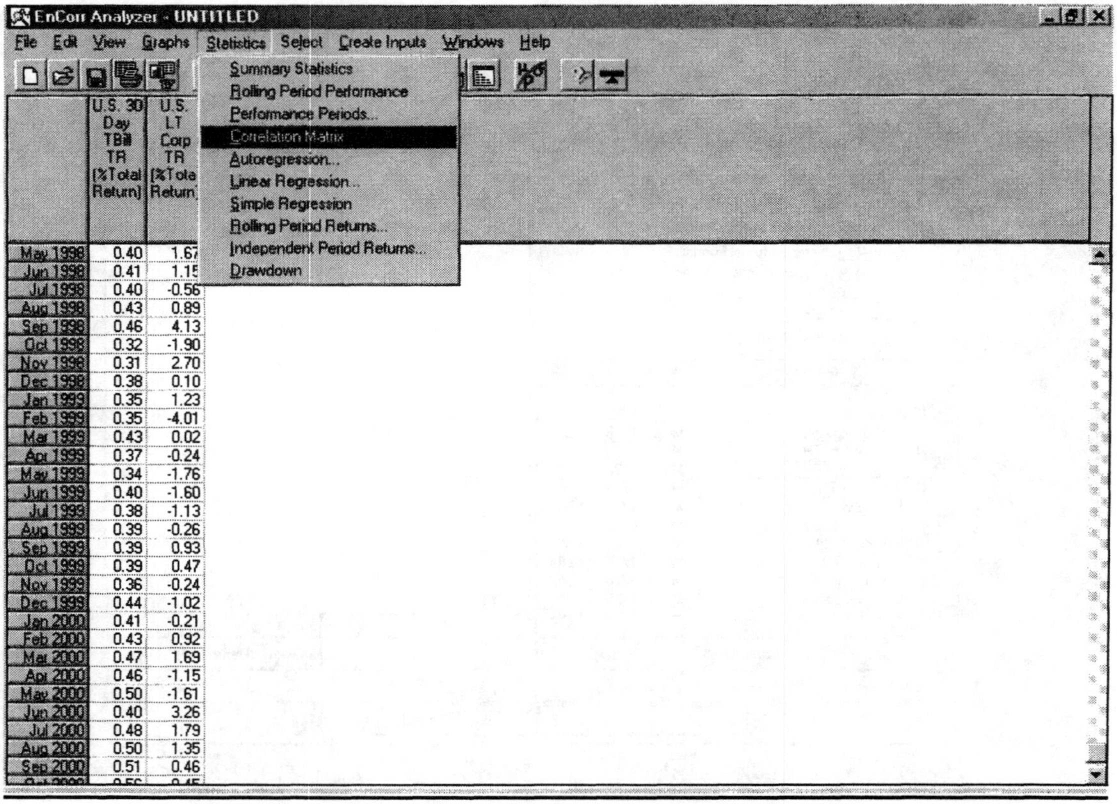

EnCorr Analyzer - UNTITLED

File Edit View Graphs Statistics Select Create Inputs Windows Help

Summary Statistics
Rolling Period Performance
Performance Periods...
Correlation Matrix
Autoregression...
Linear Regression...
Simple Regression
Rolling Period Returns...
Independent Period Returns...
Drawdown

	U.S. 30 Day TBill TR (%Total Return)	U.S. LT Corp TR (%Total Return)
May 1998	0.40	1.67
Jun 1998	0.41	1.15
Jul 1998	0.40	-0.56
Aug 1998	0.43	0.89
Sep 1998	0.46	4.13
Oct 1998	0.32	-1.90
Nov 1998	0.31	2.70
Dec 1998	0.38	0.10
Jan 1999	0.35	1.23
Feb 1999	0.35	-4.01
Mar 1999	0.43	0.02
Apr 1999	0.37	-0.24
May 1999	0.34	-1.76
Jun 1999	0.40	-1.60
Jul 1999	0.38	-1.13
Aug 1999	0.39	-0.26
Sep 1999	0.39	0.93
Oct 1999	0.39	0.47
Nov 1999	0.36	-0.24
Dec 1999	0.44	-1.02
Jan 2000	0.41	-0.21
Feb 2000	0.43	0.92
Mar 2000	0.47	1.69
Apr 2000	0.46	-1.15
May 2000	0.50	-1.61
Jun 2000	0.40	3.26
Jul 2000	0.48	1.79
Aug 2000	0.50	1.35
Sep 2000	0.51	0.46

Figure 4.5 Select the Correlation Matrix

Double click on the **Correlation Matrix**. The window with the correlation coefficient values will appear. (**Figure 4.6**)

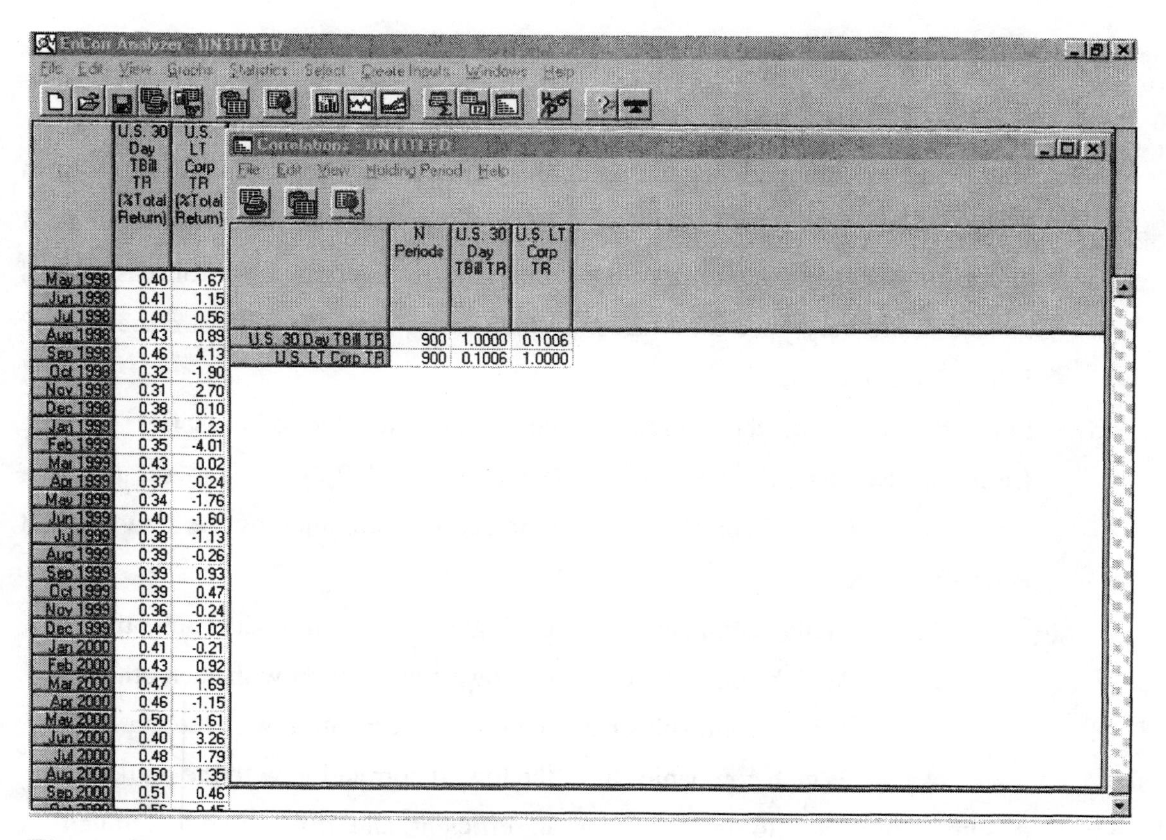

Figure 4.6 Correlation Coefficient Values

As you will observe, the variability of the Total Returns between the T-bill series and the Long Term Corporate bond Total Returns have a relatively low correlation (.1006) during the time period, 1926 to 2000. But you will also note, the relationship is positive meaning the two move in the same direction when they experienced a change in values. Yet, the low value of .1006 might make them a likely pair for a diversified portfolio.

EXERCISES

4.4 Find the correlation between the remaining series in the **Stocks, Bonds, Bills, and Inflation Series.** The resulting table that you create will give you a good indication of series that are excellent candidates to diversify a portfolio as well as those that are very poor candidates. Which series have the highest correlations? Which have the lowest?

4.5 Find the values of the correlation coefficients for the other series **Sample Company Stocks.** Be sure to include the series **S&P 500 TR** to see how the company returns were correlated to the market as represented by the Standard and Poor 500 index.

1. Which companies have the highest correlation with each other?
2. Which companies have the lowest correlation with each other?
3. Which companies have the highest correlation with the market?
4. Which companies have the lowest correlation with the market?

4.6 Assume you want to put together an efficient and diversified (as much as possible) portfolio of the Sample Company Stocks. Choose any 10 and defend your choice.

5

Equity Shares

INTRODUCTION TO EQUITY ANALYSIS

In this chapter we investigate the risk-return tools that Markowitz introduced to the investment industry. We will analyze a stock's total return and total risk and partition the risk into the diversifiable and undiversifiable segments. Our goal will be to identify the characteristics of an allocation of risky assets into an efficient portfolio that we will create in Chapter 7.

Equity Risk and Return

The Ibbotson Associates software packaged with your textbook provides a sample of historical returns for 16 American companies between 1989 and 2000. We will access these securities to perform our analyses.

From the EnCorr Analyzer Main Window click on **Select, Series, Ibbotson Database, Sample Company Stocks**. The list of 16 company stock returns will appear in the series name box. Double click on Eastman Kodak. The return series will now appear in the Selected Series window on the right side of the window (**Figure 5.1**). Click **OK**.

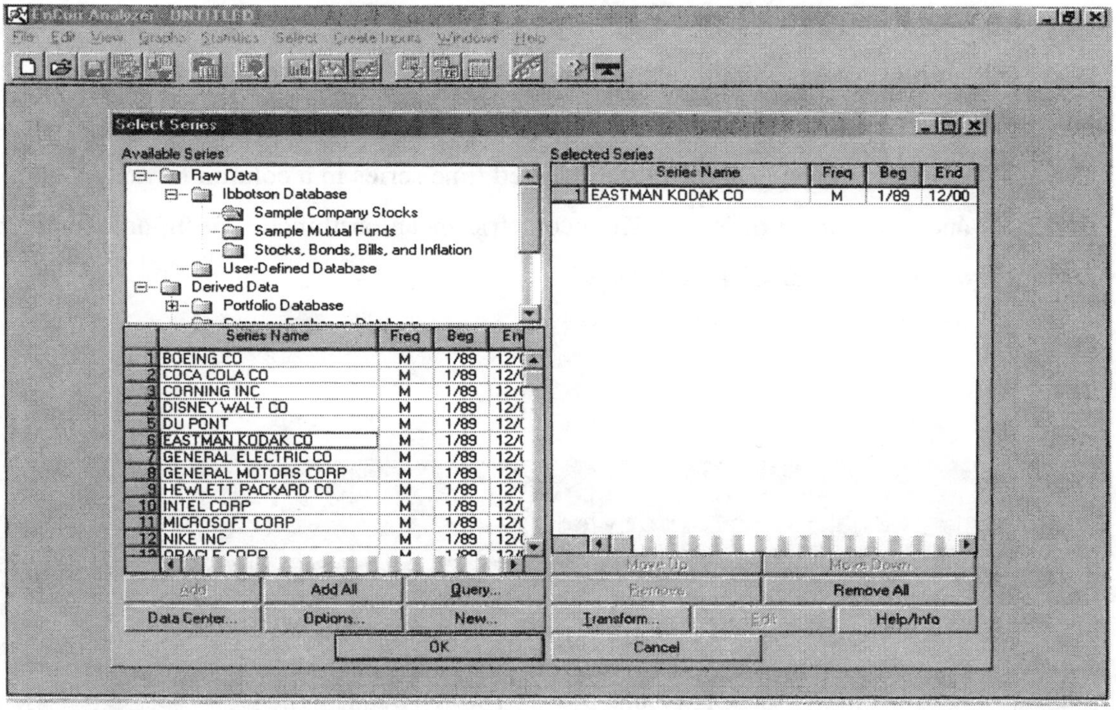

FinCorr Analyzer - UNTITLED
File Edit View Graphs Statistics Select Create Inputs Windows Help

Select Series

Available Series
Raw Data
Ibbotson Database
Sample Company Stocks
Sample Mutual Funds
Stocks, Bonds, Bills, and Inflation
User-Defined Database
Derived Data
Portfolio Database

	Series Name	Freq	Beg	End
1	BOEING CO	M	1/89	12/(
2	COCA COLA CO	M	1/89	12/(
3	CORNING INC	M	1/89	12/(
4	DISNEY WALT CO	M	1/89	12/(
5	DU PONT	M	1/89	12/(
6	EASTMAN KODAK CO	M	1/89	12/(
7	GENERAL ELECTRIC CO	M	1/89	12/(
8	GENERAL MOTORS CORP	M	1/89	12/(
9	HEWLETT PACKARD CO	M	1/89	12/(
10	INTEL CORP	M	1/89	12/(
11	MICROSOFT CORP	M	1/89	12/(
12	NIKE INC	M	1/89	12/(

Selected Series

	Series Name	Freq	Beg	End
1	EASTMAN KODAK CO	M	1/89	12/00

Add | Add All | Query... | Move Up | Move Down | Remove | Remove All
Data Center... | Options... | New... | Transform... | Edit | Help/Info
OK | Cancel

Figure 5.1 Main Window/Selected Series

The **Data Settings** window appears (**Figure 5.2**).

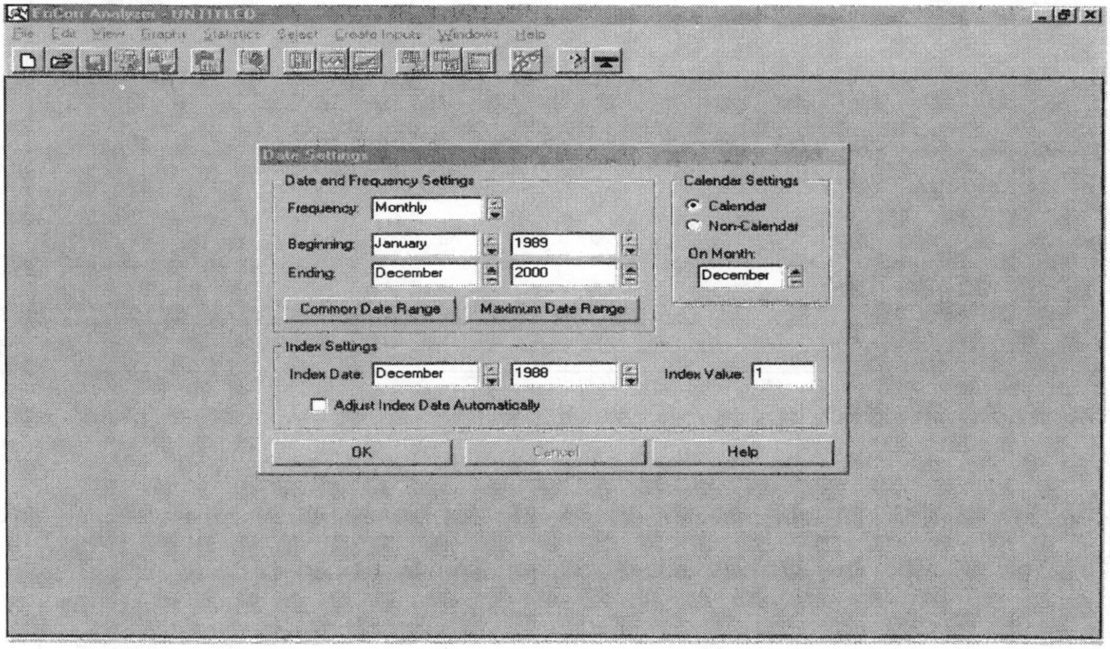

FinCorr Analyzer - UNTITLED
File Edit View Graphs Statistics Select Create Inputs Windows Help

Data Settings

Date and Frequency Settings
Frequency: Monthly
Beginning: January 1989
Ending: December 2000
Common Date Range | Maximum Date Range

Calendar Settings
Calendar
Non-Calendar
On Month: December

Index Settings
Index Date: December 1988 Index Value: 1
Adjust Index Date Automatically

OK | Cancel | Help

Figure 5.2 Data Settings

Leave the settings, years, months, etc. as you see them in Figure 5.2. Click **OK**.

The Main window now appears with the selected time series in a column format. Choose **Statistics** and click on **Summary**. The geometric mean, arithmetic mean, and standard deviation will now appear (**Figure 5.3**).

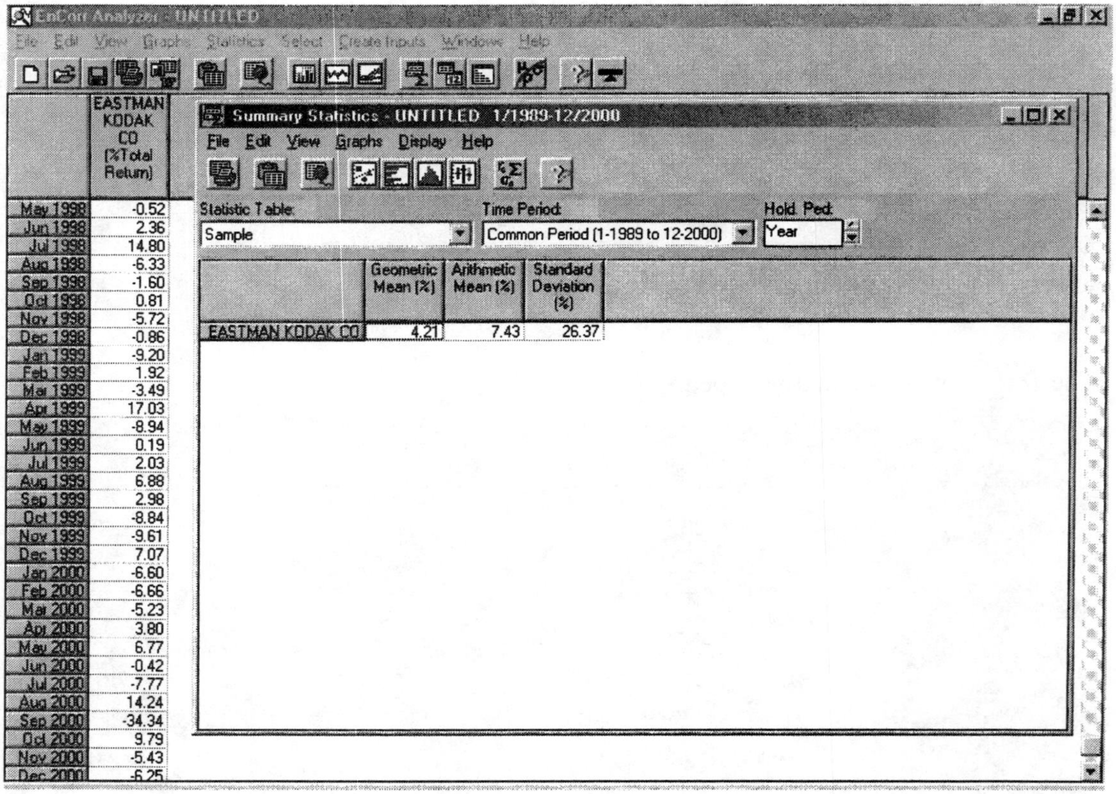

Figure 5.3 Summary Statistics for Eastman Kodak

We now have an indication of the average return and its variability for the series, but it is possible to further analyze the standard deviation, known as the risk.

RISK ANALYSIS

In the text by Francis and Ibbotson, we have learned in Chapter 2 that risk equates with variability of return. An asset is perceived as riskier when its returns fluctuate over a wider range. We can observe the range of return changes firsthand for Eastman Kodak using the graphing function.

In the Main Window with the Eastman Kodak returns displayed (**Figure 5.1**), select the **Return Line Graph** from the **Graphs** drop down. A monthly graph over the time period from 1989 to 2000 now appears (**Figure 5.4**). The ending value for monthly returns for the series indicates a return of negative 6.2%. Although we are now aware that the monthly returns appear quite variable (from a positive 25% in 1992 to a negative 35% in 2000), we are not aware of any common or expected values during the time period.

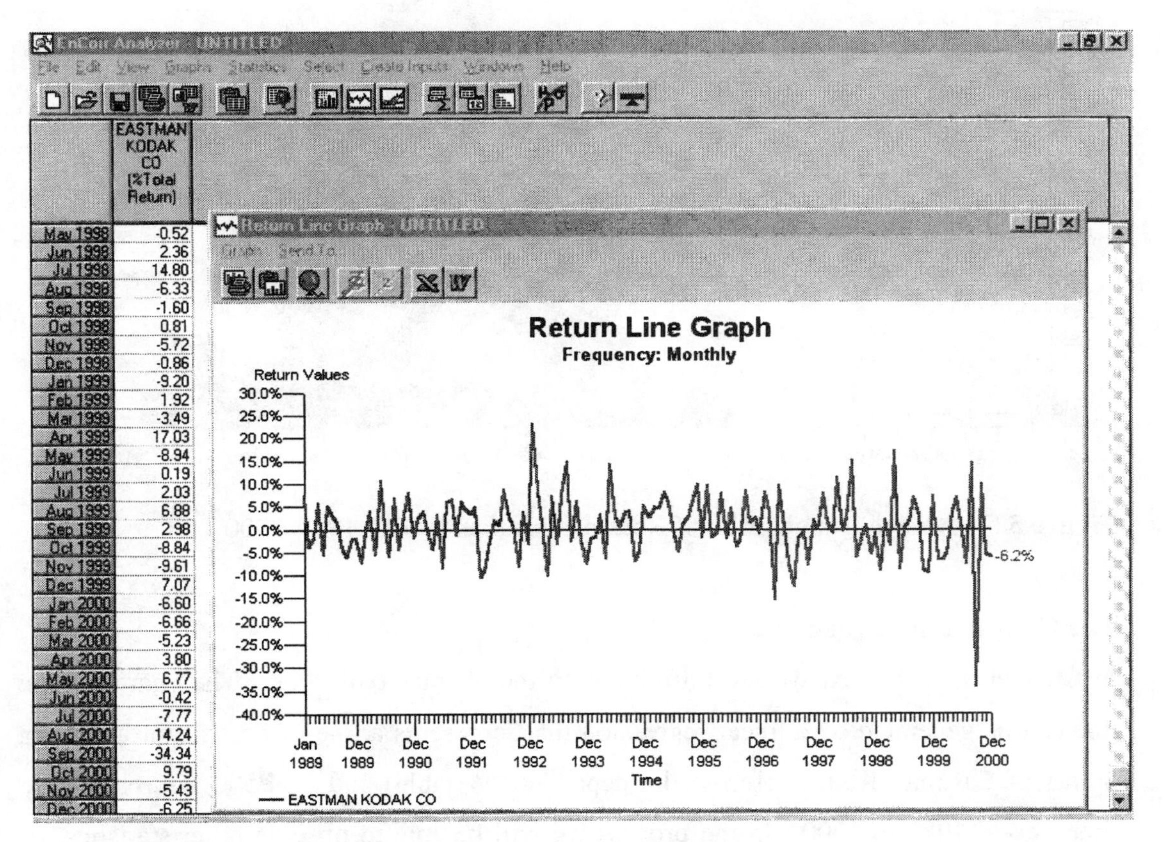

Figure 5.4 Return Line Graph: Eastman Kodak Company

The Histogram

A more precise method to observe and analyze variability is to look at the frequency of a stocks return using a histogram. To plot the histogram go to the drop down menu in the **Summary Statistics** window, select **Graphs** and click on **Histogram**. A histogram of Eastman Kodak average return frequencies is now displayed showing the most frequent return (20% probability) of around 2 to 4% on a monthly basis (**Figure 5.5**).

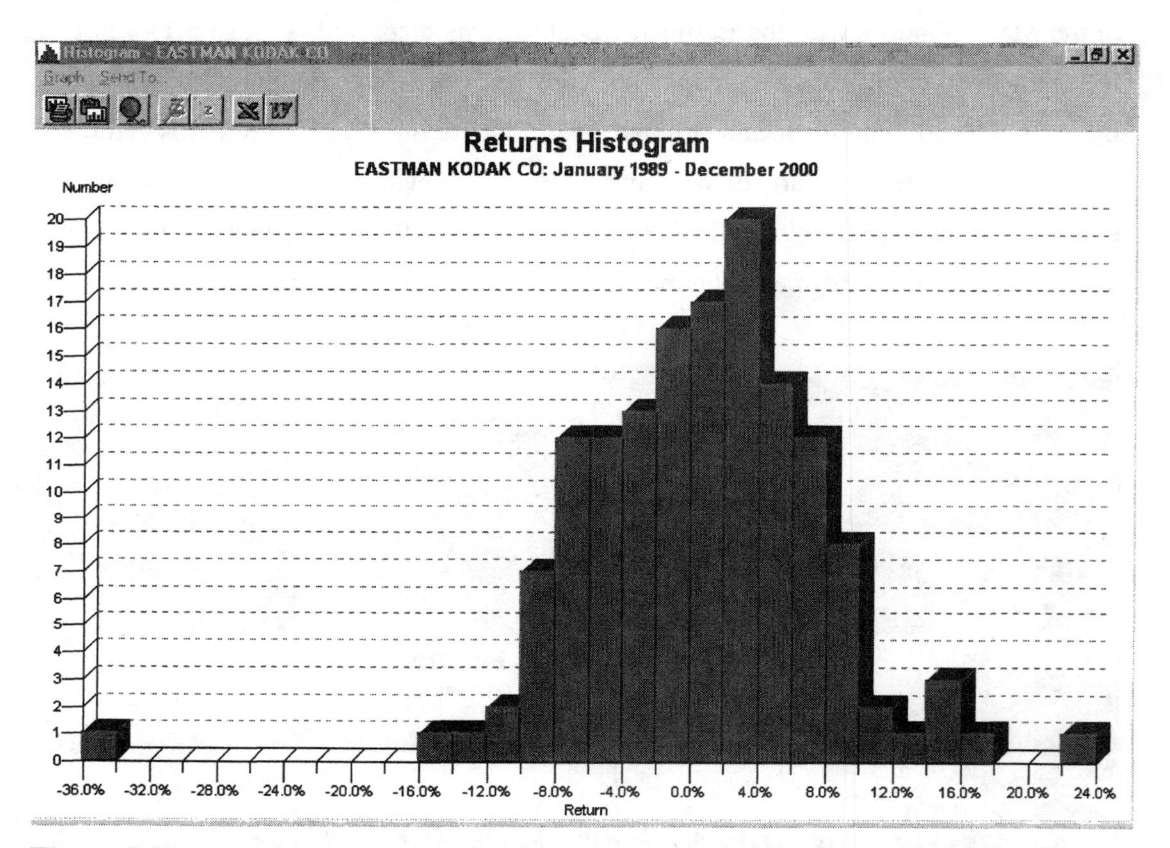

Figure 5.5 Average Annual Rate of Return: Eastman Kodak 1989-2000

The Characteristic Line

In Chapter 7 of the text we are introduced to the characteristic line. The characteristic line can be generated by a linear regression that represents a line-of-best-fit through data points of Eastman Kodak returns (the dependent variable) and S&P500 returns for the time period 1989 to 2000. In the process we will be able to observe other statistics of equity risk such as beta and residual variance.

Components of Risk

Beta

The total risk of an asset's return consists of two components: diversifiable and non-diversifiable risk. We know that the rational investor can and will eliminate diversifiable risk, but non-diversifiable risk by its basic nature is the only relevant component since it is inescapable. Using the S&P500 returns as the independent variable plotted on the horizontal axis gives a representaion of the economic forces that drive the securities market. We will plot the Eastman Kodak monthly returns as the dependent variable on the vertical axis. The beta coefficient will measure the undiversifiable risk or variability. Beta, when computed as the slope coefficient of our regression, will indicate how the returns of Eastman Kodak are related to the returns of the market. For analytical purposes, we will be a able to observe how the stock's returns respond to the economic forces of the market. The more responsive the returns, the higher will be the value of the beta and that security's risk with respect to the market. This statistic can assist the investor, his broker, or the fund manager to determine the composition of his or her portfolio and how the addition of a certain stock affects the total risk.

Computing Beta

To calculate the beta for Eastman Kodak using linear regression, we must add the **S&P500 TR** series from the Main Window. To do this choose **Select|Series**, click on **Stocks Bonds Bills and Inflaiton** series. Double click on the **S&P500 TR** series to add it to the **Selected Series** window on the right-side of the screen. Click **OK**. Next, the data settings window appears and click **OK**. In the main window, click on **Statistics|Linear Regression.** The Main Window will now display the Linear Regression window where we will choose the dependent and independent variables. (**Figure 5.6**).

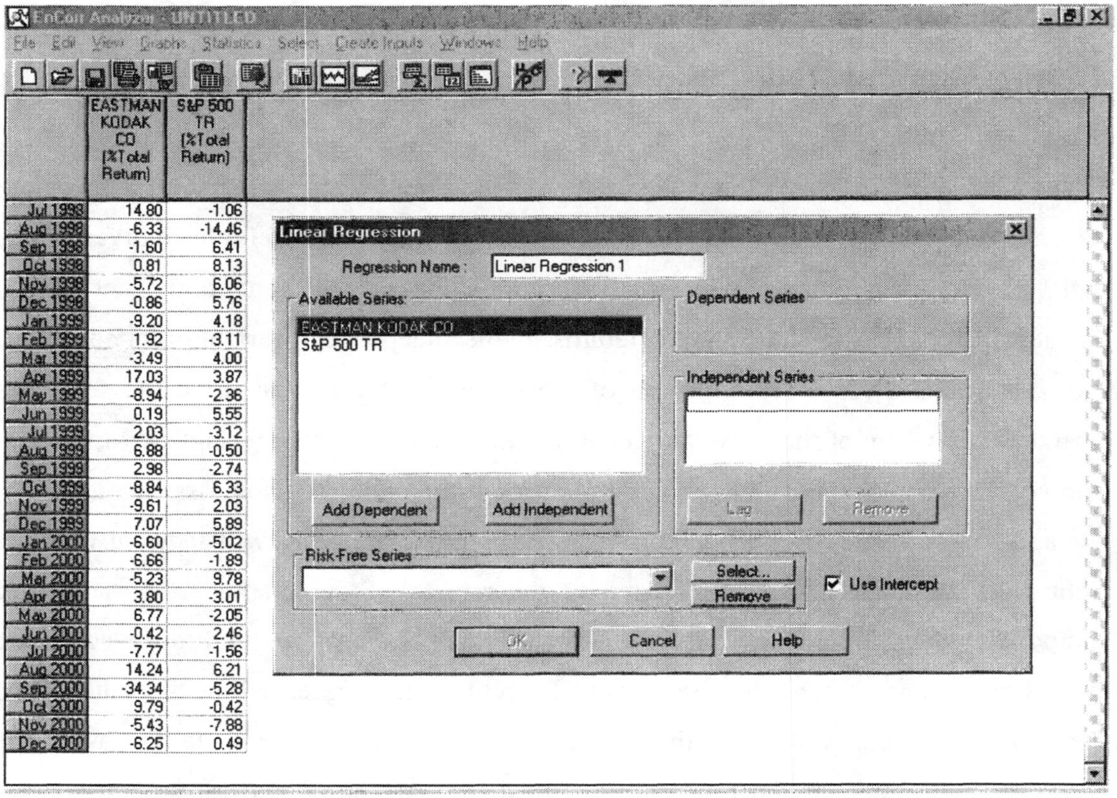

EnCorr Analyzer - UNTITLED

File Edit View Graphs Statistics Select Create Inputs Windows Help

	EASTMAN KODAK CO (%Total Return)	S&P 500 TR (%Total Return)
Jul 1998	14.80	-1.06
Aug 1998	-6.33	-14.46
Sep 1998	-1.60	6.41
Oct 1998	0.81	8.13
Nov 1998	-5.72	6.06
Dec 1998	-0.86	5.76
Jan 1999	-9.20	4.18
Feb 1999	1.92	-3.11
Mar 1999	-3.49	4.00
Apr 1999	17.03	3.87
May 1999	-8.94	-2.36
Jun 1999	0.19	5.55
Jul 1999	2.03	-3.12
Aug 1999	6.88	-0.50
Sep 1999	2.98	-2.74
Oct 1999	-8.84	6.33
Nov 1999	-9.61	2.03
Dec 1999	7.07	5.89
Jan 2000	-6.60	-5.02
Feb 2000	-6.66	-1.89
Mar 2000	-5.23	9.78
Apr 2000	3.80	-3.01
May 2000	6.77	-2.05
Jun 2000	-0.42	2.46
Jul 2000	-7.77	-1.56
Aug 2000	14.24	6.21
Sep 2000	-34.34	-5.28
Oct 2000	9.79	-0.42
Nov 2000	-5.43	-7.88
Dec 2000	-6.25	0.49

Linear Regression

Regression Name: Linear Regression 1

Available Series:

EASTMAN KODAK CO

S&P 500 TR

Dependent Series

Independent Series

Add Dependent

Add Independent

Lag

Remove

Risk-Free Series

Select...

Remove

Use Intercept

OK

Cancel

Help

Figure 5.6 Linear Regression Window

In the Linear Regression window, we will select the **S&P500 TR** series as the independent variable by highlighting the series and clicking on **Add Independent**. To add the dependent variable, highlight **Eastman Kodak Co**, then click on **Add Dependent.** In the **Dependent Series** box in the upper right side of the Window, you should now see the Eastman Kodak Co series and below in **the Independent Series** box, you should see S&P500 TR. Click **OK.** The parameter values of the regression will now appear in the lower left corner of the window. (**Figure 5.7**)

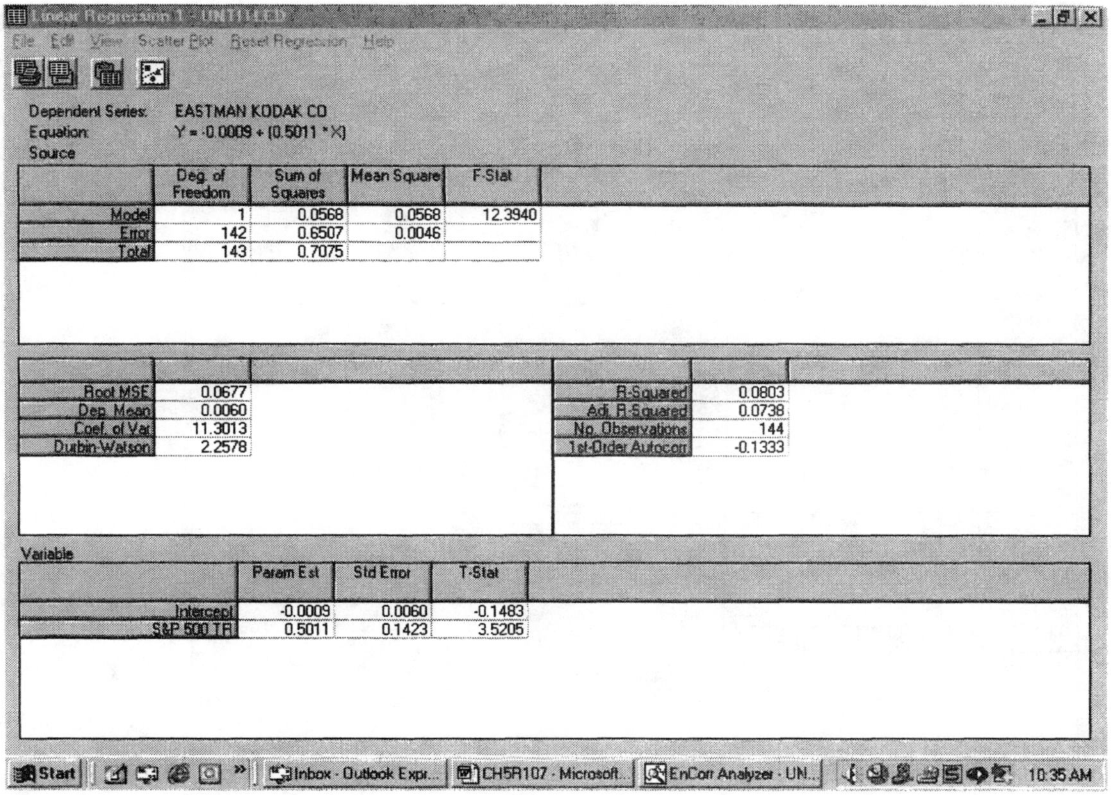

Linear Regression 1 - UNTITLED

File Edit View Scatter Plot Reset Regression Help

Dependent Series: EASTMAN KODAK CO
Equation: Y = -0.0009 + (0.5011 * X)
Source

	Deg. of Freedom	Sum of Squares	Mean Square	F-Stat
Model	1	0.0568	0.0568	12.3940
Error	142	0.6507	0.0046	
Total	143	0.7075		

Root MSE	0.0677
Dep. Mean	0.0060
Coef. of Var	11.3013
Durbin-Watson	2.2578

R-Squared	0.0803
Adj. R-Squared	0.0738
No. Observations	144
1st-Order Autocorr	-0.1333

Variable

	Param Est	Std Error	T-Stat
Intercept	-0.0009	0.0060	-0.1483
S&P 500 TR	0.5011	0.1423	3.5205

Start | Inbox - Outlook Expr... | CH5R107 - Microsoft... | EnCorr Analyzer - UN... | 10:35 AM

Figure 5.7 Linear Regression Values

The value for beta is given as the Parameter Estimate for the Independent Variable. In **Figure 5.7** we observe the beta value is .5011. To view the characteristic line, click on **Scatter Plot**. Since we are only interested in the Characteristic Line, click on the Graph Options drop-down menu, select the **Data Tab**, choose **Hide All Values**. (**Figure 5.8**) We can now modify the graph so we only observe the characteristic line.

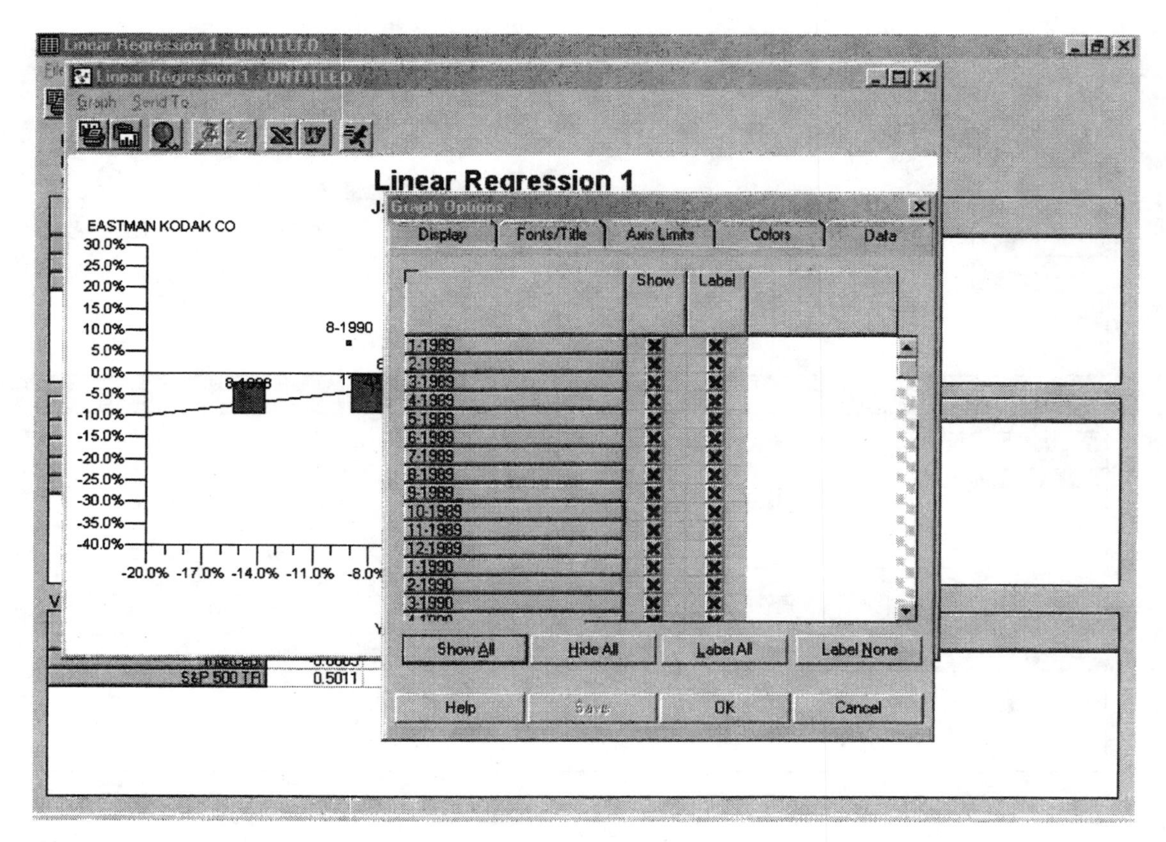

Figure 5.8 Modify the Characteristic Line Graph

Click **OK**. The characteristic line by itself as well as the equation will appear in **Figure 5.9**.

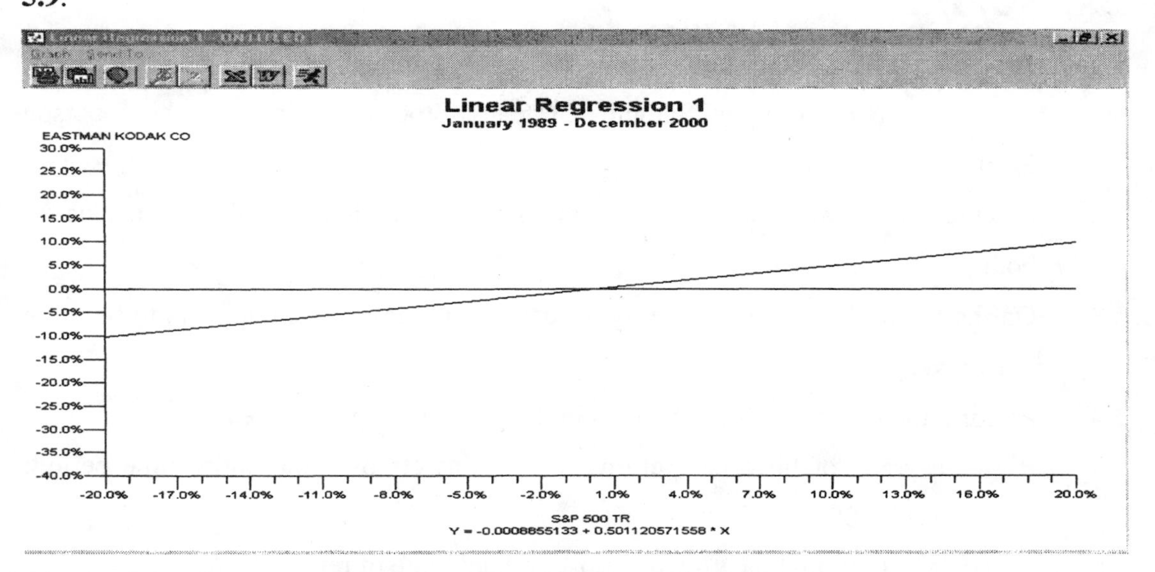

Figure 5.9 Eastman Kodak Characteristic Line and Equation

Interpreting Beta

The beta coefficient is an index of undiversifiable risk. As we observed as reflected in the equation in **Figure 5.9**, the beta value of the Eastman Kodak returns during the period from 1989 to 2000 with a value of .5011. The interpretation of this value gives some indication of how prone to systematic or undiversifiable risk the returns of this series were during the sample period. We know with a beta value larger than 1, the returns are more volatile than the market classifying the asset as *aggressive* (p 177). What we observe in the Eastman Kodak case is an asset value less than 1 that we classify as *defensive* with rates of return that were less volatile than the market's returns. But beta values change over time. The exercises below will give you an opportunity to see the changes first hand.

EXERCISES

5.1 Assume you are considering a portfolio containing two equity-based assets. Select any two from the Sample Company Stocks provided in the Ibbotson Software.

5.2 Calculate the standard deviation as well as the geometric and arithmetic means for both.

5.3 On the basis of a review of the return data, which investment appears to be more risky? Why?

5.4 Perform the risk analysis procedures in the previous pages by creating

  a. a graph of historical returns for both assets over the entire time period: 1989-2000

  b. a histogram indicating the most probable rate of return

  c. a characteristic line for each asset

  d. compute both betas

5.5 On the basis of a review of the analysis in questions 4, which investment appears to have been the more risky? Why? Compare this conclusion to your observations from questions 3.

5.6 To see the impact of how betas change over time, reset the time settings to a smaller series from 1995 to 2000 and apply the questions in 5.4 and 5.5. How different are your answers from the 1989-2000 series?

5.7 Prepare a chart with two columns, one headed AGGRESSIVE and the other DEFENSIVE. Using the Sample Company Stocks, calculate a beta for each of the remaining 16 companies and categorize and rank them by magnitude (highest value in the first row for AGGRESSIVE and lowest value in the first row for DEFENSIVE) and belonging to one or the other of the classifications.

6

Bond Performance

INTRODUCTION

In this chapter we analyze the historical record of risk, returns, and other relationships associated with fixed income securities. Employing U.S. government bills and bonds we can compare them to the historical record in the equity markets.

Risk and Return

In this section we analyze the risk involved with investing in U.S. government treasury bills, intermediate, and long-term bonds. If you recall, Treasury bills have a shorter term (less than one year) and transact in the money markets, whereas intermediate and long-term bonds are products purchased and sold in the capital markets. The theory related to the term structure of interest rates suggests there is often a direct relationship between risk and the term of the fixed-income security.

Bond Time Series

In the Main Window, click on **Select|Series|Ibbotson Database|Stocks Bonds Bills and Inflation.** The Select Series window appears (**Figure 6.1**). Double click on the following series to add them to the Selected Series box:

- S&P 500 TR
- U.S. LT Gvt TR
- U.S. LT Gvt Yld
- U.S. IT Gvt TR
- U.S. IT Gvt Yld
- U.S. 30 Day Tbill TR
- U.S. Inflation

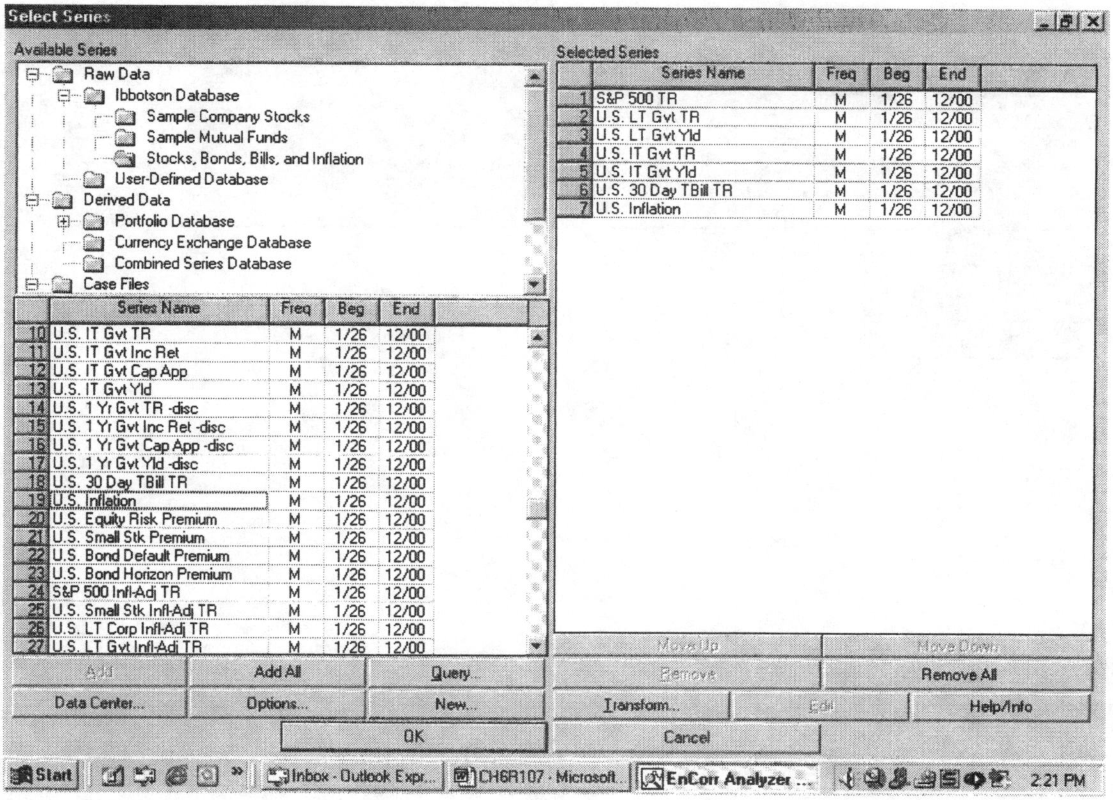

Figure 6.1 Select Series Window

Click **OK**. When the Date Setting window appears, leave the returns set for monthly and click **OK**. The Main Window appears again with the six selected series and their time monthly values arranged in columnar format.

To further analyze the picture of fixed-income risk and return, we will refer to the statistics function. In the Main Window, click on **Statistics|Summary**. The combined geometric and arithmetic means along with the standard deviation for each series now appear. (**Figure 6.2**)

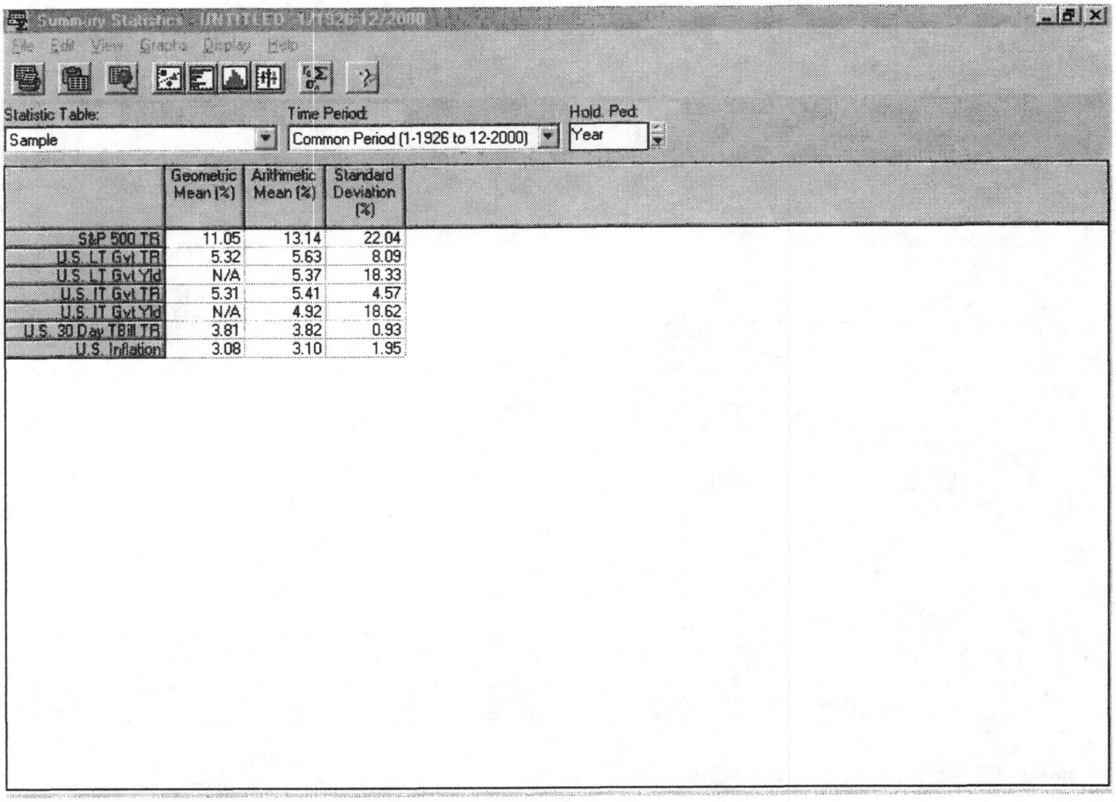

	Geometric Mean (%)	Arithmetic Mean (%)	Standard Deviation (%)
S&P 500 TR	11.05	13.14	22.04
U.S. LT Gvt TR	5.32	5.63	8.09
U.S. LT Gvt Yld	N/A	5.37	18.33
U.S. IT Gvt TR	5.31	5.41	4.57
U.S. IT Gvt Yld	N/A	4.92	18.62
U.S. 30 Day TBill TR	3.81	3.82	0.93
U.S. Inflation	3.08	3.10	1.95

Figure 6.2 Fixed-Income Securities Summary Statistics

In **Figure 6.2** we are able to compare the relative returns and standard deviation (or the risk of the returns) related to short-term (Tbills), intermediate-term (U.S. IT Govt TR), and long-term (U.S. LT Govt TR) securities.

EXERCISES

6.1 Comparing the series selected, what asset outperformed the U.S. inflation rate during the period 1926 to 2000?

6.2 What series performed the weakest against U.S. rate of inflation most during the period?

6.3 From the text we are told of the relationship between a bond's term and its yield. Is this relationship observable in the statistics? How is it represented?

6.4 Graph the series U.S. LT Gvt TR and U.S. LT Gvt Yld. What relationship (direct or indirect) do you observe? Is this expected according to what you have learned from the text? Why?

Fixed-Income Securities: Holding Periods

In Chapter 21 of the text we are told that bonds with a longer term or horizon are riskier than bonds with shorter ones. In this section, we will look more closely at the three bond series analyzed in the previous section, that is, 30-day Tbills, U.S. Govt IT TR, and U.S. Govt LT TR.

From the Main Window choose **Select|Series|Ibbotson Database|Stocks Bonds Bills and Inflation**. Choose the three series mentioned above by double-clicking on each to place them in the Selected Series window. Click **OK**. Leave Date Settings as monthly over the entire time period of 1926 to 2000.

Select **Statistics|Rolling Period** and when the window appears for the number of periods, enter 120 for a ten-year rolling holding period. The results for the three series now appear for the rolling period returns (**Figure 6.3**). Next, we will convert the reported returns on an annual basis. From the **Holding Period** drop down menu, click on **Annually**. The new window appears with annually reported holding periods.

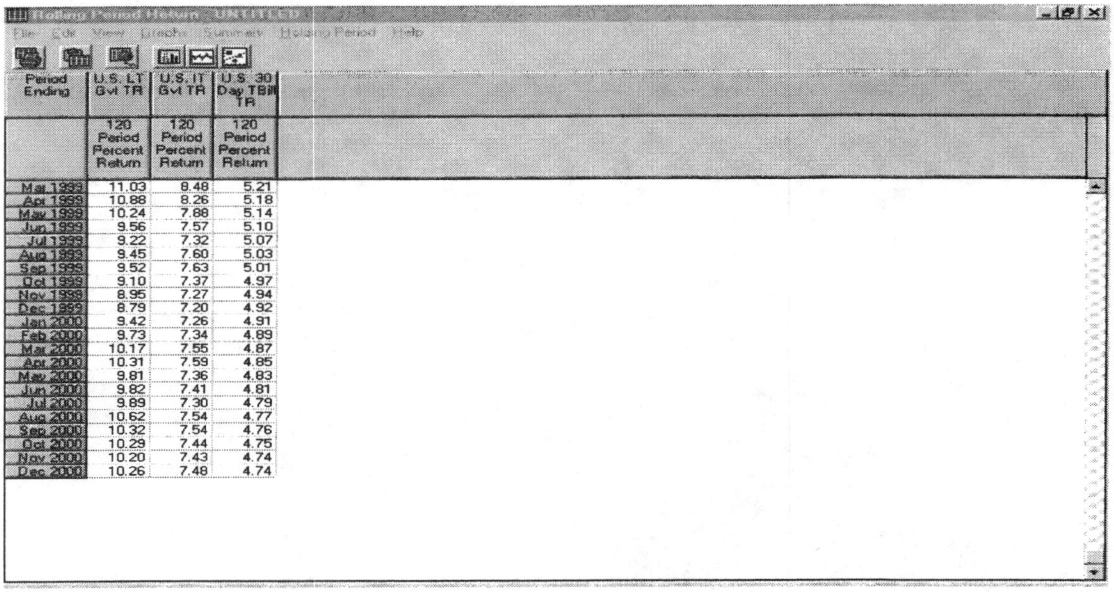

Period Ending	U.S. LT Gvt TR	U.S. IT Gvt TR	U.S. 30 Day TBill TR
	120 Period Percent Return	120 Period Percent Return	120 Period Percent Return
Mar 1999	11.03	8.48	5.21
Apr 1999	10.88	8.26	5.18
May 1999	10.24	7.88	5.14
Jun 1999	9.56	7.57	5.10
Jul 1999	9.22	7.32	5.07
Aug 1999	9.45	7.60	5.03
Sep 1999	9.52	7.63	5.01
Oct 1999	9.10	7.37	4.97
Nov 1999	8.95	7.27	4.94
Dec 1999	8.79	7.20	4.92
Jan 2000	9.42	7.26	4.91
Feb 2000	9.73	7.34	4.89
Mar 2000	10.17	7.55	4.87
Apr 2000	10.31	7.59	4.85
May 2000	9.81	7.36	4.83
Jun 2000	9.82	7.41	4.81
Jul 2000	9.89	7.30	4.79
Aug 2000	10.62	7.54	4.77
Sep 2000	10.32	7.54	4.76
Oct 2000	10.29	7.44	4.75
Nov 2000	10.20	7.43	4.74
Dec 2000	10.26	7.48	4.74

Figure 6.3 Rolling Period Returns

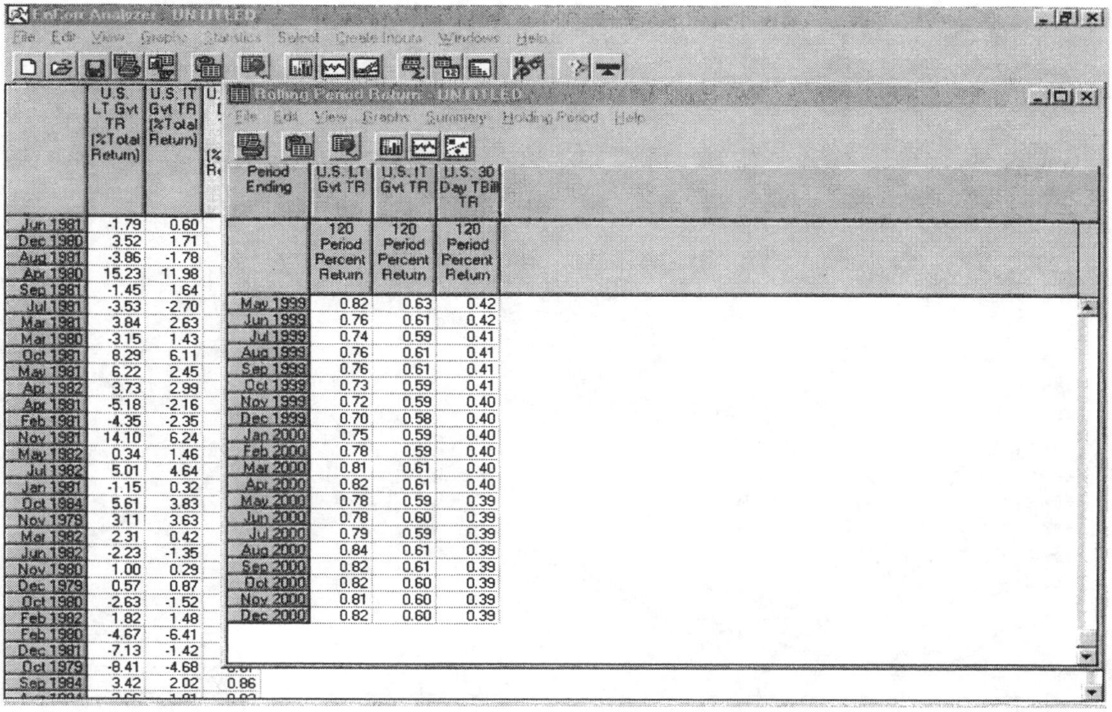

FinCen Analyzer - UNTITLED

	U.S. LT Gvt TR (%Total Return)	U.S. IT Gvt TR (%Total Return)
Jun 1981	-1.79	0.60
Dec 1980	3.52	1.71
Aug 1981	-3.86	-1.78
Apr 1980	15.23	11.98
Sep 1981	-1.45	1.64
Jul 1981	-3.53	-2.70
Mar 1981	3.84	2.63
Mar 1980	-3.15	1.43
Oct 1981	8.29	6.11
May 1981	6.22	2.45
Apr 1982	3.73	2.99
Apr 1981	-5.18	-2.16
Feb 1981	-4.35	-2.35
Nov 1981	14.10	6.24
May 1982	0.34	1.46
Jul 1982	5.01	4.64
Jan 1981	-1.15	0.32
Oct 1984	5.61	3.83
Nov 1979	3.11	3.63
Mar 1982	2.31	0.42
Jun 1982	-2.23	-1.35
Nov 1980	1.00	0.29
Dec 1979	0.57	0.87
Oct 1980	-2.63	-1.52
Feb 1982	1.82	1.48
Feb 1980	-4.67	-6.41
Dec 1981	-7.13	-1.42
Oct 1979	-8.41	-4.68
Sep 1984	3.42	2.02

Rolling Period Return - UNTITLED

Period Ending	U.S. LT Gvt TR	U.S. IT Gvt TR	U.S. 30 Day TBill TR
	120 Period Percent Return	120 Period Percent Return	120 Period Percent Return
May 1999	0.82	0.63	0.42
Jun 1999	0.76	0.61	0.42
Jul 1999	0.74	0.59	0.41
Aug 1999	0.76	0.61	0.41
Sep 1999	0.76	0.61	0.41
Oct 1999	0.73	0.59	0.41
Nov 1999	0.72	0.59	0.40
Dec 1999	0.70	0.58	0.40
Jan 2000	0.75	0.59	0.40
Feb 2000	0.78	0.59	0.40
Mar 2000	0.81	0.61	0.40
Apr 2000	0.82	0.61	0.40
May 2000	0.78	0.59	0.39
Jun 2000	0.78	0.60	0.39
Jul 2000	0.79	0.59	0.39
Aug 2000	0.84	0.61	0.39
Sep 2000	0.82	0.61	0.39
Oct 2000	0.82	0.60	0.39
Nov 2000	0.81	0.60	0.39
Dec 2000	0.82	0.60	0.39

Figure 6.4 Rolling Period with Monthly Holding Periods

To analyze the relationship of a bond's term, let's graph the three transformed series. If you choose **Graph|Rolling Period Line**, a graph of the three series appears over the entire time period (**Figure 6.5**).

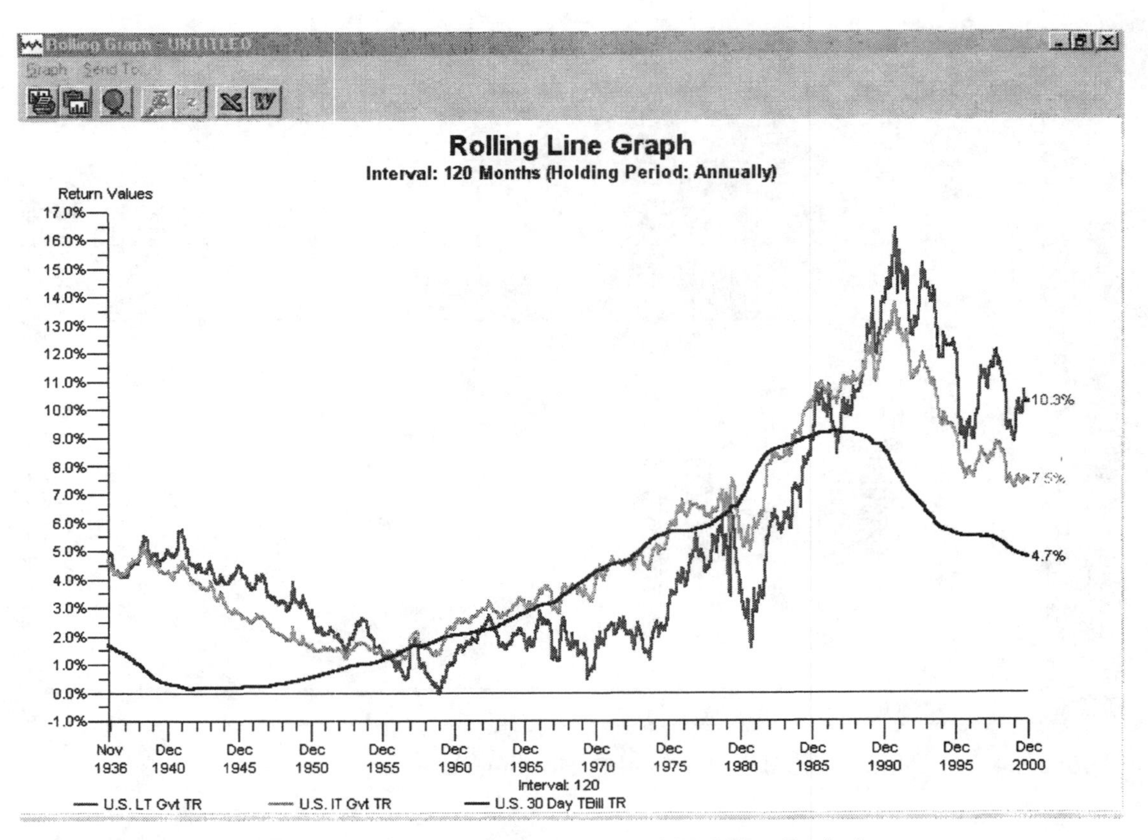

Figure 6.5 Ten-Year Rolling Period with Annual Holding Periods

EXERCISES

6.5 From what you observed in **Figure 6.5**, does the relationship hold that bonds with longer terms are riskier and have higher returns throughout the sample time period?

6.6 Using the Zoom feature, highlight t he decade of the 1980's. Review what you see and report on the term relationship of risk to return. How did the decade begin? How did it end?

6.7 Repeat the use of the Zoom feature but this time highlight the decade of the 1990's. How did the decade compare to the results you reported in 6.5 and 6.6?

Part III

Portfolio Analysis

7

Portfolio Analysis

Introduction

If you recall in Chapter 14 of your text, Modern Portfolio Theory is based on mean-variance optimization. As we know, mean-variance optimization is the process of identifying portfolios that are closest to the efficient frontier, or those that have the highest possible return for a given level of risk. The portfolio approach is another useful tool for investors who wish to analyze a combination of series.

The Ibbotson software gives you the ability to determine if your portfolio is optimal. It will assist you by supplying the Efficient Frontier to help you make your decision to add or delete securities. One way to determine whether your weighted portfolio is optimal is to plot it in relation to an efficient frontier line created from the same assets. In this chapter we will see how the EnCorr Analyzer is able to create a portfolio then paste it into the Efficient Frontier graph. We will also show how to edit a portfolio. Finally, we will show how to find the optimal portfolio in the Analyzer.

Creating a Portfolio

Portfolios created in EnCorr Analyzer can be viewed in other EnCorr products such as the EnCorr Optimizer. A popular use for Optimizer is to view a current portfolio and proposed (optimal) portfolios and their position compared to the Efficient Frontier. Ideally, the closer the proposed portfolio approaches the frontier, the more attractive it is to the investor.

A portfolio is constructed using the weighted average returns of its component securities. With EnCorr Optimizer, portfolios can be constructed with total return, capital appreciation, or income return series, as well as previously saved portfolios, combined series, and exchange rates.

Constructing A New Portfolio

1. From the Main Window, click **Select|Series** to access the Select Series window (**Figure 7.1**). Within the **Ibbotson Database** open the series, **Stocks, Bonds, Bills and Inflation** module. Double click on the following series:

- S&P 500 TR
- U.S. 30 Day TBill TR
- U.S. IT Govt TR
- U.S. Small Stk TR

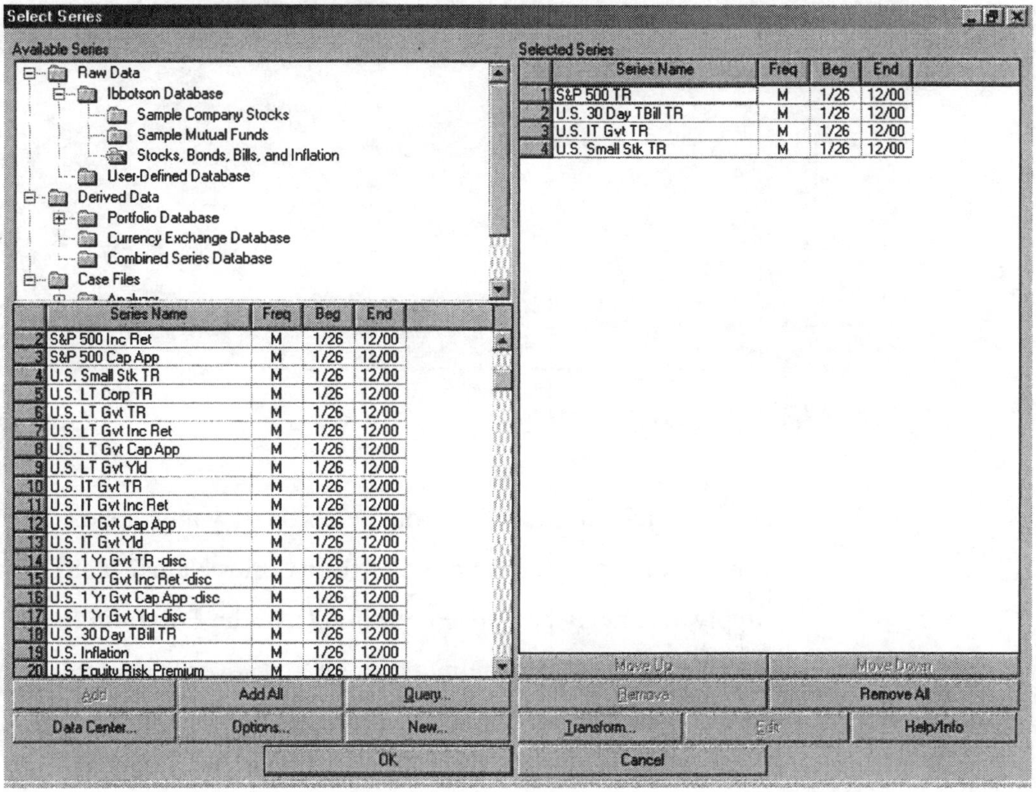

Select Series

Available Series

Raw Data
Ibbotson Database
Sample Company Stocks
Sample Mutual Funds
Stocks, Bonds, Bills, and Inflation
User-Defined Database
Derived Data
Portfolio Database
Currency Exchange Database
Combined Series Database
Case Files

	Series Name	Freq	Beg	End
2	S&P 500 Inc Ret	M	1/26	12/00
3	S&P 500 Cap App	M	1/26	12/00
4	U.S. Small Stk TR	M	1/26	12/00
5	U.S. LT Corp TR	M	1/26	12/00
6	U.S. LT Gvt TR	M	1/26	12/00
7	U.S. LT Gvt Inc Ret	M	1/26	12/00
8	U.S. LT Gvt Cap App	M	1/26	12/00
9	U.S. LT Gvt Yld	M	1/26	12/00
10	U.S. IT Gvt TR	M	1/26	12/00
11	U.S. IT Gvt Inc Ret	M	1/26	12/00
12	U.S. IT Gvt Cap App	M	1/26	12/00
13	U.S. IT Gvt Yld	M	1/26	12/00
14	U.S. 1 Yr Gvt TR -disc	M	1/26	12/00
15	U.S. 1 Yr Gvt Inc Ret -disc	M	1/26	12/00
16	U.S. 1 Yr Gvt Cap App -disc	M	1/26	12/00
17	U.S. 1 Yr Gvt Yld -disc	M	1/26	12/00
18	U.S. 30 Day TBill TR	M	1/26	12/00
19	U.S. Inflation	M	1/26	12/00
20	U.S. Equity Risk Premium	M	1/26	12/00

Selected Series

	Series Name	Freq	Beg	End
1	S&P 500 TR	M	1/26	12/00
2	U.S. 30 Day TBill TR	M	1/26	12/00
3	U.S. IT Gvt TR	M	1/26	12/00
4	U.S. Small Stk TR	M	1/26	12/00

Move Up | Move Down | Add | Add All | Query... | Remove | Remove All | Data Center... | Options... | New... | Transform... | Edit | Help/Info | OK | Cancel

Figure 7.1 Building a Portfolio: Selecting the Series

2. Click the **New** button and select **Portfolio** to display the Build/Edit Portfolio window. (**Figure 7.2**)

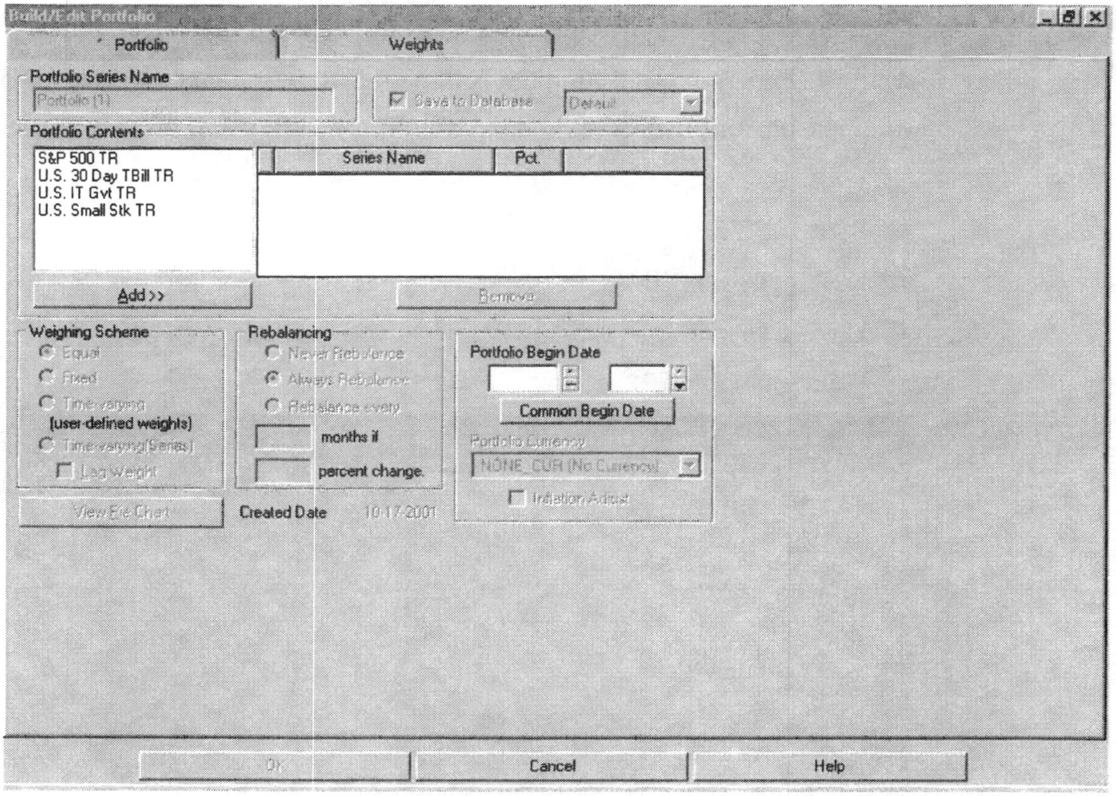

Build/Edit Portfolio
Portfolio
Weights
Portfolio Series Name
Portfolio (1)
Save to Database
Default
Portfolio Contents
S&P 500 TR
U.S. 30 Day TBill TR
U.S. IT Gvt TR
U.S. Small Stk TR
Series Name
Pct.
Add >>
Remove
Weighing Scheme
Equal
Fixed
Time-varying
(user-defined weights)
Time-varying(Series)
Lag Weight
Rebalancing
Never Rebalance
Always Rebalance
Rebalance every
months if
percent change.
Portfolio Begin Date
Common Begin Date
Portfolio Currency
NONE_CUR (No Currency)
Inflation Adjust
View Pie Chart
Created Date 10-17-2001
OK
Cancel
Help

Figure 7.2 Build/Edit a Portfolio

3. Double click on each of the four series so they now appear in the Series Name window on the right. Enter a Portfolio Series Name. The software will supply a name by default, **Portfolio (1),** in the **Portfolio Series Name** box**.** To give your portfolio a unique name, type over the default. Let's name this portfolio **Example**.
4. Check **Save to Database** if you want to save this portfolio for later use or use in other Ibbotson software. Retrieve saved portfolios from the Portfolio Database under Derived Data.

5. To add our series to the Selected Series window, double click the series name or highlight the desired series and click the **Add** button. The series appears in the **Selected Series** list box. (**Figure 7.3**)

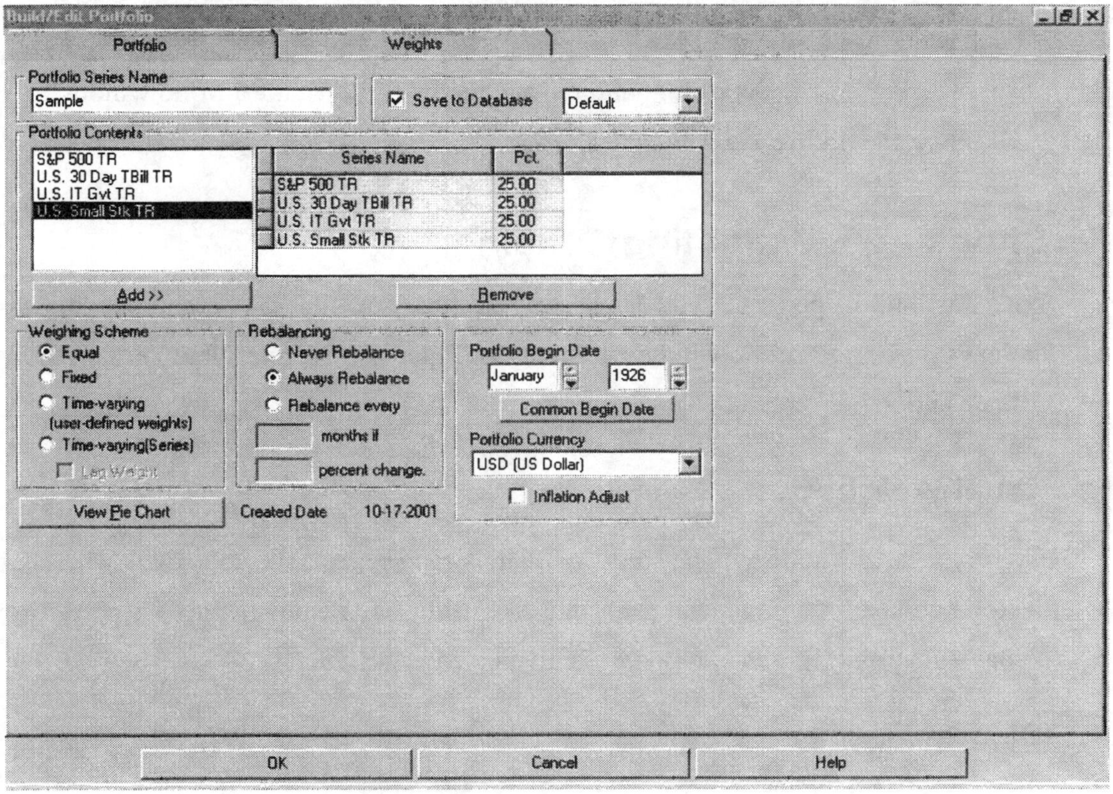

Build/Edit Portfolio
Portfolio
Weights
Portfolio Series Name
Sample
Save to Database
Default
Portfolio Contents
S&P 500 TR
U.S. 30 Day TBill TR
U.S. IT Gvt TR
U.S. Small Stk TR

Series Name	Pct.
S&P 500 TR	25.00
U.S. 30 Day TBill TR	25.00
U.S. IT Gvt TR	25.00
U.S. Small Stk TR	25.00

Add >>
Remove
Weighing Scheme
Equal
Fixed
Time-varying (user-defined weights)
Time-varying(Series)
Lag Weight
Rebalancing
Never Rebalance
Always Rebalance
Rebalance every
months if
percent change.
Portfolio Begin Date
January
1926
Common Begin Date
Portfolio Currency
USD (US Dollar)
Inflation Adjust
View Pie Chart
Created Date 10-17-2001
OK
Cancel
Help

Figure 7.3 Building the Sample Portfolio

6. Choose the desired weighting scheme (see "Choosing a Weighting Scheme," below). To designate the weights, select from Equal, Fixed, Time-varying (user-defined weights), and Time-varying (Series), and assign weights.
7. Select the appropriate portfolio rebalancing, inflation adjustment option, and portfolio begin date. By default, the software chooses **Always rebalance, Earliest Series Begin Date, USD (US Dollars)**, and no inflation adjustment.
8. Click **OK** to view the portfolio.

Editing an Existing Portfolio

1. Open the Select Series window by clicking **Select|Series** from the menu bar.
2. Highlight the desired portfolio once it has been added to the Select Series window.
3. Click the **Edit Portfolio** button to access the Build/Edit Portfolio window.
4. Edit the desired cells and click **OK**.

Choosing a Weighting Scheme

When you build a portfolio, you can assign different percentages (weights) to your assets. In the Build/Edit Portfolio window, select from Equal, Fixed, and Time-varying (user-defined and Series) weights.

Equal Weights

This is the default setting. The software assigns each series a weight of 1/n, where n is the total number of component assets in the portfolio. For example, if your portfolio contains four assets, each component is given a 25% weight.

Fixed Weights

Fixed weights are not necessarily equal but they are constant over the entire time horizon of the portfolio. You can also enter values (i.e., client's holdings or a market value) as well as a percentage in this field.

To Enter Fixed weights:

1. Click **Fixed** in the **Weighting Scheme** box.
2. Enter the desired weights in the Weight column. The Pct. Column is the relative weights, where an individual series weight reflects its proportion to the sum of weights. If the asset weights in the Weight column sum to 100, the column will be equal to the Pct. Column.

Time-Varying (User-Defined) Weights

This option allows you to create a portfolio with weights that change over time. For time-varying portfolios, this option is recommended if your portfolio weights are in percentages and they sum to 100.

To enter Time-varying (user-defined) weights:

1. In the **Weighting Scheme** box, click **Time-varying (user-defined weights)**.
2. Click the Weights tab.
3. Assign the time-varying weights. Weights must be in percentage terms and they must sum to 100. For example, select three series and split a portfolio weight with 50% to each of two series for the first ten years. Then change the weighting to 33.33% for each of three series for the next ten years. The **Fill Down** option can quickly fill the weightings for a given row down the columns for All Rows or Next Row Only.

Time-Varying Weights

This option allows you to crate a portfolio with weights that vary over time. If you want to create a market-capitalization-weighted portfolio/index, you need to have the appropriate market value series in your database. You can create a portfolio that will allocate the individual asset weights in proportion to their combined value. For time-varying portfolios, this option is recommended if your portfolio weights are values instead of percentages, or if the portfolio weights do not sum to 100.

To enter Time-varying Weights

1. Select the desired return and market value series in the Selected Series window.
2. In the **Weighting Scheme** box, click **Time-varying (Series).**
3. For each data series, select the desired value series by clicking the drop-down box in the Time-Varying Column.

You can also choose the **Lag Weight** option to assign percentage holdings based on the previous period's values.

How to Find the Optimal Portfolio

Building a Weighted Portfolio

First we will build a weighted portfolio in the Analyzer.

- Open EnCorr Analyzer. Click **File|New Folder.** The Select Series dialog box appears. Double click the **Ibbotson Database** folder; select the **Stocks, Bonds, Bills and Inflation** folder.

- Select the following asset classes :

  S&P 500 TR,
  U.S. Small Stock TR,
  U.S. LT Corp TR,
  U.S. IT Gvt TR,
  U.S. 30 Day Tbill TR

- Click the **New|Portfolio** button (**Figure 7.4**)

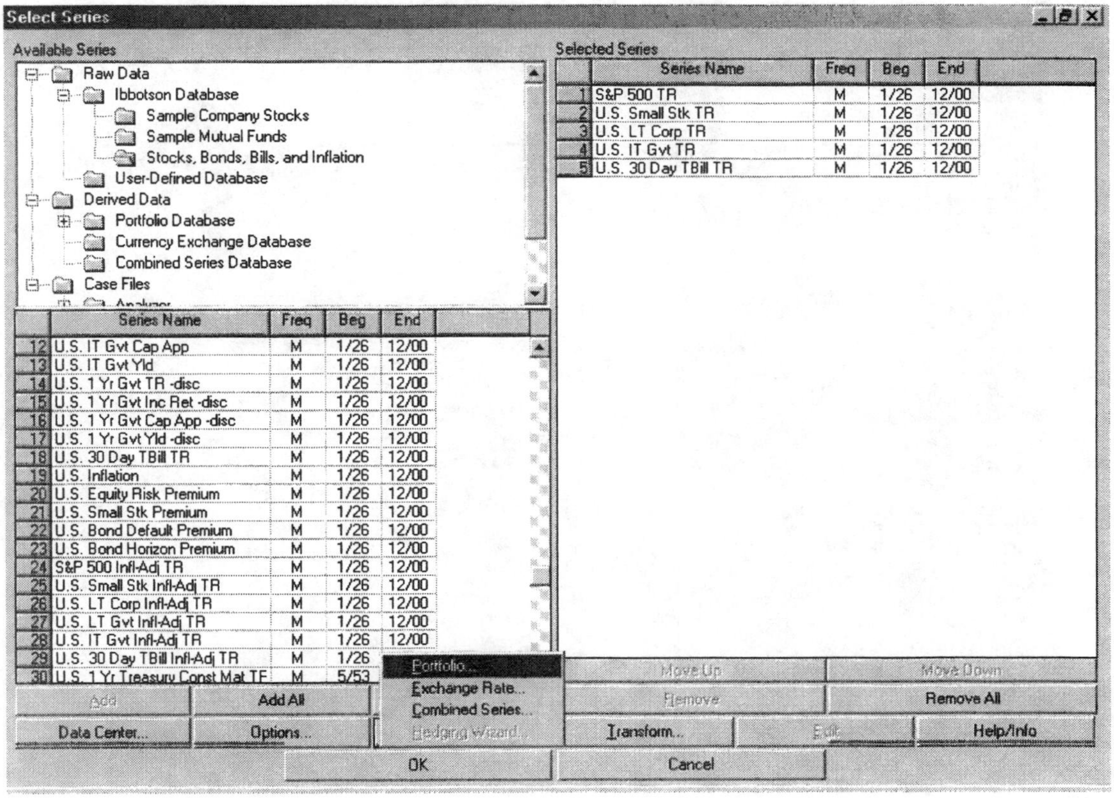

Select Series

Available Series

- Raw Data
  - Ibbotson Database
    - Sample Company Stocks
    - Sample Mutual Funds
    - Stocks, Bonds, Bills, and Inflation
  - User-Defined Database
- Derived Data
  - Portfolio Database
  - Currency Exchange Database
  - Combined Series Database
- Case Files

	Series Name	Freq	Beg	End
12	U.S. IT Gvt Cap App	M	1/26	12/00
13	U.S. IT Gvt Yld	M	1/26	12/00
14	U.S. 1 Yr Gvt TR -disc	M	1/26	12/00
15	U.S. 1 Yr Gvt Inc Ret -disc	M	1/26	12/00
16	U.S. 1 Yr Gvt Cap App -disc	M	1/26	12/00
17	U.S. 1 Yr Gvt Yld -disc	M	1/26	12/00
18	U.S. 30 Day TBill TR	M	1/26	12/00
19	U.S. Inflation	M	1/26	12/00
20	U.S. Equity Risk Premium	M	1/26	12/00
21	U.S. Small Stk Premium	M	1/26	12/00
22	U.S. Bond Default Premium	M	1/26	12/00
23	U.S. Bond Horizon Premium	M	1/26	12/00
24	S&P 500 Infl-Adj TR	M	1/26	12/00
25	U.S. Small Stk Infl-Adj TR	M	1/26	12/00
26	U.S. LT Corp Infl-Adj TR	M	1/26	12/00
27	U.S. LT Gvt Infl-Adj TR	M	1/26	12/00
28	U.S. IT Gvt Infl-Adj TR	M	1/26	12/00
29	U.S. 30 Day TBill Infl-Adj TR	M	1/26	
30	U.S. 1 Yr Treasury Const Mat TF	M	5/53	

Selected Series

	Series Name	Freq	Beg	End
1	S&P 500 TR	M	1/26	12/00
2	U.S. Small Stk TR	M	1/26	12/00
3	U.S. LT Corp TR	M	1/26	12/00
4	U.S. IT Gvt TR	M	1/26	12/00
5	U.S. 30 Day TBill TR	M	1/26	12/00

Portfolio...
Exchange Rate...
Combined Series...
Hedging Wizard...

Add | Add All | Move Up | Move Down | Remove | Remove All
Data Center... | Options... | Transform... | Edit | Help/Info
OK | Cancel

Figure 7.4 New Portfolio Window

- From the Build/Edit Portfolio window, select the following asset classes to be included in the portfolio:

  S&P 500 TR,
  U.S. LT Corp TR,
  U.S. IT Gvt TR,

  In the same window enter "FirstCase" as the portfolio series name and then also be sure to check the "Save to Database" checkbox. (**Figure 7.5** First Case Portfolio)

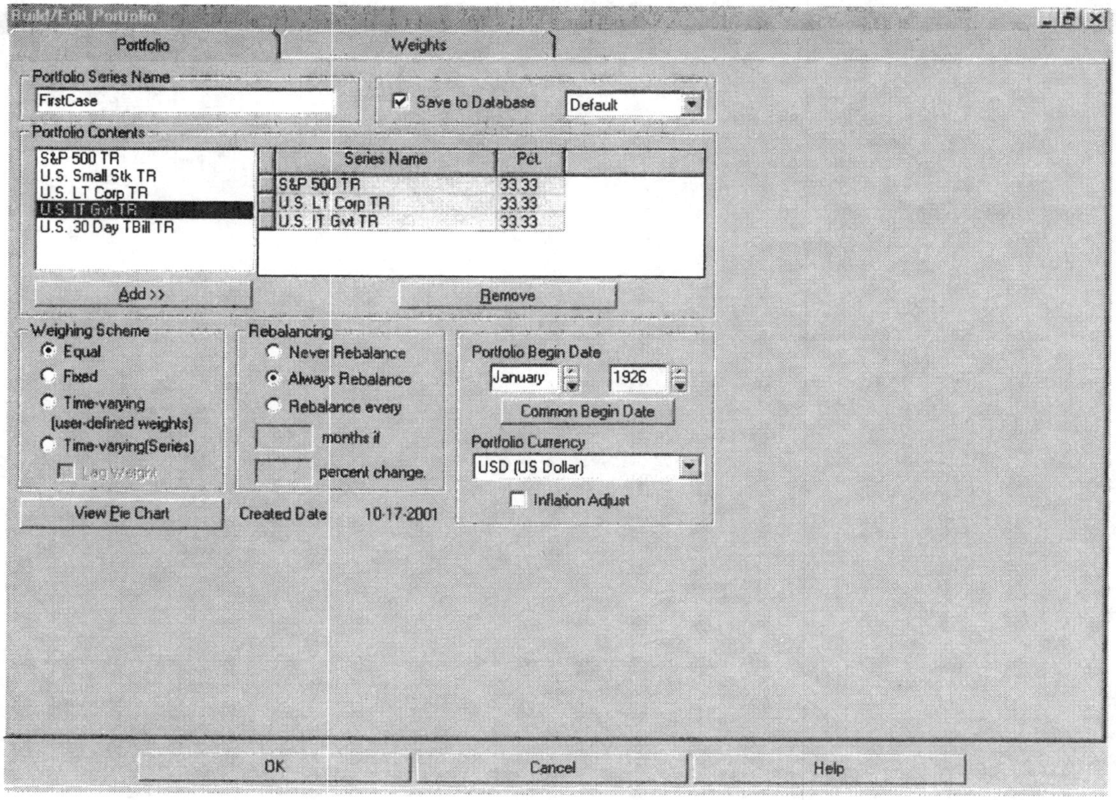

Build/Edit Portfolio

Portfolio | Weights

Portfolio Series Name: FirstCase

Save to Database: Default

Portfolio Contents

S&P 500 TR
U.S. Small Stk TR
U.S. LT Corp TR
U.S. IT Gvt TR
U.S. 30 Day TBill TR

Series Name	Pct.
S&P 500 TR	33.33
U.S. LT Corp TR	33.33
U.S. IT Gvt TR	33.33

Add >> | Remove

Weighing Scheme
Equal
Fixed
Time-varying (user-defined weights)
Time-varying(Series)
Lag Weight

Rebalancing
Never Rebalance
Always Rebalance
Rebalance every
months if
percent change.

Portfolio Begin Date
January 1926
Common Begin Date
Portfolio Currency
USD (US Dollar)
Inflation Adjust

View Pie Chart

Created Date 10-17-2001

OK | Cancel | Help

Figure 7.5 First Case Portfolio

- Click on the **Fixed** option button to assign weights. In the Weight column enter the following weights: **10%** S&P, **75%** LT Corp, **15%** IT Gvt TR. (**Figure 7.6 Setting the Weights**)

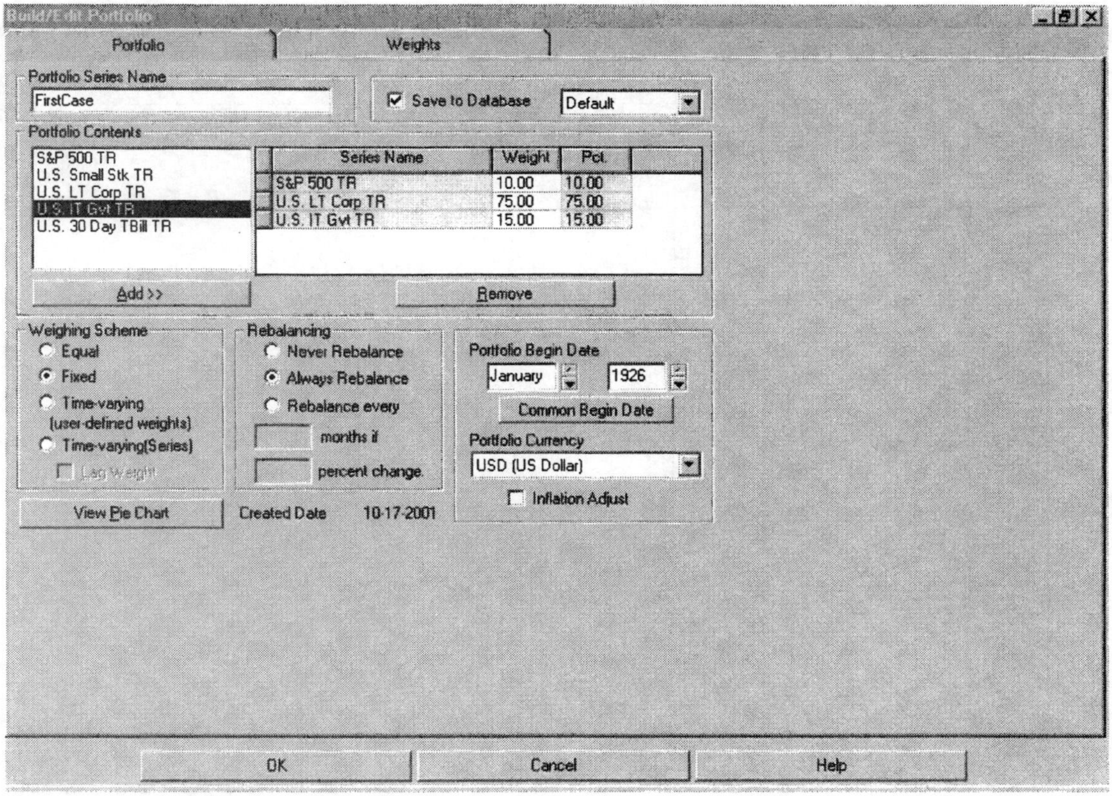

Figure 7.6 Setting the Weights

- Click **OK** when you are finished.

In the Select Series window the **FirstCase** portfolio name now appears in the Selected Series box.

- Click **OK** and the Date Settings window will appear.
- Select monthly as the frequency and click **OK**.

The Main Window with the columns of data now appears; you have created a weighted portfolio. (**Figure 7.7**)

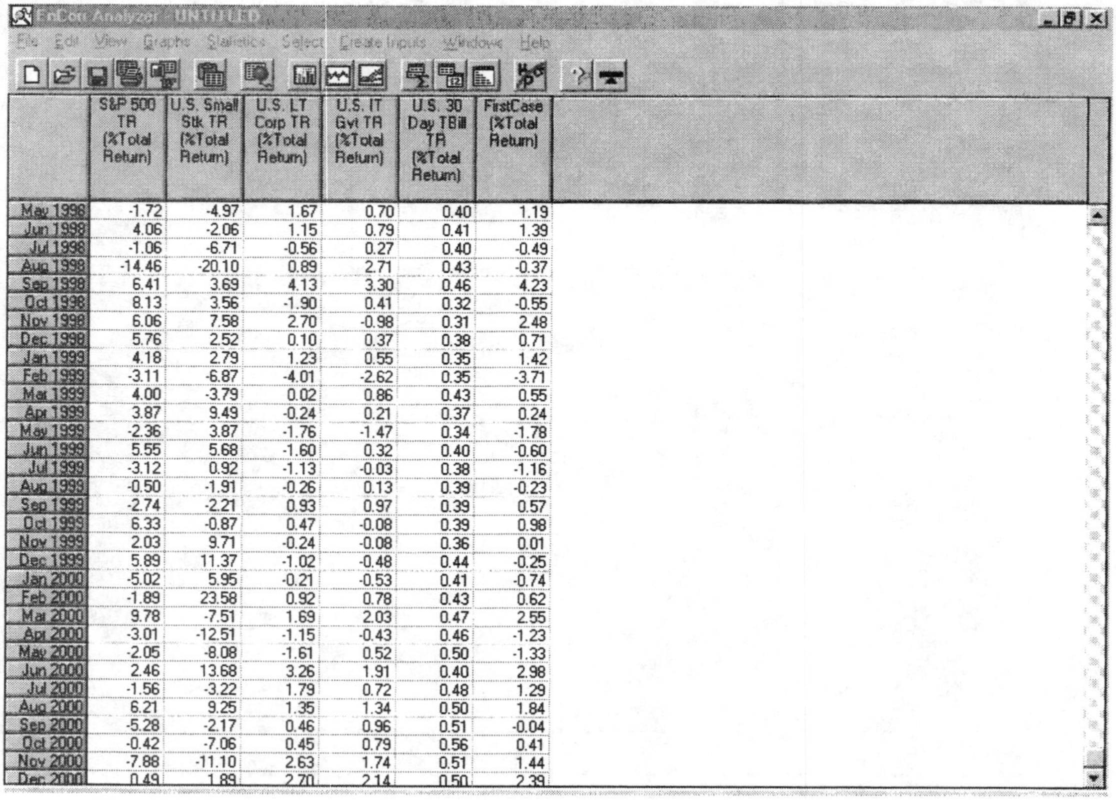

EnCorr Analyzer - UNTITLED

File Edit View Graphs Statistics Select Create Inputs Window Help

	S&P 500 TR (%Total Return)	U.S. Small Stk TR (%Total Return)	U.S. LT Corp TR (%Total Return)	U.S. IT Gvt TR (%Total Return)	U.S. 30 Day TBill TR (%Total Return)	FirstCase (%Total Return)
May 1998	-1.72	-4.97	1.67	0.70	0.40	1.19
Jun 1998	4.06	-2.06	1.15	0.79	0.41	1.39
Jul 1998	-1.06	-6.71	-0.56	0.27	0.40	-0.49
Aug 1998	-14.46	-20.10	0.89	2.71	0.43	-0.37
Sep 1998	6.41	3.69	4.13	3.30	0.46	4.23
Oct 1998	8.13	3.56	-1.90	0.41	0.32	-0.55
Nov 1998	6.06	7.58	2.70	-0.98	0.31	2.48
Dec 1998	5.76	2.52	0.10	0.37	0.38	0.71
Jan 1999	4.18	2.79	1.23	0.55	0.35	1.42
Feb 1999	-3.11	-6.87	-4.01	-2.62	0.35	-3.71
Mar 1999	4.00	-3.79	0.02	0.86	0.43	0.55
Apr 1999	3.87	9.49	-0.24	0.21	0.37	0.24
May 1999	-2.36	3.87	-1.76	-1.47	0.34	-1.78
Jun 1999	5.55	5.68	-1.60	0.32	0.40	-0.60
Jul 1999	-3.12	0.92	-1.13	-0.03	0.38	-1.16
Aug 1999	-0.50	-1.91	-0.26	0.13	0.39	-0.23
Sep 1999	-2.74	-2.21	0.93	0.97	0.39	0.57
Oct 1999	6.33	-0.87	0.47	-0.08	0.39	0.98
Nov 1999	2.03	9.71	-0.24	-0.08	0.36	0.01
Dec 1999	5.89	11.37	-1.02	-0.48	0.44	-0.25
Jan 2000	-5.02	5.95	-0.21	-0.53	0.41	-0.74
Feb 2000	-1.89	23.58	0.92	0.78	0.43	0.62
Mar 2000	9.78	-7.51	1.69	2.03	0.47	2.55
Apr 2000	-3.01	-12.51	-1.15	-0.43	0.46	-1.23
May 2000	-2.05	-8.08	-1.61	0.52	0.50	-1.33
Jun 2000	2.46	13.68	3.26	1.91	0.40	2.98
Jul 2000	-1.56	-3.22	1.79	0.72	0.48	1.29
Aug 2000	6.21	9.25	1.35	1.34	0.50	1.84
Sep 2000	-5.28	-2.17	0.46	0.96	0.51	-0.04
Oct 2000	-0.42	-7.06	0.45	0.79	0.56	0.41
Nov 2000	-7.88	-11.10	2.63	1.74	0.51	1.44
Dec 2000	0.49	1.89	2.70	2.14	0.50	2.39

Figure 7.7 Weighted Portfolio

At this point, optimize the selected asset classes in order to create the Efficient Frontier graph.

- From the Main Window, click **Create Inputs**. **Save** as FirstCase. Click **NO** when asked if you want to treat the portfolio as an asset class. (**Figure 7.8**)

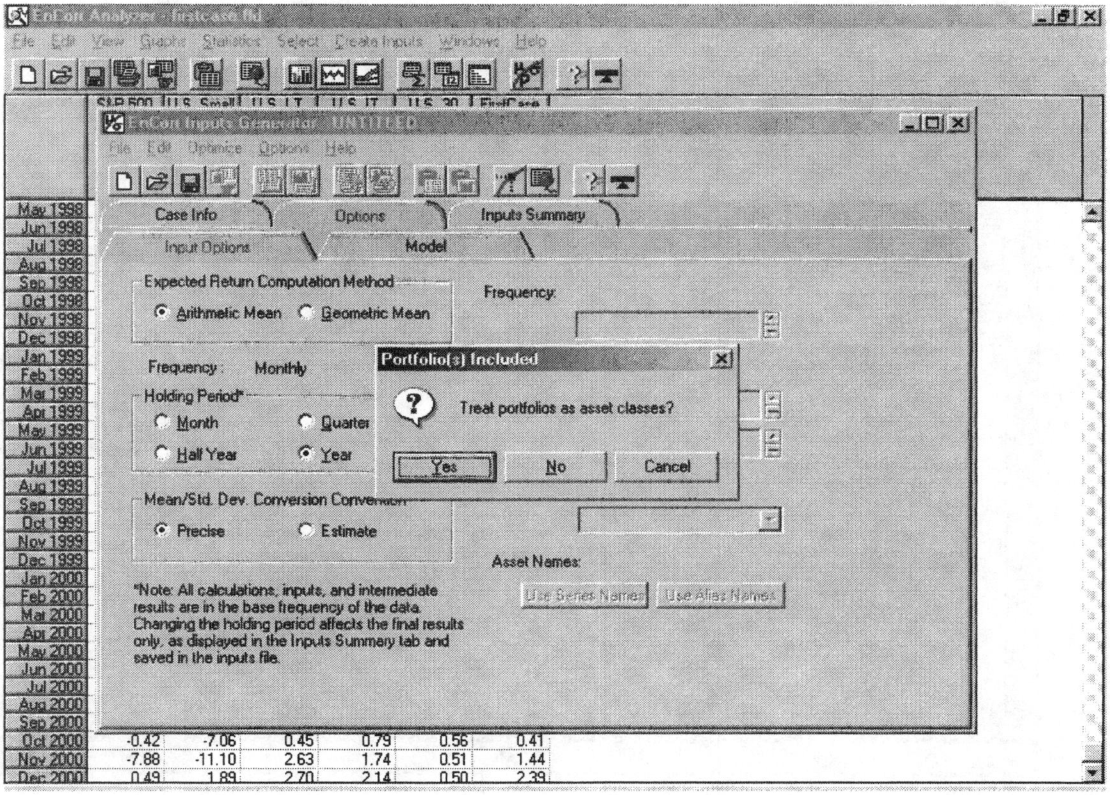

EnCorr Analyzer - firstcase.fld
File Edit View Graphs Statistics Select Create Inputs Windows Help
S&P 500 | U.S. Small | U.S. LT | U.S. IT | U.S. 30 | FirstCase
EnCorr Inputs Generator - UNTITLED
File Edit Optimize Options Help
Case Info | Options | Inputs Summary
Input Options | Model
Expected Return Computation Method
Arithmetic Mean | Geometric Mean
Frequency:
Frequency: Monthly
Holding Period*
Month | Quarter
Half Year | Year
Mean/Std. Dev. Conversion Convention
Precise | Estimate
Asset Names:
Use Series Names | Use Alias Names
*Note: All calculations, inputs, and intermediate results are in the base frequency of the data. Changing the holding period affects the final results only, as displayed in the Inputs Summary tab and saved in the inputs file.
Portfolio(s) Included
Treat portfolios as asset classes?
Yes | No | Cancel

May 1998						
Jun 1998						
Jul 1998						
Aug 1998						
Sep 1998						
Oct 1998						
Nov 1998						
Dec 1998						
Jan 1999						
Feb 1999						
Mar 1999						
Apr 1999						
May 1999						
Jun 1999						
Jul 1999						
Aug 1999						
Sep 1999						
Oct 1999						
Nov 1999						
Dec 1999						
Jan 2000						
Feb 2000						
Mar 2000						
Apr 2000						
May 2000						
Jun 2000						
Jul 2000						
Aug 2000						
Sep 2000						
Oct 2000	-0.42	-7.06	0.45	0.79	0.56	0.41
Nov 2000	-7.88	-11.10	2.63	1.74	0.51	1.44
Dec 2000	0.49	1.89	2.70	2.14	0.50	2.39

Figure 7.8 Treat Portfolio as Asset Classes?

- Click **Optimize** from the toolbar in the main Inputs Generator window and select **Yes** to save the inputs file.
- In the Save As dialog box, type in **FirstCase.inp** as the filename and click **Save.** You will now be opening EnCorr Optimizer.
- In the main Optimizer tab window, highlight all of the available assets and click on the **Add Asset** button. (**Figure 7.9**)

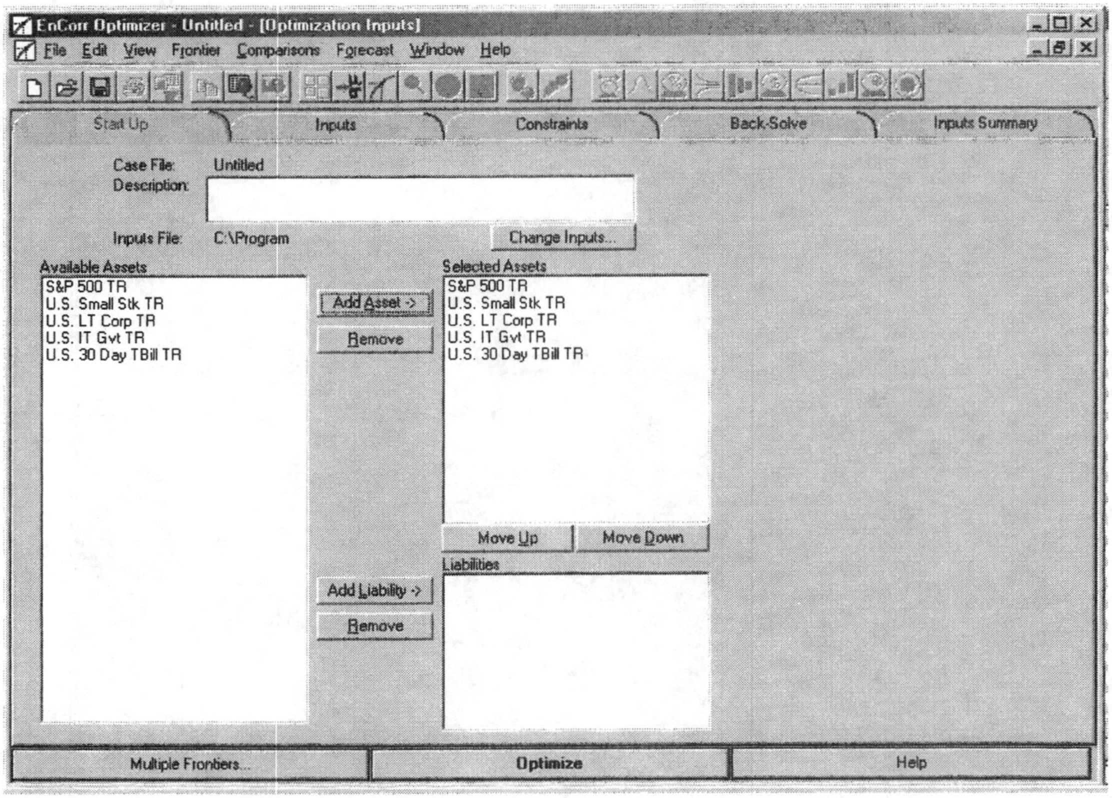

Figure 7.9 Main Optimizer Tab Window

- Now, click on **Optimize** on the tool bar at the bottom of the window and the Efficient Frontier appears as the lower right window in a four window page. (**Figure 7.10**)

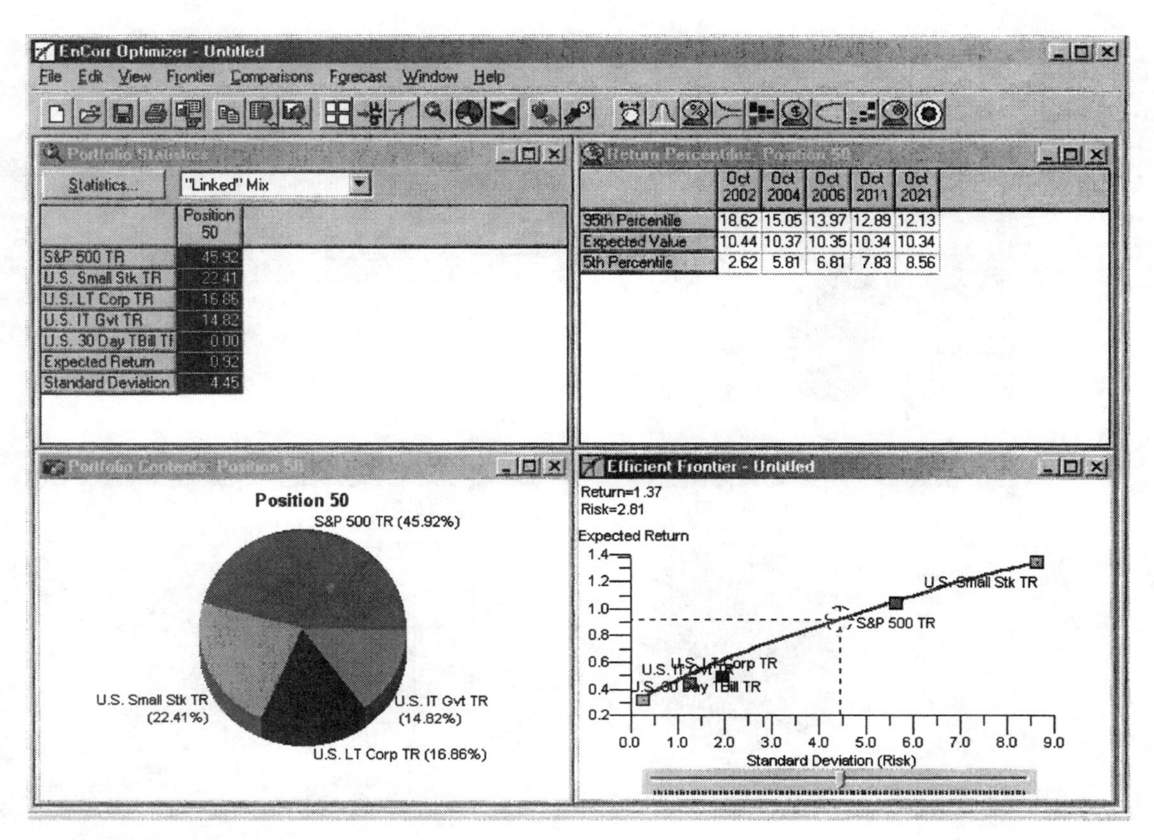

Figure 7.10 The Efficient Frontier

- Click the **Frontier** drop down menu and then click on **Asset Mixes/Classes.** Choose the **Portfolio Database** option and from the list of available portfolios, double-click on **FirstCase**; click **OK**. Then select **Close.** The Analyzer-created portfolio, FirstCase, now appears below the efficient frontier (**Figure 7.11).** You can get a better view if you optimize the Efficient Frontier window.

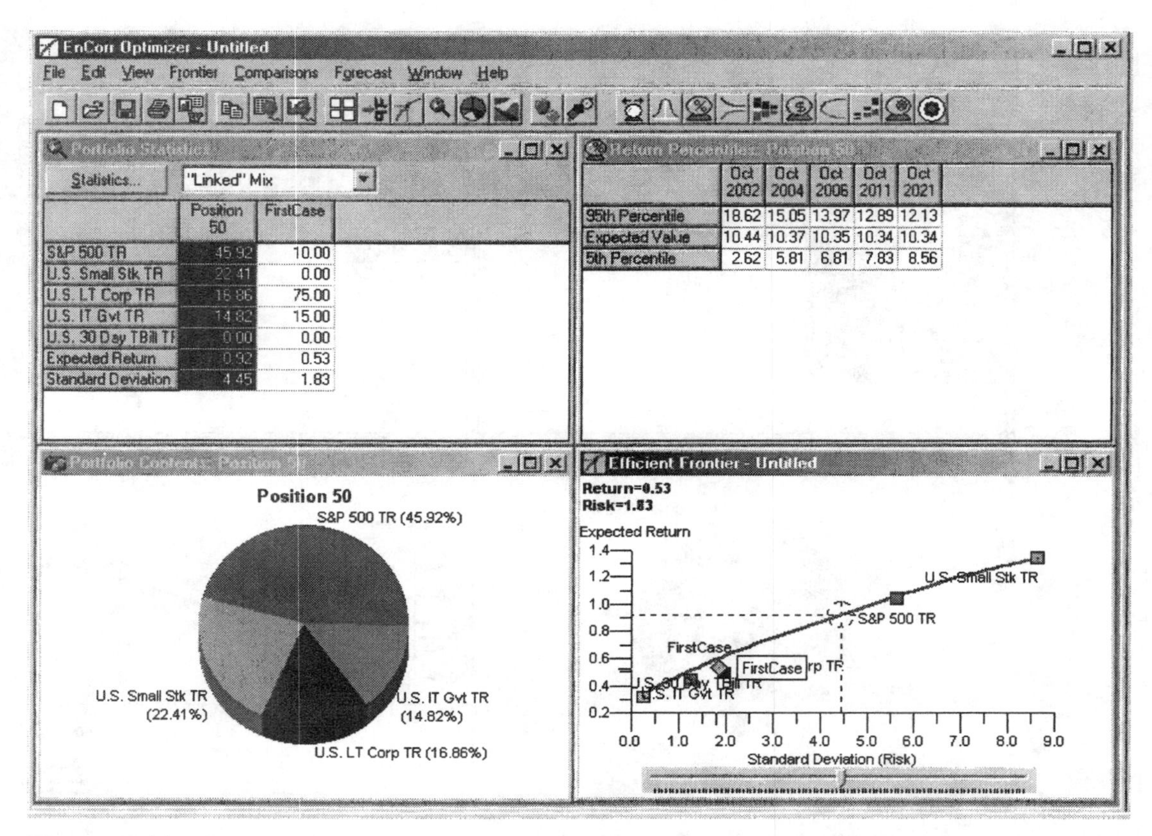

Figure 7.11 The "FirstCase Portfolio" falls below the efficient frontier

Since the portfolio falls below the efficient frontier line, the Analyzer-created portfolio, FirstCase, is sub-optimal; that is, there is an optimal portfolio that has the same level of risk as FirstCase but with a higher expected return. This new "optimal portfolio" lies directly above FirstCase on the frontier line.

We are looking for a portfolio that has the same standard deviation as FirstCase (1.83) but with a higher return than .53.
To find the "optimal portfolio":

- In the FirstCase window on the upper left corner of your screen containing the graph of the Efficient Frontier, find the Analyzer-created FirstCase portfolio's standard deviation (1.83).

- Go to **Frontier, Find/Label Point** and under the **Find By** tab, use the dropdown list to select **Standard Deviation**. Now, type in 1.83 as the portfolio's standard deviation and click **Find and Label**. The efficient point that you have specified will show in the lower left **Efficient Frontier** window. It will also appear as a column in the upper left corner of your screen under **Portfolio Statistics**. (**Figure 7.12**)

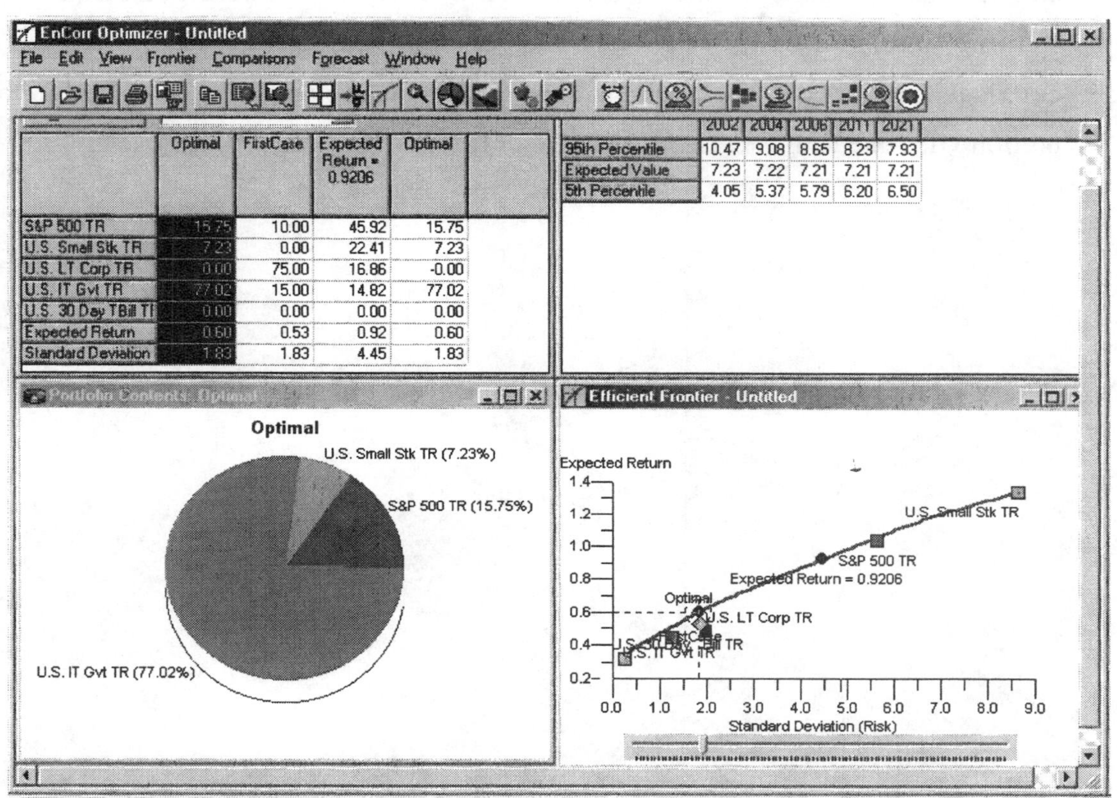

Figure 7.12 Optimal Portfolio

- In the Portfolio Statistics window, highlight the "**Optimal**" portfolio (with 1.83 standard deviation), then click **Edit, Copy as a Portfolio**.

We can now backtest this new Optimal portfolio. After pasting it back into the folder window of the Analyzer, you can compare its historical performance to the Analyzer-created portfolio in the Summary Statistics table of the Analyzer.

- Minimize the Efficient Frontier and Inputs Generator windows.
- Bring up the folder window of the Analyzer and click on **Edit, Paste Portfolio**.

- Click **Statistics, Summary Statistics**. The Summary Statistics window will appear.

The Summary Statistics table shows the comparison between both portfolios (the Analyzer-created and Optimal) in terms of historical geometric mean, arithmetic mean and standard deviation. Also, click **Display** and choose **Highest Return, Lowest Return, Number of Positive Periods** and **Number of Negative Periods** for further criteria for comparison. These criteria illustrate the superior performance of the Optimal portfolio (the one with 1.83 standard deviation) versus the Analyzer-created portfolio.

Exercises

The following problems are based on the series known as **Sample Company Stocks** found in the Available Series of the Ibbotson Database.

7.1 Choose the Sample Company Stocks for each portfolio and generate the inputs. Find the efficient frontier by using all 16 stock series. Be sure to save each portfolio after Analyzer creates it.

Portfolio A. Select the following series as the Analyzer-created portfolio:

- Oracle
- Microsoft
- Intel
- Hewlett-Packard

a. Is this an optimal portfolio? Why?
b. If not, find the optimal portfolio at this risk?
c. Backtest the new Optimal portfolio. How does its values compare to the Analyzer-created portfolio values with respect to its arithmetic mean, geometric mean, and standard deviation?

Portfolio B. Select the following series as the Analyzer-created portfolio:

- Wal Mart
- Proctor and Gamble
- Pepsi Cola
- Nike
- Eastman Kodak
- Coca Cola

a. Is this an optimal portfolio? Why?
b. If not, find the optimal portfolio at this risk?
c. Back test the new Optimal portfolio. How does its values compare to the Analyzer-created portfolio values with respect to its arithmetic mean, geometric mean, and standard deviation?

Portfolio C. Select the following series as the Analyzer-created portfolio:

- General Motors
- General Electric
- Du Pont
- Boeing
- Corning

a. Is this an optimal portfolio? Why?
b. If not, find the optimal portfolio at this risk?
c. Back test the new Optimal portfolio. How does its values compare to the Analyzer-created portfolio values with respect to its arithmetic mean, geometric mean, and standard deviation?

7.2 Using the three portfolios (A,B,C) that Analyzer created, choose the best portfolio. Give a short explanation why you made this choice and not the others.

SINGLE PC LICENSE AGREEMENT AND LIMITED WARRANTY

READ THIS LICENSE CAREFULLY BEFORE OPENING THIS PACKAGE. BY OPENING THIS PACKAGE, YOU ARE AGREEING TO THE TERMS AND CONDITIONS OF THIS LICENSE. IF YOU DO NOT AGREE, DO NOT OPEN THE PACKAGE. PROMPTLY RETURN THE UNOPENED PACKAGE AND ALL ACCOMPANYING ITEMS TO THE PLACE YOU OBTAINED THEM [[FOR A FULL REFUND OF ANY SUMS YOU HAVE PAID FOR THE SOFTWARE]]. ***THESE TERMS APPLY TO ALL LICENSED SOFTWARE ON THE DISK EXCEPT THAT THE TERMS FOR USE OF ANY SHAREWARE OR FREEWARE ON THE DISKETTES ARE AS SET FORTH IN THE ELECTRONIC LICENSE LOCATED ON THE DISK:***

1. GRANT OF LICENSE and OWNERSHIP: The enclosed computer programs <<and data>> ("Software") are licensed, not sold, to you by Prentice-Hall, Inc. ("We" or the "Company") and in consideration [[of your payment of the license fee, which is part of the price you paid]] [[of your purchase or adoption of the accompanying Company textbooks and/or other materials,]] and your agreement to these terms. We reserve any rights not granted to you. You own only the disk(s) but we and/or our licensors own the Software itself. This license allows you to use and display your copy of the Software on a single computer (i.e., with a single CPU) at a single location for academic use only, so long as you comply with the terms of this Agreement. You may make one copy for back up, or transfer your copy to another CPU, provided that the Software is usable on only one computer.

2. RESTRICTIONS: You may not transfer or distribute the Software or documentation to anyone else. Except for backup, you may not copy the documentation or the Software. You may not network the Software or otherwise use it on more than one computer or computer terminal at the same time. You may not reverse engineer, disassemble, decompile, modify, adapt, translate, or create derivative works based on the Software or the Documentation. You may be held legally responsible for any copying or copyright infringement which is caused by your failure to abide by the terms of these restrictions.

3. TERMINATION: This license is effective until terminated. This license will terminate automatically without notice from the Company if you fail to comply with any provisions or limitations of this license. Upon termination, you shall destroy the Documentation and all copies of the Software. All provisions of this Agreement as to limitation and disclaimer of warranties, limitation of liability, remedies or damages, and our ownership rights shall survive termination.

4. LIMITED WARRANTY AND DISCLAIMER OF WARRANTY: Company warrants that for a period of 60 days from the date you purchase this SOFTWARE (or purchase or adopt the accompanying textbook), the Software, when properly installed and used in accordance with the Documentation, will operate in substantial conformity with the description of the Software set forth in the Documentation, and that for a period of 30 days the disk(s) on which the Software is delivered shall be free from defects in materials and workmanship under normal use. The Company does not warrant that the Software will meet your requirements or that the operation of the Software will be uninterrupted or error-free. Your only remedy and the Company's only obligation under these limited warranties is, at the Company's option, return of the disk for a refund of any amounts paid for it by you or replacement of the disk. THIS LIMITED WARRANTY IS THE ONLY WARRANTY PROVIDED BY THE COMPANY AND ITS LICENSORS, AND THE COMPANY AND ITS LICENSORS DISCLAIM ALL OTHER WARRANTIES, EXPRESS OR IMPLIED, INCLUDING WITHOUT LIMITATION, THE IMPLIED WARRANTIES OF MERCHANTABILITY AND FITNESS FOR A PARTICULAR PURPOSE. THE COMPANY DOES NOT WARRANT, GUARANTEE OR MAKE ANY REPRESENTATION REGARDING THE ACCURACY, RELIABILITY, CURRENTNESS, USE, OR RESULTS OF USE, OF THE SOFTWARE.

5. LIMITATION OF REMEDIES AND DAMAGES: IN NO EVENT, SHALL THE COMPANY OR ITS EMPLOYEES, AGENTS, LICENSORS, OR CONTRACTORS BE LIABLE FOR ANY INCIDENTAL, INDIRECT, SPECIAL, OR CONSEQUENTIAL DAMAGES ARISING OUT OF OR IN CONNECTION WITH THIS LICENSE OR THE SOFTWARE, INCLUDING FOR LOSS OF USE, LOSS OF DATA, LOSS OF INCOME OR PROFIT, OR OTHER LOSSES, SUSTAINED AS A RESULT OF INJURY TO ANY PERSON, OR LOSS OF OR DAMAGE TO PROPERTY, OR CLAIMS OF THIRD PARTIES, EVEN IF THE COMPANY OR AN AUTHORIZED REPRESENTATIVE OF THE COMPANY HAS BEEN ADVISED OF THE POSSIBILITY OF SUCH DAMAGES. IN NO EVENT

SHALL THE LIABILITY OF THE COMPANY FOR DAMAGES WITH RESPECT TO THE SOFTWARE EXCEED THE AMOUNTS ACTUALLY PAID BY YOU, IF ANY, FOR THE SOFTWARE OR THE ACCOMPANYING TEXTBOOK. BECAUSE SOME JURISDICTIONS DO NOT ALLOW THE LIMITATION OF LIABILITY IN CERTAIN CIRCUMSTANCES, THE ABOVE LIMITATIONS MAY NOT ALWAYS APPLY TO YOU.

6. GENERAL: THIS AGREEMENT SHALL BE CONSTRUED IN ACCORDANCE WITH THE LAWS OF THE UNITED STATES OF AMERICA AND THE STATE OF NEW YORK, APPLICABLE TO CONTRACTS MADE IN NEW YORK, AND SHALL BENEFIT THE COMPANY, ITS AFFILIATES AND ASSIGNEES. HIS AGREEMENT IS THE COMPLETE AND EXCLUSIVE STATEMENT OF THE AGREEMENT BETWEEN YOU AND THE COMPANY AND SUPERSEDES ALL PROPOSALS OR PRIOR AGREEMENTS, ORAL, OR WRITTEN, AND ANY OTHER COMMUNICATIONS BETWEEN YOU AND THE COMPANY OR ANY REPRESENTATIVE OF THE COMPANY RELATING TO THE SUBJECT MATTER OF THIS AGREEMENT. If you are a U.S. Government user, this Software is licensed with "restricted rights" as set forth in subparagraphs (a)-(d) of the Commercial Computer-Restricted Rights clause at FAR 52.227-19 or in subparagraphs (c)(1)(ii) of the Rights in Technical Data and Computer Software clause at DFARS 252.227-7013, and similar clauses, as applicable.

Should you have any questions concerning this agreement or if you wish to contact the Company for any reason, please contact in writing: [give name, address, email address for Company or customer service representative]